BUSINESS
Intermediate GNVQ

BUSINESS
Intermediate GNVQ

Jon Sutherland

and

Diane Canwell

PITMAN
PUBLISHING

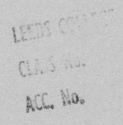
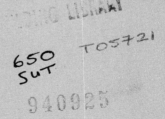

PITMAN PUBLISHING
128 Long Acre, London WC2E 9AN

A Division of Longman Group Limited

First Published in 1994
© Jon Sutherland and Diane Canwell 1994

A CIP catalogue record for this book can be obtained from the British Library

ISBN 0 273 60298 5

Typeset by Create Publishing Services Ltd, Bath, Avon
Printed and bound in Great Britain by Clays Ltd, St Ives plc

10 9 8 7 6 5 4 3

The Publishers' policy is to use paper manufactured from sustainable forests.

For Joshua

Contents

Unit 1: BUSINESS ORGANISATIONS AND EMPLOYMENT
Intermediate Level

Unit 2: PEOPLE IN BUSINESS ORGANISATIONS
Intermediate Level

Introduction

This book contains a wealth of practical and above all, relevant, activities and tasks which are designed to meet all the criteria required to complete a GNVQ Intermediate Award in Business.

We have attempted to follow all the Performance Criteria, Ranges and Evidence Indicators, Element by Element, across the four Units of the learning programme. At all times, we have endeavoured to use the most up-to-date documentation from BTEC and GNVQ in the preparation of the material.

Successful completion of all Student Activities and Element Assignments will provide candidates with sufficient evidence for their portfolios. Throughout these assignments and activities, we have attempted to use the three Core Skills as often as is practicable. We are sure that those responsible for the delivery of this programme at various institutions will find their own ways of organising the candidates' portfolios. You will find some guidance on this matter in the section headed 'Portfolio building'.

The ten multiple-choice questions printed at the end of each Unit should form the basis of a useful summative test in the style of the BTEC-designed Unit Tests. We have also included sets of short answer questions at the end of each Element to provide a focus for revision.

A few last words, to the candidates themselves. We are sure that your institution will have created its own way of undertaking this programme of study. Whichever method it has chosen, the key to success is to be systematic and take each Element independently. You will be required to show that you understand the coverage of the range of subject matter before being considered to have successfully completed the Element.

We hope that you will find the text interesting and informative and the Student activities useful and practical.

Jon Sutherland and Diane Canwell
January 1994

Portfolio building

Gathering evidence for the Portfolio

Throughout the book we have designed a series of Student Activities and Element Assignments which are both formative and summative in nature. Formative means that students will be learning while they are doing, summative means that the student will be tested after a specific block of information to ensure understanding. In addition, at the commencement of each Element, we have listed the Performance Criteria and Range as specified by GNVQ.

The Student Activities and Element Assignments not only cover the GNVQ Performance Criteria and Range, but also the Core Skills – i.e. students apply technology, are asked to communicate in a variety of ways, and show application of number.

Because these Activities and Assignments cover all the necessary criteria and Core Skills, it is therefore possible to use these to build up the Student Portfolio of Evidence.

What the Portfolio should contain

The Student Portfolio should contain evidence that they have either achieved outcomes or proved competence in the past, or have carried out tasks which test both their knowledge and competence during their GNVQ programme. In effect, this means that the Portfolio can contain both evidence obtained within the institution of study, as well as any external activities.

Examples of evidence which a student could use to claim accreditation for prior learning or experience might be:

- Certificates from qualifications already gained
- A reference from an accredited assessor stating that the student has carried out a certain task competently on a number of occasions
- A log of visitors which a student may have dealt with on a regular basis over a period of time
- Evidence based on the student's part-time work experience

This is not an exclusive list. Other evidence may be negotiated with an External Verifier.

The Portfolio *must* contain evidence of assessment of all the GNVQ Elements.

The Range and Evidence Indicators assist in suggesting how this could be carried out.

The Portfolio *must* contain evidence of achievement of the three Core Skills. It is not essential that Additional Core Skills be contained in the Portfolio, as they will not be required to prove competence at Intermediate Level. If, however, these Additional Core Skills have been assessed, then obviously the evidence should be included in the Portfolio.

The Student Activities and Element Assignments in this book are designed to assist in the preparation of the Evidence Portfolio, although naturally additional evidence will also be required or preferred. When students have to prove competence on a number of different occasions, then obviously the centres involved in delivering the Programme will need to provide additional means of assessment.

Core skills

GNVQ Core Skills

When we designed the learning and assessment activities it was essential to be familiar with the Unit Specifications demanded within the programme. When considering the Core Skills, think about these as being a separate issue. The Core Skills coverage should be mapped on a Programme Assessment Sheet. The Core Skills in themselves require continuous assessment throughout the programme of study. There should be sufficient evidence generated from the Student Activities and Element Assignments to confirm the candidate's ability to fulfil the specific Elements of each Core Skill. In practice, you will be assessing not only the same Core Skills on more than one occasion, but you will also find that the particular Elements which make up that Core Skill are similarly tested repeatedly. This process is perfectly acceptable, since it re-affirms the candidate's ability to reproduce a particular achievement on a number of occasions. In this respect, the candidate has shown a consistent performance.

1 Communication Intermediate Level

- Element 2.1 – Take part in discussions with a range of people on routine matters.
- Element 2.2 – Prepare written material on routine matters.
- Element 2.3 – Use images to illustrate points made in writing and in discussions with a range of people on routine matters.
- Element 2.4 – Read and respond to written materials and images on routine matters.

2 Information Technology Intermediate Level

- Element 2.1 – Set up storage systems and input information.
- Element 2.2 – Edit, organise and integrate information from different sources.
- Element 2.3 – Select and use formats for presenting information.
- Element 2.4 – Evaluate the features and facilities of given applications.
- Element 2.5 – Deal with errors and faults at Intermediate Level.

3 Application of Number Intermediate Level

- Element 2.1 – Gather and process data at Core Skill Intermediate Level.
- Element 2.2 – Represent and tackle problems at Core Skill Intermediate Level.

- Element 2.3 – Interpret and present mathematical data at Core Skill Intermediate Level.

Presently approved Additional Core Skill Units (not required for the award, although the achievements should be recorded on the NRA):

Working with Others Intermediate Level

- Element 2.1 – Work to given collective goals and responsibilities and provide information to help with the allocation of responsibilities.
- Element 2.2 – Use given working methods in fulfilling own responsibilities and provide feedback to others on own progress.

Improving own learning and performance Intermediate Level

- Element 2.1 – Contribute to the process of identifying strengths and weaknesses and of identifying short-term targets.
- Element 2.2 – Make use of feedback in following given activities to learn and improve performance.

Acknowledgements

The authors would like to thank the following individuals and organisations for their help and support in the preparation of this book:

Tracey Birkbeck (British Nuclear Fuels plc)
Julie Conneely (Marks and Spencer plc)
Theresa Gibson (Avon Cosmetics Ltd)
Richard Garbutt (Peugeot Talbot Motor Company plc)
Paul Hallett (Department of Trade and Industry)
Her Majesty's Stationery Office
Steve McIvor (British Union for the Abolition of Vivisection)
R C Newstead (Mobil Oil Company Ltd)
Amanda Smee (Woolworths; Kingfisher plc)
Edmund Staples (Mercury Communications Ltd)
Tracey Suett (The British Petroleum Co plc)

We acknowledge the copyright of illustrated materials as detailed below:

Name of organisation	Figure numbers
Avon Cosmetic Ltd	4.5, 4.18
Bank of Education	3.3, 3.9–3.17, 3.26
British Nuclear Fuels plc	1.5, 1.11, 1.14, 1.25, 2.16, 2.25, 2.27, 4.8, 4.28, 4.35
British Petroleum Co plc	1.2, 1.16, 1.18, 3.2, 4.31, 4.32, 4.33
BUAV	1.8, 4.7
Department of Trade and Industry	1.23, 1.29, 2.1, 2.28, 2.29, 3.4, 3.27, 4.16, 4.30
Inland Revenue (Her Majesty's Stationery Office)	1.20, 1.21, 1.22, 2.23*
Kingfisher plc	1.13, 2.15, 2.21, 2.26, 4.4, 4.6, 4.19 (also p. 1.20)
Marks and Spencer	1.17, 2.20, 4.1, 4.2, 4.3
Mercury	2.22, 2.24, 4.9, 4.15, 4.34, 4.40
Mobil Oil	2.14, 4.12, 4.13, 4.14, 4.17
Peugeot Talbot	2.5–2.12, 4.20–4.27, 4.36–4.39

*These illustrations are reproduced with the permission of the Controller of Her Majesty's Stationery Office

Unit 1
BUSINESS ORGANISATIONS AND EMPLOYMENT
Intermediate Level

Element 1.1
Explain the purposes and types of private and public sector business organisations

Element 1.2
Investigate business organisations and products

Element 1.3
Investigate the UK employment market

Element 1.1
The purposes and types of private and public sector business organisations

PERFORMANCE CRITERIA

1 **Purposes of different types of business organisations are explained**
2 **Industrial sectors are described and examples given**
3 **Local and national business activities are identified**

RANGE

1 **Purposes: profit-making, public service and charitable**
2 **Types of business organisation: sole trader, partnership, private limited company, public limited company, co-operative, franchise, charitable, state-owned industry or service, and local government**
3 **Industrial sectors: primary, secondary and tertiary**

EVIDENCE INDICATORS

Examples of different local and national business organisations to illustrate the different purposes, different industrial sectors and different types of business activity. Evidence should demonstrate understanding of the implications of the range dimensions in relation to the element. The unit test will confirm the candidate's coverage of the range.

PURPOSES OF BUSINESS ORGANISATIONS

The types and role of the economy

All resources are said to be scarce compared to our wants and needs. The main problem is how resources are managed. Different countries have different solutions to this problem, but they all address the same three questions:

1   What should be produced?
2   How should it be produced?
3   Who should have what is produced?

The four main factors of production are:

1   Land
2   Labour
3   Capital
4   Enterprise

Land

This includes all of the physical resources like coal, timber, minerals and crops.

Labour

This includes all the available physical and mental efforts of people.

Capital

This includes not only money but anything which is used to make other things, e.g. machines.

Enterprise

These are the skills which people have and the risks they take in bringing the other three factors together.

As we have said, not all countries use the same methods to organise their economy. One of the ways of looking at the different economies is to measure the amount of influence the Government has on decision making.

Free market

In a free market the Government is not involved in controlling the resources. All decisions are made by buyers or sellers. Buyers will only buy goods that they believe offer value for money. If buyers or consumers think they would get better value from buying something else then they will buy that. Those that make the goods, known as producers, have to constantly adjust their output of goods to match consumer demands. In the real world there is not a single country that can claim to be a truly free market. To a greater or lesser extent, all governments meddle with the economy.

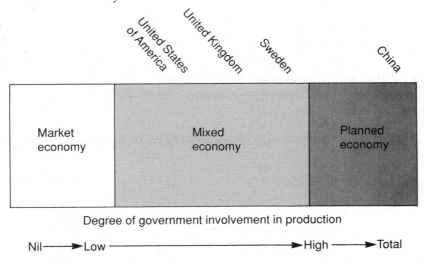

Degree of government involvement in production

Nil──►Low ────────────────────────────►High ──►Total

Fig 1.1 Types of economy

Advantages and disadvantages of a free market

Advantages

■ Consumers will buy what they think will give them the most satisfaction and value for money

■ The most popular goods are likely to be produced in huge quantities and at low prices

■ Most resources will be channelled into goods which are popular. It is unlikely that unpopular goods will be widely available

■ Scarce resources are not wasted on goods which will not sell

■ The free market can respond to change very quickly when buying trends make the producing of old fashioned goods unprofitable

Disadvantages

■ Large and powerful companies have much more influence than smaller companies

■ Although all production is linked to consumers' willingness to buy, those consumers with more money have more influence

■ The free market does not guarantee that the poorest consumers will have their basic needs provided for

■ In a free market it is common for some large companies to be the only producer of particular goods (these are known as monopolies)

■ The free market only really works when consumers know exactly where and at what price they can buy goods, in other words the consumers do not always know where the best bargain is

■ Advertising in a free market is very powerful. The information given to the consumers is often misleading. It is difficult for consumers to know when they are being told the truth

1.5

Planned economy

This is a system on the opposite side of the scale from a free market system. The Government, through central planning, needs to know how much each region of the country is able to produce and exactly what its needs will be. From this information it can give out the available resources. This system has not worked very well in the long run, and only China and Cuba still operate this way.

Advantages and disadvantages of a planned economy

Advantages	Disadvantages
■ The combined effort of the whole country can be used to achieve targets of production	■ Since there is no competition then the quality of the products suffers. This also removes the rewards that individuals would normally get for their own effort and enterprise
■ All parts of the country are dependent upon one another, and this is a powerful way of ensuring all areas of the country remain united in their efforts	■ Factory managers and regional planners will always over-estimate what they need to complete a project so that they can obtain more than their fair share of the resources. Resources are therefore wasted because the regions of the country like to think that they are more important
■ Basic needs of the people can be fulfilled. If there is high unemployment these basic needs can be reduced in price so that they are affordable	■ Because everything is centrally planned a lot of paperwork needs to be completed. This is known as bureaucracy, and means that the cost of running a planned system is high
■ Long-term planning can be made for all resources and all industries	■ Because all decisions must go through the bureaucracy decision making is slowed down
■ There is no wasteful duplication of production	■ When the planned economy fails to produce enough particular goods individuals who can obtain these goods sell them at high prices themselves. This is known as a black market
■ All goods and services can be distributed fairly	

Mixed economy

Mixed economies have features of both the free market and planned systems. The mixed economy is also the most common. There is a level of government involvement, but also a large element of private enterprise. Most Western

European countries use this system, where three main groups are of equal importance: the producer, the Government and the consumer.

The producers are private owners who are free to decide how their own resources are used. They decide what to produce, how many to produce (quantity), and the quality of the product.

The Government has control over some resources and runs most of the services needed by the country, e.g. healthcare, welfare services and defence. It has the power to influence producers and consumers. This is usually done by imposing laws or high rates of tax to discourage the over-buying of certain goods, e.g. alcohol and tobacco products.

The consumers are a very powerful but disorganised group. Individuals have their own needs and wants. They have the choice of buying from a range of goods on offer. Their decisions are heavily influenced by price, availability and advertising.

Advantages and disadvantages of a mixed economy

Advantages

- The mixed economy combines the best elements of planned and free markets

- The Government should be able to influence how resources are used

- The Government also provides a 'safety net' for the weaker members of society who are unable to provide for themselves, e.g. the unemployed, the elderly and the sick

- The Government, with the help of the producers, is able to make sure that the market runs smoothly and that there is effective competition within the market to keep prices low

Disadvantages

- The mixed economy also combines the worst elements of the free market and planned economies

- The government interferes with initiative and enterprise by imposing restrictive laws

- Competition will always favour the strong at the expense of the weak. Larger businesses will always be able to offer what appears to be a better deal as they are in a position to buy the resources they need at lower costs

Group activity

Research and identify at least five examples of each type of economy. Is one particular type of economy more common than another? Is one type of economy more successful than another? Do certain types of economy tend to be in one area of the world? Research this activity in pairs and feedback your findings to the remainder of the group.

FUNCTIONS OF ORGANISATIONS

There are a wide variety of different forms of business organisations, each with a broad range of different goals.

Perhaps a good start is to look at how different many organisations are at their very core.

Formal and informal organisations

Formal organisations can be defined as those that have established the express purpose of achieving particular goals, aims or objectives. These types of organisation have clearly defined rules and instructions as well as quite highly developed communication between different parts of the organisation.

Good examples include most businesses, governments and international institutions.

The opposite to these are informal organisations, also known as socia organisations.

These do not tend to have clearly defined goals, and examples include families or communities.

Productive and non-productive organisations

Because there are so many different types of formal organisation, this large group needs to be carefully classified.

One of the easiest ways is to separate them into productive and non-productive categories.

Productive organisations are those which are concerned with producing something, or production. These can be privately or publicly owned, they do not necessarily have to make a product, they could provide a service.

All the industries mentioned so far tend to sell something, or offer their services to the community. There are a number of publicly-owned services, such as health and education. These are still considered to be productive organisations, but they do not trade. Therefore this large category can also be sub-divided into trading and non-trading.

There are many organisations which do not make goods or offer any services at all. These are called non-productive – but they are still important.

Good examples are courts, unions or churches. They all play an important role in our lives.

Group activity

In threes, discuss the following statement:
'The purpose of businesses is to make a profit.'
How far do you think this is true? Do all organisations have this goal? Can you identify some organisations which do not have this goal?

PURPOSES OF ORGANISATIONS

The purpose of any organisation is to be successful. Successfulness is measured in many different ways, depending upon the type of organisation concerned. A good starting point for any organisation is to set down guidelines for activity, which serve as a form of standard from which it can measure performance.

There is always likely to be a major difference between the organisation itself, how it operates, and what the ideal type of organisation would be to achieve success. It is only when the organisation has clearly set out its goals and objectives that it can identify shortcomings or problems and seek solutions to solve them.

Business plans

Many businesses begin with setting out their aims, purposes and objectives in a Business Plan, which is a formal statement of their goals. However, in reality, the day-to-day achievement of these goals may differ from the business plan. Organisations do not exist in isolation. The environment in which they operate is constantly changing, therefore organisations must be flexible. Any change may require organisational change, when old ways of operating are no longer efficient or advisable in the new circumstances.

Individual activity

What would you expect to find in a business plan? How would you expect a business plan to be organised? Who would be responsible for putting a business plan together? Who would wish to see the business plan? How closely do businesses adhere to their business plans?

Mission Statements

A Mission Statement differs from a business plan in that it looks at what the organisation actually stands for. Generally, this is an agreement of both managers and employees. These agreed goals are often more valuable as they have the common consent of all those involved in the organisation. The individuals involved have a shared point of view and perhaps some common ideas of how to achieve it.

Individual activity

The institution in which you are studying this course will have a mission statement. Discover what it is and try to describe in your own words what it actually means.

Goals to action

Once an organisation has established its goals, it must then find methods of achieving them. These are known as the Strategies and Tactics.

Strategies are the major ways to achieve the objectives and tend to be fairly long term in their approach, e.g. to increase turnover by 50 per cent in 10 years.

Tactics, on the other hand, are more short term and flexible. These are the individual parts of the main strategy, e.g. in order to increase turnover by 50 per cent in 10 years the product range needs to be increased and cheaper suppliers found.

So, strategy answers how the organisation intends to get where it wants to go, and tactics are the means by which it achieves the strategy.

As we have said, businesses exist for many different reasons, and perhaps the most common is profit, but certainly not the only one. Being happy and satisfied is as strong a reason for running an organisation, and this is why many people like to work for themselves. The freedom to make one's own choices is good compensation for not having to work for an organisation that is only interested in profit.

The following are some of the main objectives of organisations.

Maximising profits

This is when there is the largest possible difference between how much something has cost to produce, and how much it can be sold for. In order to achieve this the organisation needs to know as much about the customer and the market as possible. It needs to know where to get its supplies at the cheapest possible rate, the most economical way of getting the product to the customer and the maximum price the customer would be prepared to pay for the product.

Being the Market Leader

A Market Leader is an organisation that tries to sell more products than any of its rivals, or perhaps all of its rivals combined. There are considerable advantages to being a market leader, since every other organisation's products are compared to its own products. Once this status has been achieved, profit maximisation may also follow as each product can be produced cheaper than a rival's as so many more are being produced.

A part-way stage of achieving market leadership is to set an achievable level of market share. In other words, the organisation may not directly seek to be the market leader straight away, but will move towards this in stages by gradually increasing their market share.

Maximising sales

On the face of it, this would appear to be similar to maximising profits, but this is not the case. It does not necessarily follow that achieving high sales results in achieving high profits. There may be only a small profit to be made from each product. It is only when many thousands of a product are sold that a reasonable profit is made. This particular objective is most common in the retail trade, when different branches of the same organisation 'compete' with one another to achieve high sales figures. After all, the employees of the branches may be given considerable cash bonuses to encourage them to sell more.

Organisational growth

The larger an organisation is, the more likely it is to attract investors and to be able to produce products on a vast scale. Being big brings its own particular problems. Keeping track of business activity such as sales, stock and profit require many extra employees. Should a company grow too quickly and over-take its ability to keep track of things, it runs the risk of 'over-trading'. It is therefore very important to be able to monitor all activities when an organisation is growing fast.

Providing a steady income

In some ways, this is the opposite to sales and profit maximisation. An organisation which states that providing a steady income is its principal objective is saying that it would rather attain realistic goals than overstretch itself. This is perhaps a cautious approach to business, but it is one which is often the most workable. Being able to easily meet sales targets, deliver goods on time and maintain high quality standards may mean the difference between survival and failure in an uncertain business world. Many of the organisations which grew very quickly in the 1980s over extended themselves in pursuit of short-term profits. It can now be seen that companies which 'plodded along' throughout the 1980s are still trading successfully, having provided themselves with a steady income in good times and bad (*See* Fig 1.2).

The British Petroleum Company p.l.c. is one of Britain's biggest companies. It is also the third largest oil company in the world, and one of the world's largest industrial corporations.

BP owes its origin to one man, William Knox D'Arcy, who shortly after the turn of the century invested time, money and labour in the belief that worthwhile deposits of oil could be found in Persia (now known as Iran).

Today, BP's key strengths are in oil and gas exploration and production; the supply, refining and marketing of petroleum products; and the manufacturing and marketing of chemicals. It supports all its businesses with high quality research and technology.

BP operates in over 70 countries. In recent years, it has established a major presence in the USA, where about one-third of its fixed assets are now located.

Fig 1.2 From relatively humble beginnings BP now operates world-wide and is one of Britain's foremost companies

Expanding the range of products or services

The more products or services an organisation offers, the more likely that organisation is to survive and succeed. Organisations which only offer a single product or service can often find themselves in great difficulty if demand for what they offer reduces or disappears.

There are dangers of offering too wide a range of products or services as the company may not be considered to be expert or a market leader in any of them. In addition, it is exposing itself to the risks of several markets failing.

Freedom

As we have already mentioned, many people set up a business in order to work for themselves. They prefer the opportunity to make their own decisions and be their own boss, and, of course, take all the profits and risk all the losses.

Providing a return for shareholders and owners

This objective aims to provide a steady and acceptable level of profit to those who own the organisation. In this sense a distinction is made between owners and shareholders. This will be covered in greater detail later.

Shareholders are owners of the business, but may only have a small stake in it and look for profits in the form of dividends from the shares they own.

The term 'Owners', on the other hand, may refer to either Sole Traders, Partners or major Shareholders, who again are looking for income from the organisation related to how much of that organisation they own.

Beating the competition

In a sense this objective is similar to being a market leader. However, beating the competition may just relate to achieving higher sales. Measuring this objective in terms of success is difficult, but can usually be assessed by the level of profit or reputation.

Survival

When times are bad and the economy is in recession, a company may simply seek survival. Measuring this may mean having the ability to maintain existing staff levels, keeping customers and not having to close branches or retail outlets.

Breaking even

This objective can often be used to describe the attitude of a charity or non-profit making organisation (e.g. a Local Authority or a Government Department). Any profits that are made are simply ploughed back into the organisation to cover running costs and purchase more products in order to continue the cycle. This can be termed as 'ticking over' and is another objective often adopted by organisations in times of recession.

Individual activity

Ten main objectives of organisations have been identified, but which are the most important? Put the 10 in ranking order of importance, then look at the top five and give reasons why you have decided the order of them. Compare your decision with those of your fellow students.

TYPES OF ORGANISATION

There are many ways in which a business can be organised, from a small one-man business to a multinational.

The sole trader

The sole trader is perhaps the most common, although in recent years this is declining due to a number of reasons which will be looked at later.

The sole trader is responsible for all actions that the company undertakes. This individual is responsible for borrowing all the money required and actually running the business day to day. Perhaps the most common sorts of sole traders are craftsmen – plumbers, decorators, electricians, mobile hairdressers, window cleaners and chiropodists.

Fig 1.3 Examples of sole traders

Perhaps the most common feature of all sole traders is the way they get started, and they can always normally be run by one person, although that person has to be very flexible, in other words they need to be willing to work very long hours.

There are quite a number of advantages of setting up as a sole trader.

Advantages and disadvantages of being a sole trader

Advantages

- There are no real legal formalities to complete before commencing to trade

- There are no real legal requirements governing the layout of their accounts

- The annual accounts do not have to be audited

- Decisions can be made quickly since only the individual is involved

- All the profits and, indeed, losses belong to the owner

- The owner has the freedom to run the business in their own way

Disadvantages

- Capital is limited to the owner's savings or profits or any other money they can borrow

- The owner has sole responsibility for debts – if they do fall into financial difficulties they may have to sell their own personal possessions to meet the business debts

- Responsibility for a range of expertise falls upon the shoulders of the one person which runs the business. So in other words they are responsible for running the business – dealing with paperwork, customers, filling in tax returns and dealing with day-to-day contact with employees or sub-contractors they might use

- The success of the business is always dependent on how hard the sole trader wishes to work

- Any unforeseen accident or illness could seriously affect the business since all responsibilities rest on the shoulders of the one person

Individual activity

Using the local newspaper and *Yellow Pages*, try to identify at least a dozen sole traders. What kind of occupations are they in? Do you know any sole traders? Or do you regularly buy products or services from sole traders? Do they offer a valuable personal service despite the fact they may be more expensive than larger organisations? Compare your opinions with the rest of your group.

The partnership

To overcome the problems a sole trader may have in raising capital, they may enter into a partnership. This can be between two and 20 people who set up in business together and share the responsibilities for that business. Each partner is required to contribute some capital and they share out the profits and the losses between each of the partners. The control of the business is the responsibility of all the partners and decisions made by one partner are always binding on the others.

In partnerships, though, all partners have what is known as unlimited liability. This means that any debts incurred by the company have to be met by all the partners.

Individuals enter into a partnership with one another without any real formal written agreement, but in practice it is usually the case that they would draw up a partnership agreement. Essentially this is a set of rules which will hopefully help avoid disagreements between the partners (Fig 1.4).

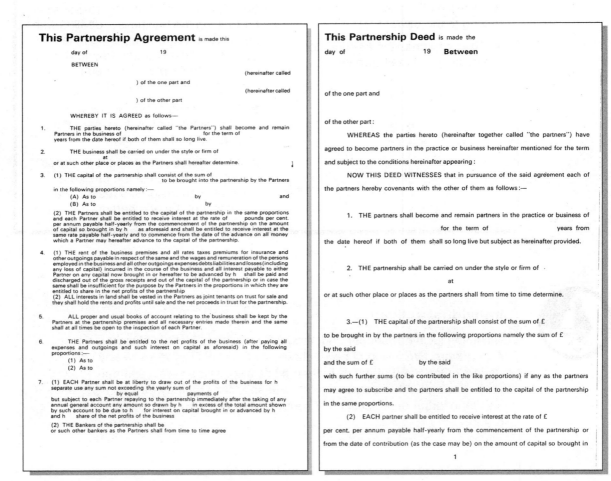

Fig 1.4 A partnership agreement and partnership deed
(Courtesy of the Solicitor's Law Stationery Society plc)

Items usually included in a partnership agreement

- The amount of capital that is to be contributed by each partner

- The ratio in which the profits and losses are to be shared, usually worked out in relation to the amount of capital each partner has put in. So, in other words, the more capital each partner has put in, the more profits they will be entitled to

- The salaries, if there are any, to be paid to specific partners

- Rules for admitting and expelling partners

- Voting rights, where partners have either an equal or unequal share of the decision making

- The rules which will end the partnership

On the question of limited liability, there is an option that allows a partnership to have limited liability for some members of the partnership – this is known as a limited partnership.

In this case a partnership is set up where some partners are known as sleeping partners. They take no part whatsoever in the decision-making process of the business, and should the business fail they stand to loose no more than their original investment in the business. Therefore, they have a limited liability.

In contrast, the others, known as the general partners, still face unlimited liability. In law there must always be at least one partner with unlimited liability.

The most common form of partnership though, is the ordinary partnership where all partners play an active role in the running of the business. In the event of losses being incurred, each partner has unlimited liability.

It is very important when setting up a partnership where unlimited liability is a factor that the other partners are trustworthy, hardworking and honest. Otherwise the mistakes made by one partner can financially affect all the others.

The most common sorts of partnerships are found in the accounting and legal professions, where specialists will join together in a partnership to make the business more attractive to prospective clients.

There are a number of advantages and disadvantages in setting up a partnership.

Advantages and disadvantages of a partnership

Advantages	Disadvantages
■ As we have said earlier, the capital is more easily raised because each partner can pool their resources and have access to more capital	■ A partner is personally liable for all of the firm's debts
■ Partners can share their expertise and their efforts	■ Disagreements can arise between partners about the amount of effort each puts in

Advantages	*Disadvantages*
■ Partners can arrange to cover one another at times of illness or holidays, or even lunch breaks	■ Partnerships can only raise limited amounts of capital when compared to businesses like limited companies, which will be looked at later
■ A partnership, like a sole trader, has the advantage of not having to publish its accounts or have them audited by anybody	■ Decision making can be slow since all partners have to be consulted
■ Additional capital can be raised by introducing more partners to the actual partnership	■ The death or retirement of a member can bring a partnership to an end if that is written into the deed of partnership

Individual activity

Using the same sources of information, identify 10 partnerships in your local area. Which occupational groups do these belong in? What advantages do they have over sole traders? If you were starting a business, what kind of qualities would you be looking for in partners? Compare the list qualities with another member of the group who is interested in a similar business occupation.

The Limited Company

The Limited Company is rapidly becoming one of the most common forms of business organisation.

A limited company is a separate organisation in law from its shareholders and Directors.

As with a partnership, individuals – known as shareholders – provide capital for the business; and they own part of the business and will share any profits which are earned.

They elect a number of directors who will actually run the business on their behalf.

The law requires a meeting of shareholders once a year, and minuting of things that may be called is required. Shareholders really play little part in the day-to-day running of the business; however, they may also be directors.

A number of Companies Acts have been passed over the years which protect the interests of shareholders, and indeed creditors who are owed money by limited companies.

In order to set up a limited company two documents must be drawn up.

The first is known as a Memorandum of Association. This is really the company's rule book. The kinds of thing that are in a memorandum of association are:

- *The name of the company*
- *The address of the registered office*
- *The company's activities*
- *The type and amount of capital which has been invested to set the company up*

The second step is to draw up what is known as The Articles of Association. This deals with the inside working of the company. It details the following:

1 The procedures that have to be followed at an Annual General Meeting, known as an AGM

2 The duties of the Directors of the company

3 The voting rights of the shareholders

4 How profits and losses are distributed amongst shareholders

5 Details of how accounts will be kept and recorded

6 Details of how company officers will be appointed

7 The rules and procedures of issuing shares and transferring shares to other people.

Once these two documents have been written up the next step is to send them to Companies House. If everything is in order, the Registrar of Companies will issue a Certificate of Incorporation, which in effect is like a Birth Certificate.

It is relatively simple and reasonably cheap to set up a company.

There are essentially two different types of limited company. Both of them, though, have a minimum of two shareholders. The first is known as a Private Limited Company.

A company is a private limited company when the word 'Limited' or 'Ltd' is written after the company name.

The shares in a private limited company are not freely available to the general public and the transfer of shares are agreed only by the Directors. It is usually the case that private limited companies are family concerns, or were originally.

This is the form of organisation often chosen when a sole trader wants to expand, or wishes to remain in control of the company.

The second type of limited company is a Public Limited Company. These tend to be larger concerns.

They are allowed to raise capital through selling their shares on the stock exchange. This enables them to have greater flexibility in terms of raising capital.

Only two people are needed to form a limited company, and there is no stated number of maximum shareholders.

The process of becoming a public company is very similar to that of becoming a private company. Once a public company has received its Certificate of Incorporation it will prepare a prospectus, which is basically an invitation to the public to buy shares. How those shares are sold is then decided, and how many shares will be allocated to each prospective buyer is also decided.

WOOLWORTHS

One of the UK's longest established and still most favoured variety store chains, Woolworths has been revitalised over the last decade. It is the high street market leader in confectionery, toys, Christmas decorations, gift wrap, greetings cards, chart music and pre-recorded videos.

Woolworths posted another excellent all-round performance. Profits were up 13.3%, again achieved from reduced selling space.

The VAT increase took its toll in the early part of the year but did not prevent Woolworths reporting a first half profit for the first time in a decade. All key product groups made sound sales and market share gains. There was a particularly strong final quarter performance from entertainment (up 11% over the year) and throughout the year from kidswear and confectionery. Sales in both were up by 8%.

There were five store openings, most in city centres. Stores continued to be refurbished as part of a major investment programme aimed at creating a friendly, spacious and comfortable ambiance in the stores.

Productivity gains were once again a keynote of Woolworths' performance. The year saw a much more effective advertising and promotional spend, based on more precise targeting of customer groups. An increase of 5% in sales per sq ft saw space productivity continuing to rise, alongside reductions both in overall selling space and in linear footage within new, more open-style stores. Gardening recorded a healthy 13% gain in sales per sq ft.

Sales per employee again rose as Woolworths reaped rewards from its highly committed approach to developing its 27,000-strong workforce.

The commercial development training programme, aimed at improving the skills of the company's buying and marketing teams, won a National Training Award for excellence.

There were also significant improvements in cost control, cash flow monitoring and control of working capital together with further efforts to restructure and simplify all elements in the supply chain. These were designed not only to enhance the system's capability to handle current demand – especially seasonal variations – but also to handle consistently high volume all year round.

Woolworths is working ever more closely with its suppliers to improve productivity. New efforts are being made to speed up every aspect of response to customer demand – ordering, manufacture and delivery – using information gathered by increasingly accurate stock monitoring systems.

Thanks to such systems, the distribution element too has been able to achieve significant productivity advances. It is now focused on just two major warehousing facilities all year round. Woolworths became the first retailer to reach the British Standard Institution's BS5750 quality standard in distribution.

The company continued to build on its considerable success in establishing specialist ranges – such as the immensely popular Ladybird brand of children's clothing – and to match this with efforts to promote cross-purchasing between the different product areas.

Woolworths – a division of Kingfisher plc. This retail operation may be found in most towns and cities in the UK

The Registrar of Companies will then issue a Trading Certificate. This means that the business is now up and running.

One thing in common with both types of limited company is that they must file a set of audited accounts with the Registrar of Companies. Within this set of accounts they will include:

- *A Directors' Report*
- *An Auditor's Report*
- *A Balance Sheet*
- *The source of application of funds*
- *An explanation of the accounts*

(*See* Fig 1.5.)

Consolidated Profit and Loss Account

For the year ended 31 March	Note	1992 £M	1991 £M
Turnover	2	1082	1042
Less net operating costs and expenses	3	754	703
Operating profit	2	328	339
Less research and development not specifically recoverable directly from customers		50	34
		278	305
Income from associated undertakings		2	2
		280	307
Less financial charges	6	119	151
Profit on ordinary activities before tax		161	156
Tax on profit on ordinary activities	7	15	17
Profit on ordinary activities after tax		146	139
Profit attributable to minority interests		3	3
Profit for the financial year		143	136
Dividends	8	52	50
Retained profit for the year		91	86

Statement of retained profit/reserves

	Profit and loss account	Exchange differences
Balance at the beginning of the year	521	2
Profit retained for the year	91	—
Exchange differences	—	—
Balance at the end of the year	612	2

Fig 1.5 BNFL's consolidated profit and loss account

These items are dealt with later.

It is also necessary for a limited company to file an Annual Return. This gives the details of the Directors, shareholders and any other information that is actually required by law. All this information is kept on file at Companies House, and is always open to inspection by members of the public for a small fee.

There are a number of advantages and disadvantages in setting up a limited company.

Advantages and disadvantages of a limited company

Advantages

- Shareholders have limited liability

- It is easier to raise capital through shares

- It is often easier to raise finance from the bank

- It becomes possible to operate on a larger scale since when additional capital is required, additional shares are offered

- It is possible to employ specialists

- Suppliers tend to feel a bit more comfortable in trading with legally established organisations

- Directors are not liable providing they follow the rules

- It is easy to pass a company down from one generation to another by passing on the shares

- The company name is protected by law

- There are tax advantages attached to giving shares to employees

- A company pension scheme can give better benefits when compared to those available for the self-employed

- The ill health of shareholders does not affect the running of the business

Disadvantages

- The formation and running costs of a Limited Company can be expensive

- Decisions tend to be slow since there are a number of people involved

- Employees and the shareholders are actually distanced from one another

- All the affairs of the company are public, with the audited accounts and annual returns which the company makes being produced

- Legal restrictions are fairly tight with the various Companies Acts and there are very heavy penalties for companies which break the rules

- Large companies are often accused of being impersonal to work for and to deal with

- Rate of tax on profits are often higher than sole traders and partnerships have to pay

Group activity

In pairs, one person taking PLCs and the other taking Ltds, list the main advantages. Take just five minutes to do this, then together try to agree which has the most advantages. If you agree that PLCs are better than Ltds, think about why some companies remain Ltds. If you think that Ltds are better than PLCs, why do some companies bother to become PLCs?

Co-operatives

Co-operatives are an increasingly popular type of business organisation.

In the past Co-operatives were only found in agriculture or retailing. One of the biggest areas of growth in co-operatives has been in services and in small-scale manufacturing.

Fig 1.6 A Co-op Superstore

A co-operative means that all the people that are part of that organisation join together to make decisions, share the work and also share the profits.

The first successful co-operative was the retail Co-operative. It was set up at the end of the last century in Rochdale when weavers joined together to start their own shop selling basic grocery items. Their profits were shared as was the amount of money that they spent, and everyone had an equal say on how the shop was run.

The basic idea behind the Rochdale Co-op is still to be seen in the high streets today with the Co-ops which are found throughout the country.

Nowadays, the Co-ops are registered as limited liability companies although the basic ideas still stand.

Another major area for co-operatives is in production, whether it is manufacturing or food production. In this type of organisation all the members share the responsibility for the success or the failure of the business and work together, making decisions together and taking a share of the profits.

These co-operatives do suffer from a number of problems:

1 They often find it difficult to raise capital from banks and other bodies because co-operatives are not just in business to make a profit

2 The larger co-operatives have discovered that they must set up a solid management structure in order that decisions can be made.

   In food production, several farmers will set up what is known as a marketing co-operative, where each farmer takes responsibility for a particular part of the production of a food, whether it is packaging, distribution or advertising.

Individual activity

Research the local business community, excluding Co-operative retail stores, try to identify at least another five. What kind of business activity are they involved in? Why do you think they have chosen to become a co-operative?

The franchise

The Franchise is a form of organisation which has been imported into the UK and the rest of the world from America, where over a third of all retail businesses are operating on what is known as a franchise agreement (or franchisee). Again, this is becoming a very popular form of business organisation in the UK.

Franchising really amounts to hiring out or licensing the use of product lines to other companies. A Franchise Agreement allows another company to trade in a particular name in a particular area.

The person that takes out the franchise needs a sum of money for capital and is issued with a certificate from the franchising company.

The firm which sells the franchise is known as the Franchisor.

The person which is buying the franchise is known as the Franchisee.

The franchisee usually has the sole right of operating in a particular area.

Some examples of franchises can be seen in many high streets – Fastframe, Pizza Hut, Prontaprint, Body Shop and Spud U Like.

Fig 1.7 A Fastframe franchise

Another important feature of the franchise agreement is that the franchisee agrees to buy all of its supplies from the franchisor who makes a profit on these supplies.

The franchisor also takes a share of the profits that the business makes, without having to risk any capital or be involved in the day-to-day management of the business.

The franchisee, on the other hand, does benefit from trading under a well-known name and enjoys a local monopoly. In other words they are the only business to operate under that name in that area.

The Franchise Agreement allows people to become their own boss without the normal kind of risks of setting up a business from scratch.

Individual activity

Franchises have become a very popular way of starting a new business quickly. How many franchises can you find in your local business community? Using research methods, where would you find details concerning franchises? If possible, obtain a brochure and application for the setting up of a franchise. How much money, on average, would you need to buy a franchise operation?

Charities

These organisations are often called non-profit making organisations in the sense that their sole purpose is not to provide a profit for the shareholders or owners. Many charities do indeed make a profit, but this is channelled to whichever deserving cause they represent.

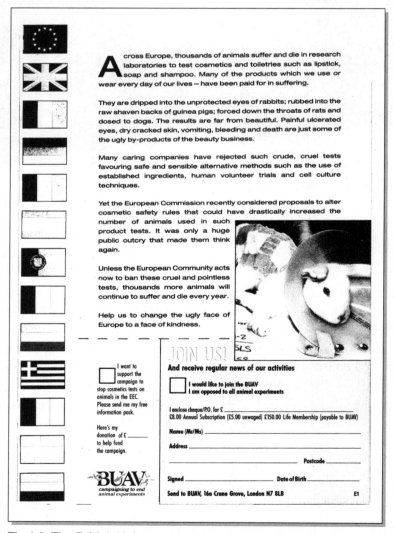

Fig 1.8 The British Union for the Abolition of Vivisection is a registered charity

An organisation with a 'charitable status' is exempt from many of the legal obligations of a normal organisation. This is not to say that they must not comply with such things as health and safety or contracts of employment, but that any profits they make are not taxable.

In recent times, in addition to the standard charities like Dr Barnados, Oxfam and Help the Aged, many schools have adopted this form of organisation.

Individual activity

Identify five major national charities which operate in your area, then find five local charities. How do they differ? Which part of the community benefits from the operations of these charities?

We have now looked at the main types of business organisation but there are a number of others which are worth mentioning.

Multinational

Most people will have heard of this term, examples of which are McDonald's and Woolworths.

These are private sector companies which have got divisions or subsidiary companies in various countries. They may well be PLCs.

Multiple

These are usually found within retailing, where a chain of businesses can be found in numerous high streets, stores or branches across the country.

Nationalised

Nationalised Industries are state owned like British Coal and British Rail

Many other businesses were nationalised industries in the past and have been privatised by the Conservative Government and are now public limited companies.

Another type of nationalised industry is known as a Public Corporation. These are large operations like the Energy industries which are now in the process of being privatised.

Perhaps the strangest form of business organisation is known as a Quango. (quasi autonomous non-governmental organisation). These are organisations which have been set up by the Government to carry out a specific task. In other words, they have been set up to take responsibility for a certain area of the Government's business. A good example is The Equal Opportunities Commission.

Individual activity

Identify three examples of a Quango. Why do you think Quangos exist? Why are their activities not operated by the Government directly? Are there any multinationals operating in your area? Find out where their head offices are located.

THE PUBLIC SECTOR

There is a vast range of Public Sector organisations, with an equally vast range of objectives.

Three main areas are:

■ *The Government*

■ *People who operate and work in the public sector, and*

■ *How they relate to the public*

The Government is very deeply involved in the business life of this country, as indeed are Governments throughout the world.

Depending upon the kind of policies that governments adopt, the prosperity of the country, which is measured by the success of the businesses in that country, can either be helped or hindered. The influence of the Government is far-reaching. Increases in Government expenditure or the creation of controls over businesses, or, indeed, support for business in a particular area, can have a marked affect.

The Government has the means to create wide-scale changes in business activity. Here are some examples:

1 If the Government increased interest rates this would reduce the general level of spending in the economy, and at the same time it would make it difficult for businesses which have borrowed money to finance projects

2 When the Government gives the contract to one firm rather than another, it can make the future of the business very secure, or indeed destroy its possibility of surviving

3 If the Government reduced personal taxes, this may, in fact, prove to be beneficial. The more money a person takes home, the more inclined that person is to work harder. This is known as increasing productivity

4 If the Government reduced taxes on a particular product, for example lead-free petrol, this could affect demand for that product. This in turn could lead to changes in how the product is supplied since the supply would need to be increased to match the increased demand.

The Government plays a massive role in the economy in general. Here are some examples:

1   Some particular goods and services are actually provided by the Government because it is felt that every single person is entitled to that product or that service. A good example is health or education

2   Some goods or services from which everyone benefits can only be produced by the Government if they are actually going to be provided for properly. A good example is the Police.

3   The Government is interested in reducing inequality. This could mean that people who are relatively well-off pay a higher tax. This in turn generates money to give to those who are less well-off. The alternative is that many people think inequality is a good thing as it is an incentive for people to help themselves. Any increases in taxation, of course, will mean that those earning higher salaries are taxed higher, and in turn may be less motivated

4   The Government needs to make sure that the economic system as a whole is running well. It will pass laws to protect consumers or to prevent companies from controlling particular goods or services. It will take measures against polluters or those involved in anti-social behaviour.

In other words the Government really sets the rules by which all businesses must comply.

Over time, as situations change, the Government finds itself required to make amendments to the rules. How to they change? Who loses and who benefits when they change? This will be dealt with later.

Group activity

In pairs, consider the following problems:

1   What would the Government do if a company produced a product which was harmful to the public?

2   What would the Government do if a company was found to be deliberately polluting a river?

3   What would the Government do if a particular area of the country was suffering from a very high level of unemployment?

Public Enterprises

When thinking about the Government, Downing Street, The Houses of Parliament and Whitehall come to mind. Although these are important and are examples of the Government, in action, parts of the Government, or at least organisations which are controlled by the Government in some way, are known as Public Enterprises, or Public Corporations. Here are some examples:

- *British Rail*
- *British Coal*
- *The Bank of England*
- *The Post Office*

Since 1979, however, many public corporations have been privatised. Examples of these are:

- *British Telecom*
- *British Gas*
- *Electricity generation*

But why did the Government get involved in running these organisations in the first place? Here are some examples:

1 One of the main reasons is to avoid waste and duplication. In the past many services have been offered by different companies. Essentially they were offering the same thing. For example, in the past, private railways ran similar services from the same towns, often having lines running parallel to one another

2 Many of these organisations offer services which could not be run profitably. The big debate here is would a private company invest in supplying gas or electricity or water to a remote village when even in the long term it would not be able to make a profit?

3 The larger the organisation the more benefits there are in terms of production. Organisations which produce lots of output are able to buy their raw materials cheaper, their labour can be more concentrated and consequently their prices can be lower

4 The Government is always interested in the level of employment. In setting up a public corporation the Government might be taking this into consideration. Good examples are Tax Offices and Social Security Offices, where vast head-quarters have been set up in relatively remote areas of the country that are suffering high unemployment

5 One of the biggest arguments in favour of public corporations is that the Government needs to control the vital basic goods and services that every-body needs. This is known as the infrastructure. This includes the transport network, water and energy. It is argued that the Government has a responsi-bility to make sure that this is supervised and maintained well.

The process of privatisation which turns these public corporations into com-panies owned by shareholders is carrying on apace and is sure to step up in the 1990s.

Ever since 1979 the process of privatisation has been continuing at a pace.

There are two reasons for this privatisation process:

1 Many people argue that state-run businesses are not very efficient, perhaps because they have no competition, and they never have a threat of going bankrupt because the Government will always bail them out

2   It is believed that as many people as possible should have shares in busi-
    nesses. The idea is that everyone, no matter how rich or poor, should be
    encouraged to buy a few hundred pounds worth of shares in major enter-
    prises like British Telecom. And indeed they have.

As privatisation rolls into areas which have not been affected so far, such as the
National Health Service, where Trust status is almost another word for privatisation, there have been considerable worries. Competition itself in areas such as
health can often lead to cost-cutting policies which will only mean the deterioration of standards.

One of the major arguments against privatisation is the debate whether it is right
to sell people's shares in industries which are already owned by them. The
theory behind this is that if the Government is representative of the people of the
country and runs services for the people then those services are owned by the
people, since they are state owned.

One of the ways of safeguarding the running of a public corporation is to set up
an independent body which keeps an eye on it. This organisation copes with
complaints which are made against the enterprise and tackles the enterprise
should it wish to put up prices or cut services.

Although these public corporations operate independently, they are controlled to
some extent by Government at all times. It is the Government's responsibility to
make decisions about closing down parts of the business or investing large sums
of money to improve it.

On a day-to-day basis the Chairperson of the enterprise and the other managers
will make decisions about wages, prices and industrial relations, but the
Government does still interfere when these areas affect the public.

We have seen that a limited company needs to make an annual report to its
shareholders. So too does a public corporation, but it presents its annual report
to the Government Minister responsible for taking care of it. This Government
Minister makes a report in Parliament to the Members, who will then make criticisms or support the corporation and how it is being run. At the same time a
Committee made up of Members of Parliament meets on a regular basis to keep
an eye on the day-to-day running of the corporation and reports back to
Parliament on how it is being operated. This is known as a Select Committee.

In addition to public corporations, there are two other areas in which the
Government gets involved in the business world. The first is when an activity is
actually run by a Government Department. A typical example of this is Customs
and Excise, which deals with the supervision and collection of taxes due to products entering and leaving the country.

The second area is where the Government has a shareholding in a public
company.

Perhaps the most common form of Government organisation is one which
touches our lives the most, and this is Local Government. In the UK certain
services are run by locally elected councillors. These Councils usually run business organisations such as swimming pools, sports centres, bus services, car
parks, shopping centres and public conveniences.

Just like public corporations, Local Council activities have also been affected by privatisation. The particular process that is used in this respect is that of Tendering.

The Local Council details the service which it wishes to offer for tender. Companies interested in running the service put sealed bids into the Council explaining what it would cost to run the service and what they would be providing. The company that offers the lowest tender is given the job. It is then the Council's responsibility to monitor how effective the company is in providing the service. If a company fails to reach certain standards then the contract is taken away from it. Local Government pays for this by receiving a grant direct from Central Government and by collecting local taxes. These are variously known as Rates, Community Charge (Poll Tax) and Council Tax.

The Local Council also subsidises loss-making activities such as parks and leisure centres which obviously provide benefits to the community.

Group activity

In pairs, try to answer the following questions:

1 What is meant by nationalisation?

2 What is meant by privatisation?

Identify four public corporations and four recently privatised corporations.

In the role of a group of people who use a local swimming pool on a regular basis, try to decide whether it would be good or bad for you, as users, if the swimming pool were to be privatised.

The government and public sector organisations

There is always a conflict in the relationship between the Government and the managers of public sector organisations. The Government has one set of objectives and the organisation might have another. The Government usually states its objectives to public organisations in terms of providing a good service. The Government may see its job as cutting costs. It also may have other reasons for demanding that the service be run in a particular way. For example, there may be an election soon.

Public sector organisations, just like any other, are interested in survival, expansion and efficiency. It may not always be possible to reach these three main targets. The bottom line is often that the service should give value for money. When public sector organisations have been starved of investment, as many claim nowadays, the managers of these organisations find it very difficult to offer an efficient value for money service.

Group activity

Do you think that prisons should be directly controlled by the Government, or privatised? Discuss this in pairs and decide whether you agree or disagree.

As a second task, try to agree with what is meant by the term 'Municipal Enterprise'. Try to give at least three examples of a Municipal Enterprise.

TYPES OF INDUSTRY AND INDUSTRIAL SECTORS

All types of organisation which actually produce something are also known as industry.

Industry comprises all those organisations which make things or produce raw materials, but they also include banking, insurance and retailing.

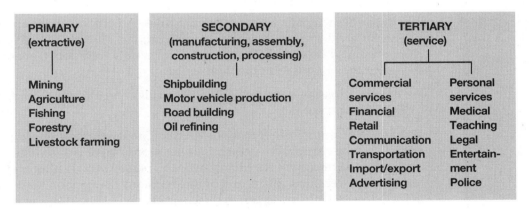

Fig 1.9 Types of production

The Government splits different sorts of organisation into 111 different types, which go under three categories.

The first is known as Primary. These industries are concerned with producing raw materials. They include agriculture, fisheries, forestry and mining.

The second major group is known as Secondary. These industries are concerned with the manufacturing or processing of products. These include car making, food processing and iron and steel working.

The third group is known as tertiary. These include service industries which do not actually produce the goods, but sell them.

The tertiary group is commonly known as the Service Sector. In this category are included banking, all of the retailing and distribution businesses and tourism.

Characteristics of organisations

Every organisation has eight main characteristics. Some are more obvious than others.

The first is that all organisations have a name. Some of these names are protected by law, others are simply the name of the person who actually runs or owns the business.

The second characteristic is that of having objectives. Some businesses are purely interested in profit whereas other organisations may be interested in providing a service or perhaps information.

The third characteristic is that of having rules. All organisations are governed to a lesser or greater extent by rules and regulations. They do not have to be written rules, they may be verbal. They may be just purely tradition. Generally speaking, the larger the organisation the more rules.

An organisation can develop both its own rules and also those imposed upon it by the Government.

The fourth characteristic is that of structure. Most organisations have what is known as a hierarchical structure, in other words there is a definite chain of command. At the top of the hierarchy is the person who is ultimately responsible for all of the decisions. But many of the decisions that person makes have been delegated to people lower down the chain. We will look at this in more detail in the section, Structure, resources and communications, in Element 2.1.

The fifth characteristic is related to the fourth because within every organisation someone has a particular role to fulfil. In smaller organisations one person may have many roles, but in a larger organisation people tend to be more specialised.

The sixth is that all organisations have a particular chain of authority. This means that someone ultimately has the right to make a decision and expect it to be carried out by those lower down in the chain of authority.

The seventh is that of power. Some individuals within an organisation have a legal right to take decisions. This could be a Director or perhaps shareholders. In the case of public corporations, this is ultimately the Government.

The eighth is that of maintaining records. All organisations have to have some record of what they have actually done. This can range from audited accounts and company reports to simply taking minutes of a particular meeting. Some of these are legal requirements and others are not.

Individual activity

Do you think that all organisations are willing and able to fulfil the eight points above? In the role of Managing Director of an organisation, which of the eight would you be particularly concerned with? Are there any that you would think are difficult to achieve?

BUSINESS ACTIVITY

Now that the purposes and types of organisation have been considered and which sector each belongs to identified, we should now look at the exact nature of organisations' business activities.

Essentially, these fall into six major categories:

- *Transport*
- *Distribution*
- *Retail*

- *Wholesale*
- *Manufacturing*
- *Service*

It should be noted that although there are six different areas of business activity, in most cases they are all interdependent. In other words, a manufacturing industry relies on transport and distribution organisations to convey both raw materials and finished goods to a wholesaler, who will then sell the goods on to a retailer. All of these organisations may require the expertise of a service industry, perhaps a cleaning company or computer software designer, advertising agencies or legal advice from a solicitor.

Group activity

In groups of three, try to decide which of the above types of business activity is the biggest. Which of the above do you think employs the most people? Which generates the most money? Which is the most important to the region in which you live?

Let us now consider the six categories in more detail.

Transport

Most organisations, particularly manufacturing ones, rely on transport and distribution to move their raw materials and finished goods around the country or even the world. Exactly how the organisation's goods and materials are transported, depends on a number of key factors.

The type of goods or materials involved:

- *What is the size of the goods or materials concerned?*
- *What is the weight of the goods or materials concerned?*
- *Are the goods or materials perishable?*
- *What is the value of the goods or materials concerned?*
- *Does the nature of the goods or materials restrict the mode of transport?*

The distance the goods or materials will have to travel:

- *Is the destination local?*
- *Is the destination regional?*
- *Is the destination national?*
- *Is the destination within Europe?*
- *Is the destination international?*

The urgency of delivery of the goods or materials involved:

- *Is the delivery required immediately?*
- *Is the delivery required on the same day?*
- *Is the delivery required by the next day?*
- *Is the delivery required within a week?*
- *Is the delivery required within a month?*

The alternative costs of transport for the goods or materials involved:

- *Is it cheaper for the manufacturers themselves to deliver the goods or materials?*
- *Does the manufacturer have a regular external delivery service?*
- *Will the goods or materials have to travel by air?*
- *Will the goods or materials have to travel by boat?*
- *Will the goods or materials have to travel by rail?*
- *Will the goods or materials have to travel by road?*
- *Can the goods or materials be delivered by hand?*
- *Can the goods or materials be delivered by messenger?*

The travel preferences of the customer:

- *Has the customer got an approved and recommended mode of transport in mind?*

- *Would the customer be concerned if a particular carrier were used?*
- *Has the customer had a previously bad experience with a particular form of transport?*
- *Will the choice of transport depend on where the customer would like delivery to be made?*

Individual activity

In the role of Transport and Distribution Manager, list any resources which you think would be vital in order to carry out the job. What sort of resources would be needed readily to hand?

In pairs, discuss how the Euro Tunnel will affect the various types of transportation to and from the UK.

Although there is a wide variety of different types of transportation system, they essentially come within three main methods: land, sea and air. Let us look at these in more detail:

Land

In the UK, land transport is mostly by road. At present, lorries are restricted to 38 tonnes. However, the Government has recently agreed to fall in line with European standards and allow lorries to carry 44 tonnes. This will be restricted, however, to transporting goods and materials from one rail system to another. Road transport is often seen as more useful to the manufacturer and the customer as goods and materials can be delivered door to door. Another distinct advantage is that lorries and other vehicles carry the logo of the transportation company or manufacturing organisation around the country (Fig 1.10). Increasingly, the strain upon our road network is leading to evermore serious traffic congestion, accidents and long delays. All of these, and our unpredictable weather, add a great deal of cost to transport. It has been estimated that poor road networks and congestion alone costs UK businesses some £15 billion per year!

Fig 1.10a Use of transportation company's logo on a vehicle

In order to ensure that drivers are not put under unnecessary strain they are restricted in the number of hours they can drive each day. For this reason, manufacturers tend to use road haulage companies. Imagine the costs of transporting goods or materials from London to Aberdeen and having the truck driver return with an empty container. Road haulage companies have the capacity to match up loads which need to travel to a particular destination with loads that have to come back to a point close to the starting point. Some vehicles are refrigerated in order to facilitate the transportation of perishable goods such as flowers and food. Once the goods or materials are in the refrigerated container they may remain safe whether the vehicle is travelling by road or being transported across the sea by a ferry or container ship.

Individual activity

Road haulage companies are dotted all over the UK. In which parts of the UK are there greater concentrations of road haulage companies? Why is this so?

Sea

The standard method of transporting goods and materials by sea is in a container. Basically, a container is a huge metal box which holds a variety of individual packing cases safely secured for the trip. This container can be lifted efficiently on and off ships and may be transferred to and from lorries on the dockside for the final leg of its journey. More specialised ships, such as oil tankers or coal steamers, are employed to carry these specific types of load (*See* Fig 1.10b).

Fig 1.10b One of BNFL's purpose-built ships for the transportation of spent nuclear fuel from overseas reactors

Individual activity

Transporting goods by sea is perhaps the slowest method for long distance. In the role of a buyer of electrical goods from the Far East, list the factors to be taken into consideration when deciding whether to transport televisions, stereo systems and refrigerators into the UK.

Air

Air transport is considerably more expensive than any other type of transportation. The two key factors here are weight and size of the goods or materials. These factors are much more crucial in the case of aircraft as they are severely limited in what they can carry. Air transport is ideal for goods and materials which need to be delivered quickly, or perhaps are of a perishable nature. Surprisingly, it is cheaper to insure goods or materials being transported by air than sea. This is because there is less danger of damage to the goods or materials in transit and handling.

Group activity

In pairs, research four major air freight carriers. If you required goods to be delivered to your local area via an airport, which airport is the most convenient for easy transit from the airport. Do any of these air freight carriers operate from your most local airport?

Fig 1.11 Use of transportation company's logo on an aircraft

Distribution

Before the transportation method can be decided, the manufacturer or supplier of raw materials needs to decide how to distribute their goods and materials. The ultimate goal, of course, is to get the goods or materials to the customer. This may be done in a number of different ways:

Wholesaler – retailer – customer

This is the most common method. This distribution system allows the manufacturer that produces goods and materials in bulk to distribute large quantities to a wholesaler. The wholesaler will 'house' or store sufficient quantities of the goods or materials to supply a number of retailers. These retailers in turn will then take smaller quantities in order to supply their customers directly.

Manufacturer – customer

Increasingly, manufacturers have recognised that there are much greater profits to be made by supplying to the customer directly. This, of course, takes out all of the 'middlemen' such as the wholesaler and retailer, who expect to take a profit for merely handling the goods or materials. The growth in the 'factory shop' method of distribution is seen as a very good way of disposing of overstocked items at reduced prices. Both the manufacturer and the customer benefit from this for obvious reasons.

Another system of manufacturer to customer distribution is mail order. Mail order purchasing has become popular and manufacturers see this as an ideal way of increasing sales as well as receiving much needed immediate cash, rather than relying on wholesalers or retailers which will expect favourable credit terms from the manufacturer. Some manufacturers have taken another step towards directly supplying the customer by opening retail outlets across the country.

Manufacturer – retailer

This distribution system effectively cuts out the need to use wholesalers. Some larger retail chains are, in effect, wholesalers and distributors themselves. They have hundreds of shops across the country and can buy in sufficient quantities to encourage the manufacturer to deal with them directly. Retail chains which fall into this category are all the major supermarkets and companies such as Dixons.

Fig 1.12 Retail chain stores

Manufacturer – wholesaler

A popular way of buying products is from a Cash and Carry outlet. In effect, these cash and carry outlets are wholesalers. They may sell to both the retailer and the customer, although, to some extent, there are restrictions upon who can buy from these outlets. In order to use a cash and carry, a customer needs an identity card which gives them the right to shop. These establishments have recognised that there is a large demand, even from customers, to buy in comparative bulk. Customers welcome the opportunity to buy in bulk for particular occasions, such as weddings, when they may spend on one particular visit several hundred pounds.

Manufacturer – specialist

This distribution system refers to manufacturers who supply specialist merchants catering for tradesmen. A builders merchant, for example, would supply a wide variety of different materials to plumbers, carpenters, electricians and bricklayers. Rather like a cash and carry, the ability to shop at a specialist merchant can be restricted. In most cases, the tradesman will have an account with the specialist merchant, and pay their bill on a monthly basis. This avoids the need to pay every time they visit the merchant.

Group activity

In pairs, consider the best method of getting the following products to the customer. Which route would you use – direct to the customer, via wholesalers, via specialist shops or a completely different route?

- Fresh salmon
- Tulip bulbs
- Bricks
- Computer disks
- Refrigerators

Retail

Retailing is all about selling goods, materials and services to the customer. The retailer is usually the last link in the distribution chain. There are some seven different sorts of retailer, these are:

- *Independent small retailers*
- *Multiples*
- *Co-operatives*
- *Department Stores*
- *Supermarkets and hypermarkets*
- *Mail order companies*
- *Vending machines*

Let us look at these in more detail:

Independent small retailers

These retailers are often sole traders. They are local and convenient and give personal attention to their customers, they will often know their customers' names. As they are working for themselves, they tend to open for long hours and offer a wide range of different goods and services. However, they may be comparatively expensive and only really offer a fairly limited range of goods. It would be difficult to buy in bulk as their stock levels are relatively low.

Multiples

These retailers, which often operate nationally, fall into two subcategories. The first are the multiples which offer a wide range of different goods from fashion to food (e.g. Marks and Spencer and Woolworths). The other category is the single-trade multiple. These traders tend to concentrate on a relatively specialist area of retailing. They may, for example, only sell electrical goods, e.g. Dixons. Or they may only sell clothes, e.g. C & A. The advantages of multiple traders is that they have a consistent image nationwide. The quality will be consistent in every shop in the chain. They can be relatively cheap as they have the opportunity to buy in bulk from manufacturers. Some customers do not favour multiples as there is less likelihood of receiving personal service and as they have bought in bulk the choice may be restricted. Other customers will never use multiples as they do not wish to be seen wearing or using a product that has been sold to thousands of other people (*See* Fig 1.13).

Fig 1.13 (Opposite) B & Q – part of Kingfisher plc – offers a wide variety of products and services to the home DIY market

Co-operatives

Co-operatives have been in existence for over 150 years and were originally set up to sell surplus production from a group of tradesmen who had joined together for this purpose. Retail co-operatives, to all intents and purposes, are very similar to supermarkets or hypermarkets, but offer the additional advantage of discounts in the form of trade stamps. These may be redeemed for goods.

Department stores

Whether the department store is a single-site independent outlet, or one of a chain of stores throughout the country (e.g. John Lewis Partnership) it will deal in a wide variety of goods. Department stores offer the advantage of being able to shop for many different items under the same roof. They are often very pleasant to shop in with additional services such as restaurants or coffee bars. Within the store are helpful and specialist staff, in-store demonstrations, credit facilities and special offers. Many of these stores will also offer free or reduced cost delivery services. The prices within a department store tend to be higher and the credit terms expensive and it is often the case that it is hard to find staff at all. Many customers will avoid department stores for these reasons and the fact that with such a bewildering variety of goods on offer, they are tempted to spend too much.

Supermarkets and hypermarkets

Over the past few years there has been a trend in retailing towards the massive out-of-town superstore. Here customers find relatively low prices, extended shopping hours and many special offers. Supermarkets and hypermarkets do not tend to offer a delivery service, and since the stores are not conveniently located, customers need their own transport. Some outlets have recognised this problem and lay on regular bus services to and from city centres. A customer tendency which is taken great advantage of is impulse buying. Although a customer may walk into the store with a shopping list, they may walk out with a shopping trolley full of goods they had not intended to buy. Supermarkets and hypermarkets always have long rows of cashier tills, despite this, many are not manned and queues are inevitable.

Another recent feature of supermarkets and hypermarkets is to offer an increasing range of customer services. Some have installed banking facilities, post offices, dry cleaners, coffee bars, shoe repairers, cigarette kiosks, hairdressers, petrol stations and small franchise outlets specialising in a variety of different goods. In effect, they have become shopping centres in their own right.

Mail order companies

As we mentioned earlier, mail order companies are taking an increasingly large part of the market in retailing. Mail order companies do not require expensive city-centre premises. They do not have to spend money on customer facilities such as parking or restaurants, and may often be located on unattractive industrial estates. Some mail order companies have begun to bridge the gap between strict mail order retailing and direct customer retailing by opening retail stores, e.g. Pastimes and Cosmetics To Go. The most popular form of mail order is via the enormous catalogues produced by such companies as Kays, Littlewoods, Great Universal Stores and Grattans.

Although we may not think of it as mail order retailing, operations such as Avon Cosmetics, Betterware and Oriflame supply by mail order via representatives who take their commission on the sales. An alternative form of mail order is direct selling, which involves a chain of distributors working on a part-time basis, who all share in the profits made from the sales of the product.

Vending machines

Soft drink machines, pool tables, arcade and fruit machines, confectionery and crisp machines, and hot drinks machines are a familiar sight. These machines are either run and owned by the site-owner or, in most cases, are owned and maintained by another organisation which pays the site-owner a percentage of the sales made from the machine. Organisations which supply and maintain these machines only need a mobile service and delivery operation as they have no direct contact with the customer at all. All the problems associated with these machines have to be dealt with, at least in the first instance, by the site-owner.

Wholesale

Wholesalers are basically 'middle men' between the manufacturer and the retailer or, in some cases, the customer. A wholesaler will offer or perform many of the following functions:

- *Buys in bulk from the manufacturer*
- *Sell smaller quantities to the retailer*
- *Predict potential demand*
- *Store sufficient goods or materials to cater for immediate demand*
- *Act as a bridge between manufacturers and small traders*
- *Give small traders the opportunity to buy goods and materials which they could not normally purchase direct from the manufacturer*
- *Offer a range of credit facilities*
- *Sort goods and materials into alternative packs sizes and grades*
- *Offer a local delivery service*

The traditional wholesaler is now in decline, as many retail outlets are either part of a multiple chain or buy their goods direct from the manufacturer. One of the main areas that still remains in the control of wholesalers is the import market where overseas companies prefer to deliver their goods to one location and rely on the import wholesaler to do the distribution for them.

Manufacturing

Manufacturers are involved in the transformation of raw materials and components to finished goods for the customer. In effect, manufacturers produce goods for either the consumer market or the industrial market. The former category relates to the following:

■ *Consumable goods – items used immediately, such as food and drink.*

■ *Consumer durable goods – items which have a longer life, such as refrigerators, dishwashers and washing machines.*

The second category, in which manufacturers produce for other organisations, covers such items as heavy goods vehicles, tractors, barrels of beer, components and in certain cases raw materials (coal, oil, paraffin and gas).

Many manufacturers offer a wide range of different goods. Sometimes this is a result of several smaller companies merging with one another to form a large organisation which can enjoy the benefits of mass production, distribution and purchasing power. Although they may sell their products to a variety of different markets, some of the essential raw materials and components are common for all.

Service

Most organisations use service organisations in the course of their business. In this respect, the term 'service' can refer to a multitude of different businesses. In fact, we can even say that retailing and wholesaling are service industries themselves. More commonly, service industries refer to the following:

■ *Advertising agencies*

■ *Communications specialists*

■ *Employment agencies*

■ *Export companies*

■ *Financial services*

■ *Import companies*

■ *Professionals such as solicitors, accountants, architects and surveyors*

The central feature of all service industries is that they provide some sort of assistance to organisations. They tend to be specialists in a particular area and can offer expertise which would otherwise be unavailable to the organisation from their existing workforce. In most cases, service industries are employed by organisations on a short-term basis, either for a particular project, or for a fixed period of time. In this way, the organisation does not have a long-term commitment to the service industry and may select an alternative company if it discovers the company not to be suitable.

Group activity

Working in pairs, identify three examples of organisation in your local area that fall into the following categories:

- Independent small retailers
- Multiples
- Co-operatives
- Department stores
- Supermarkets and hypermarkets
- Mail order companies
- Vending machine operators

Element assignment

LOCAL ORGANISATION REVIEW PROJECT

In groups of no more than three, research two local types of business organisation from different sectors of the economy.

Your research should include the following:

- The name of the organisation (including any trading or brand names)
- A list of the main types of business activity in which each company is involved
- A short history of each organisation
- The organisations' main sources of finance
- The comparative size of the organisations in terms of turnover etc.
- The number of employees in each organisation
- To which sectors of the economy each organisation belongs

The findings from your research should be presented as a 15-minute oral presentation to the remainder of your group (remember that presentations are much more interesting when visual aids are used – if you need assistance with this refer to Unit 4 of this book.

In addition to the oral presentation, you should prepare a two-page summary of the main points of research. This should take the form of a series of points which compare the purposes, activities and type of organisation and should be prepared using a word processor.

Potential sources of information

1 Direct contact with chosen companies

2 The local press

3 Local libraries

4 Local chamber of commerce or trade association

5 Personal contacts (i.e. family, friends of yourself or your colleagues)

UNIT TEST   Element 1.1

1 What is meant by the private sector of the economy?

2 What is meant by the term limited liability?

3 How is a partnership set up and run?

4 Give three major decision-makers of an organisation.

5 What is meant by franchising?

6 Why does the Government interfere in the running of the economy?

7 Who are the decision makers in a public corporation?

8 What is meant by the primary sector?

9 What is meant by the secondary sector?

10 What is meant by the tertiary sector?

11 What are the major differences between a planned economy and a free market economy?

12 Ignoring profit, give three other objectives of a private company.

13 What is meant by privatisation?

14 What is meant by nationalisation?

15 How does a wholesaler differ from a retailer?

16 Which transportation system is the cheaper in terms of insurance, sea or air. Why?

17 Identify three major differences between a private limited company and a public limited company.

18 Identify three advantages enjoyed by a partnership over a sole trader.

19 What is the difference between a multinational and an international organisation?

20 Give three advantages of being part of a co-operative organisation.

Element 1.2
Business organisations and products

PERFORMANCE CRITERIA

1 Reasons for the location of business organisations are explained
2 Scale and scope of business organisations are described
3 The product of business organisations is identified
4 Different markets are identified
5 New products which meet identified markets are proposed

RANGE

1 Reasons for location: natural resources, labour supply, local and national government incentives, proximity of other businesses, transport services
2 Scale: number of employees, market share
3 Scope: local, national multinational
4 Product: manufactured goods, services
5 Markets: needs, wants

EVIDENCE INDICATORS

Examples of three business organisations indicating their scale, scope, product of businesses and reasons for location. Proposals for two new products which would meet market needs. Evidence should demonstrate understanding of the implications of the range dimensions in relation to the element. The unit test will confirm the candidate's coverage of the range.

LOCATION OF BUSINESS ORGANISATIONS

Where an organisation chooses to establish its main site of operations can have long-term implications as to its success. The costs of establishing the head office or main factory can be very high, so before any decision is made a large number of factors need to be considered. The larger the organisation, the greater the potential pitfalls in setting up in the wrong place. A small business, which may only need relatively small premises, has more flexibility and the exact location is probably less crucial. Whereas almost any area would provide enough work for a small business offering services such as plumbing or electrical installation work, a larger business needs to consider the fact that they may have to cater for regional, national or international customers.

Some of the major factors a medium to large organisation would need to consider follow.

Transport and distribution

In situations where an organisation needs large amounts of bulky raw materials, it must consider being as close to the source of the raw materials as possible. Cities such as Sheffield have become a natural choice for manufacturers of steel and other metal works, due to the city's close proximity to the coal fields needed for smelting, and the quarries from which the metals are mined.

Fig 1.14 BNFL's purpose-built marine terminal at Barrow-in-Furness

Several ports have been the automatic choice of oil and gas industries for the construction of their rigs and the siting of their terminals as the main fields are located close to the coastline. Examples of these are Aberdeen and Great Yarmouth. Coastal towns have, of course, always been the ideal place for fishing industries as similarly many market towns have flourished close to main centres of agriculture.

In cases when it is more expensive to transport the finished product to the market than it is to transport the raw materials to the factory, organisations have established themselves nearer the market. A good example would be the production of food where an additional factor is the need to get the product to the market in its freshest state.

Group activity

In pairs, try to agree the ideal location in terms of transportation and distribution for the following organisations:

- A sand and ballast quarrying organisation
- A steel foundry
- A cotton mill
- An electrical components manufacturer

Availability of services

The five main services which nearly all industries require are:

- *Water*
- *Electricity*
- *Gas*
- *Drainage*
- *Waste disposal*

We can assume that other essential services such as telecommunications are available throughout the country. To a greater or lesser extent, each of the five main services are of importance to different industries. An industry which produces large amounts of waste would consider waste disposal the most important. A papermill, for example, uses vast amounts of water and would place considerable strain on the local water system if not carefully planned.

Group activity

In pairs, use the four types of organisation given in the previous activity and put the five main essential services in ranking order of importance for each organisation. Compare your list with those of your partner.

Government incentives

The Government is keen for organisations to establish themselves in areas of high unemployment. Some of these areas were previously the sites of now out-dated and unwanted types of industry. The Government offers a comprehensive package of incentives, often with the help and guidance of local authorities, to attract as many new businesses to the area as possible. Incentives might include financial assistance for relocation, low rents and rates and subsidised retraining programmes for the local population. There has been considerable argument over which cities, towns and regions are eligible for Government assistance.

Individual activity

Research your local area to determine whether there are any Government incentives for businesses to locate there.

Availability of labour

The availability of labour (workers) and skills is not evenly spread through the country. Certain areas, having been the site of out-dated industries, have considerable numbers of experienced workers who are available for work. In some cases, they may need additional training for new working practices, but the basic skills are there. If an organisation wishes to move large numbers of its existing workforce to a new location, this can prove to be extremely expensive (*see* the section, Housing, below). It is often the case that only key personnel are moved and the bulk of the new workforce are recruited locally.

Individual activity

Research and find a company which has relocated in your area within the last year. Why did it move to your area? What proportion of employees did it bring with it from its previous location?

Availability and cost of housing

One of the main blocks which prevent large numbers of workers from moving with the organisation to a new location is the cost and availability of housing in the new area. The regional differences in house prices and, indeed, the number of houses which are immediately vacant is enormous. The process of workers moving from one area to another is known as labour mobility. In times when it is hard to sell homes, or when house prices are very high, labour mobility is low.

Individual activity

Research the housing prices in your local area. What are the average prices for a two-bedroomed and three-bedroomed house? How do these prices compare to the national average? How do house prices in your town compare with those in your nearest large city?

Availability and cost of land or premises

The availability and cost of land will vary from region to region. Factors which affect the price of land will include such things as proximity to good road and rail networks, nearness to cities, towns or ports, or the general demand for land in the area. If the area is popular as a location for both housing and industry, land prices will be considerably higher. In cases where organisations move into existing premises, the costs are usually calculated on a square foot basis. This means that organisations with a need for extensive production line or warehousing space will be seeking premises with a low square footage price. On the other hand, offices or headquarters of organisations which may not need so much floor space are prepared to pay the higher prices which town or city centre premises attract.

When considering a potential site, an organisation must also consider the need to provide customer and employee parking space and the availability of adjacent vacant land for future expansion. In certain cases, the geological structure of the land itself may be unfit for the construction of high-rise or extremely heavy industrial buildings.

Individual activity

In the role of Managing Director of a company which wishes to relocate in your local area, research the availability of vacant land and existing premises. The organisation requires a minimum of 3,000 sq ft.

Communications

As we have mentioned, the proximity of roads, rail, ports, airports and towns and cities have been an increasingly important factor in the location of industry. Many organisations have established their headquarters in the South of England, where telecommunications and infrastructure (support services, housing, amenities, market and workforce) are more fully developed. At the same time, they have been forced to set up their factories in the North where the price of land is cheaper and they are closer to the raw materials and suppliers.

There have been moves recently, particularly with the building of new towns such as Milton Keynes, Telford and Peterborough, to offer a full range of infra-structure requirements while still being close to raw materials. To some extent this has been successful and has attracted a large number of organisations that would not have otherwise considered moving to these areas.

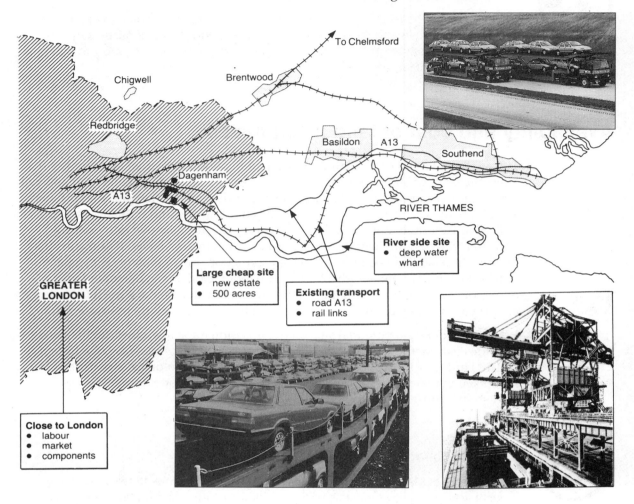

Fig 1.15 The location of the Ford plant at Dagenham

Individual activity

Prepare a brief report detailing the infrastructure of your immediate locality. This should include the following:

- Support services available

- Housing availability and average price

- Amenities available

- Whether the local market, in terms of potential sales, is healthy

- Whether there is an available pool of potential employees. These may not necessarily be experienced in one particular area of work

The environment and pollution

Certain industries are quite rightly considered to be undesirable for various reasons. They are, therefore, not usually established near local housing. Chemical plants may produce noxious fumes, other heavy industries may be very noisy and nuclear power stations or factories which produce weapons or ammunition are considered dangerous for obvious reasons. The memory of disasters such as Chernobyl in the Ukraine, or Three-Mile Island in the United States, where radiation leaks severely damaged the local population and environment, has led to the siting of these industries in remote areas.

Group activity

In pairs, look at a detailed map of the UK. Try to identify areas which are not close to major centres of population. These areas should have good communication links with the rest of the UK, but be relatively remote. You should also consider the immediate availability of a workforce. Where would you site a nuclear power station, or another organisation with potentially hazardous operations?

Location of organisation's other sites and competitors

It may be important to the organisation to establish a new factory or offices close to existing premises. Certain businesses rely on the regular inter-site communication and exchange of ideas and personnel to function efficiently. Equally, the proximity of similar types of businesses, perhaps competitors, may be an important feature in the decision-making process. London attracts the majority of financial institutions for this reason, among others. Other towns or cities may have similar attractions, such as Norwich, which has become a relatively important insurance centre.

Group activity

In groups of three, investigate a local business of your choice. This business should have a number of sites located either regionally or nationally. Why has it chosen to site its premises in this particular pattern? Are the premises convenient for easy communication? When you have located all of the premises – in the role of Development Manager for that organisation – plan the siting of three further premises. Take into account any of the criteria which you have discovered to be important as far as the organisation is concerned.

Present your findings and recommendations to the rest of your group.

Regional differences

Some industries are specific to one region only, maybe for the reasons previously mentioned. Each region has its own peculiarities and may have a reputation for being an established centre of excellence in its own field, e.g. Silicon Valley in California, USA. Not so crucial in the UK, but certainly important abroad, is the climate. This factor would particularly influence the processing of food and other products which may suffer from extreme weather conditions.

Group activity

In groups of four or five, investigate the regional specialities in your particular area. When you have identified your regional specialities, consider why they should be associated with your area, as opposed to another. How long have these specialities been associated with your area? Are they likely to continue in your area? Are there any other specialist organisations not presently operating in your area which could locate in the future?

Present your findings to your group.

Your presentation should include the use of visual aids and last approximately 15 minutes.

SCALE OF BUSINESSES

When we talk about the scale of the business, we are in fact referring to the size of the operation in terms of how much of the total market for a particular product or service the company dominates, and the number of people it employs. What this consideration does not address, is whether the organisation is profitable or, indeed, whether it is better in any way to its competitors.

It is impossible to compare two companies which offer goods and services to radically different markets. We must look at the market share and the nature of the employees in a little more detail.

Number of employees

Trying to assess the scale of an organisation in terms of the number of people it employs is a very dangerous thing to do. Being given crude figures such as total number of employees simply serves to cloud the reality of the situation. Employees may not necessarily be either full time or directly employed by the organisation.

The question is, do you count someone who pops in for a couple of hours a week to clean the staff kithcen? Or do you count a person who works on a part-time basis for a subsidiary company? Obviously, if you do, the number of employees will certainly look impressive. However, including all these additional members of staff proves in one way that you are not very efficient. Efficiency is often measured by comparing profit, turnover and number of employees and coming up with a figure which shows how much profit is generated from each employee. If you include all of these other people, then this figure will fall drastically.

Perhaps a more accurate way of determining the number of employees is to add up the total number of hours worked by all members of staff and divide it by the average working week. This will give (although a false figure) a slightly more accurate picture of the scale of operations (*See* Fig 1.16).

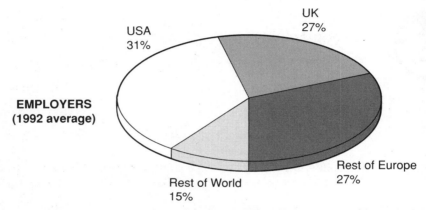

Fig 1.16 *A pie-chart showing the number of employees working for British Petroleum world-wide* (*Courtesy of BP*)

Group activity

As a group, contact your local Chamber of Commerce or Trade Association and try to obtain a detailed breakdown of the size of organisations within your local area. Having acquired this information, construct a bar chart showing the spread of employment throughout the area.

Market share

An organisation may claim to be the dominant force in a particular market. It may quote figures and statistics to back up its claim. In the final analysis, its evidence is only figures and statistics. They really do not prove anything. To say 'we have a 40 per cent market share' is meaningless if the true size of the market is not known. It is probably the case that no one knows the true size of the market; after all, we can only refer to the market as it is seen at the present. It does not include potential customers or customers who use products which are strictly outside of our definition of the market. For example, a soft drink manufacturer may claim a certain percentage share of the market. What the manufacturer is claiming is that it sells x number of cans and bottles of fizzy drink. The manufacturer is only comparing with like companies. In reality, soft drinks also compete with tea, coffee, ice-cream, hot chocolate, beers and alcoholic drinks.

On the question of comparing like with like, the other factor to consider is that markets themselves are different sizes. Again, the soft drinks market is a different size to the computer games market. It would be foolish to try to compare Coca-Cola with Sega. Although they may be market leaders in their own right, their turnover, profit and success nationally or internationally is entirely different. At the end of the day, we are probably talking about a difference of billions of pounds and not millions!

Group activity

In groups of three, investigate one of the following areas of business activity:

- Car production
- Frozen foods
- Sport and leisure wear manufacturers

- Breweries
- Soft drinks manufacturers
- Confectionery manufacturers

Try to identify the top 10 organisations engaged in one of these business activities. Organise your top 10 in ranking order in terms of market share.

Present your findings in a report format, written for an organisation which wishes to establish itself in the UK.

SCOPE OF BUSINESSES

The scope of businesses refers not necessarily to the internal elements of the organisation, but to where it actually operates. This list will include the following:

- *Local*
- *Regional*
- *National*
- *International*
- *Multinational*

These categories require a little more explanation.

Local

When a business is both based in and trades in a relatively immediate area, it can be called a local business. Typical examples are corner shops, local tradesmen and other small independent companies. Even though the majority of small business may be called 'local', this does not necessarily mean that they do all their business locally, it just means that they do the majority of it locally.

Regional

Organisations which offer an exclusive service, either in terms of products stocked or services offered, could be considered to be regional in nature. All that is meant by 'regional' is that customers are prepared to travel a reasonable distance in order to visit the premises. Companies which are the sole stockists of particular products will enjoy a regional status as a result.

The obvious alternative interpretation of the word 'regional' is a company which has a number of outlets within a particular county or city. These will often be independent traders which have grown over a number of years and have made logical moves to open stores or premises in towns or areas close to their existing sites. They may perhaps be unwilling to stray outside their regional area as they may consider themselves to be experts on local requirements.

Fig 1.17 Marks & Spencer have a 17 per cent market share of UK clothing sales. This accounts for nearly £2.5bn per year

National

We have already identified a number of national companies, which are also known as multiples. These organisations have gradually opened stores in most major concentrations of population and offer a similar range of products and services at all sites. The distinct advantage with a national company is that the customer knows that if they purchase goods or services from it they have the backing of a national organisation should they encounter any problems.

International

These organisations have premises in several different countries. The nature of work which each premises undertakes in the various countries is, of course, dependent on the nature of the organisation's type of business. In some cases a company may wish to have 'a presence' in a particular country for advisory and information purposes only. On the other hand, the organisation may actually be trading in several different countries. In this case, a version of the 'home organisation' exists which would include all the functions carried out by the 'parent' company. Some good examples of the latter are McDonald's, Burger King, Pizza Hut, Benetton and Marks and Spencer.

Multinational

You might think that a multinational is an international company. To some extent it is. The major difference is that a multinational company will actually produce goods and services in all, or most, of the countries that it operates in. Good examples of organisations which produce, on a massive scale, in various different countries, are Ford, General Motors, Mars and Nestlé/Rowntree. It is estimated that multinationals will account for nearly 50 per cent of the world's output of goods by the year 2000. This is even more significant if you consider that there are really only 250 multinationals of any major size (*See* Fig 1.18).

Group activity

In pairs, using the following list, try to identify at least five organisations from each of the categories. Do not use any of the examples which are mentioned above.

■ Local   ■ Regional   ■ National   ■ International   ■ Multinational

When you have completed this task, compare your list with those of the rest of the group.

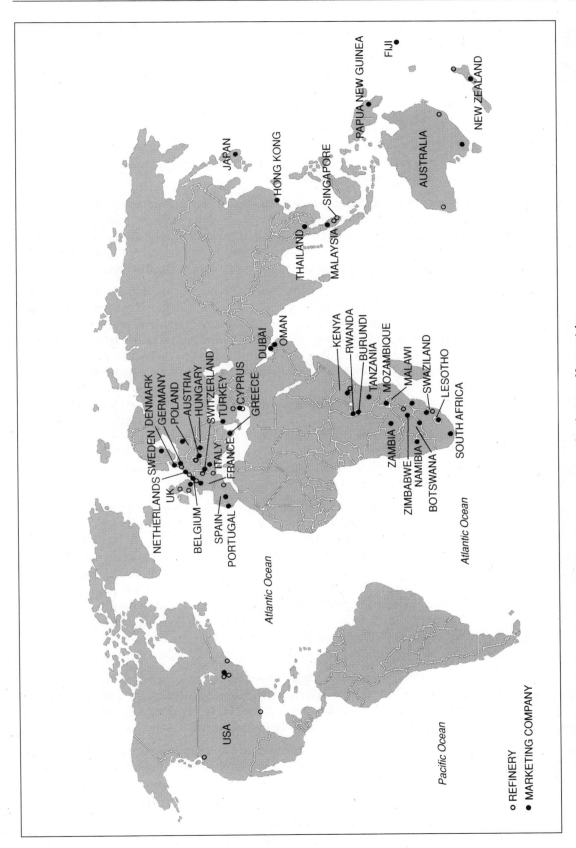

○ REFINERY
● MARKETING COMPANY

Fig 1.18 British Petroleum is a world-wide petrochemical group operating in over 40 countries

PRODUCTS

If, for the moment, we ignore raw materials and concentrate on manufactured goods and services, we can investigate how relatively few organisations share international markets and the ease to which a product manufactured in one country may be suitable for use in another.

Companies are always looking to move into markets which are expanding. This has been somewhat difficult in recent years due to a global recession. However, by looking into the recent past we can see that a number of organisations, which have seized upon a good idea – and manufactured a product or service to cater for potential demand – have grown enormously as demand for the product has increased.

There is an obvious link between the number of products an organisation sells and its potential to grow. When a company needs to grow quicker, it may choose to buy or merge with another company. However, most early growth is made by identifying and exploiting a gap in the market. If traditional markets for products are in decline, a company which is well-positioned to sell the excess production elsewhere is less likely to be seriously affected. An alternative way of dealing with this problem is to look for another way customers can use the product which is made. In the case of whisky distilleries, which have seen a gradual decline in demand, they have found it impossible to discover an alternative use for their product. They had, to some extent, coped with earlier declines in demand by exporting the majority of their whisky to the Far East. In Japan, however, which had been a huge market for Scottish whisky, the tables were turned as enterprising Japanese businessmen started producing their own version of whisky.

As mentioned earlier, a good way of expanding a business is to increase the number of products it produces. As the number of products manufactured gradually increases, so do the profits, as the individual cost for each product falls. This fact is known as 'an economy of scale'. It basically means that companies can buy in greater bulk, they can use their premises and employees more efficiently, and all their 'overheads' are spread more thinly. Overheads refer to such things as heating, lighting, insurance, rent, rates and loans. In addition, with this increased profitability, they are able to keep pace with technological changes and invest money on research and development and always be in a position to raise additional money for emergencies or the purchase of another company.

When an organisation becomes a large-scale manufacturer, it is able to mass produce goods at relatively low prices, will always be catering for comparatively stable markets (in other words the future demands for its products are fairly safe), but it will have had to invest very heavily in machinery.

The ideal situation for a large-scale producer of manufactured goods, is to create a global market for its products. It would be even more ideal if this product did not have to be substantially changed before it could be sold in various countries. The fewer the changes, the lower the cost to the manufacturer.

On the other hand, a large-scale manufacturer, involved in various different countries, is likely to suffer quite badly if there is a recession across the world. Some of the largest organisations have had to contend with losses running into billions of pounds as a result of over extending themselves. The growth process needs to be carefully considered and must not outstrip the real demand for the product.

These companies, which have suffered massive losses, have blamed various features of their organisation, including:

- *The more widespread the company is, the harder it is to manage efficiently*

- *Organisations tend to have what is known as an 'optimum' size. In other words it would have been better to have created another company to handle the production and not to have produced the goods themselves*

- *Large organisations with huge numbers of staff tend to suffer from poor communications*

- *There is a tendency for considerable numbers of employees to feel they have no real power in the organisation, and they are therefore not well motivated*

These reasons, taken together, are known as 'diseconomies of scale'.

Increasingly, the service sector is dominated by large companies. We have already pointed out that the service sector is, indeed, a large one. Many of the same problems that face a large-scale manufacturing organisation will be faced by service organisations. The major difference is that they do not necessarily produce products, but provide services. In effect, if they suffer problems, they will have to shed staff and dispose of premises.

Individual activity

In the role of Managing Director of an organisation which wishes to rapidly expand, identify three local organisations operating in a similar business activity. Your organisation is involved in manufacturing children's toys. The organisation is not interested in retailing and operates purely on a manufacturing and wholesaling basis. The organisation is interested only in businesses which are producing their own ranges of children's toys.

Compare the three local organisations that you have chosen with those of the rest of the group.

MARKETS

The ultimate success of any company is related to providing for the needs and wants of the customer. Indeed, to be really successful an organisation must stay ahead of all its competitors. Having a large 'market share' is one thing, but being a market leader is equally as important.

Let us return to the question of customers' needs and wants. Just what is the difference between the two? A need is to require something essential. This, of course, includes the need to eat, drink and keep warm. On the other hand, a want is a specific desire for something not necessarily needed. If you are hungry, this is a need, but you may want a McDonald's.

Organisations spend huge amounts of money on trying to assess and manipulate the wants of customers. What customers want, there would be no choice in products at all. Marketing experts know this and attempt, by various means, to influence what customers want.

As we have already seen, the nature of the goods that make up the consumer market are limited to just three different types of goods or services. Within each of these three categories there is a vast array of alternatives, all of which would satisfy our needs. The simple fact that one product or another has slightly different features, colours, taste or smell means that our essential need is transformed into a want.

The same can be said, to some extent, for the industrial sector of the market. Companies will purchase consumer durables (in their case capital goods like machines), consumables (in industry these will be oil, raw materials and office stationery) and services (perhaps the services of an advertising agency or an accountant). Perhaps the choice is not so great as in the consumer market, but there are definite differences between similar products and services offered by a range of companies.

Technology, design, research and development are continually introducing new products and services onto the market. In many cases, new products or services simply replace older ones, making them obsolete. Occasionally a new product or service may enter the market which offers possibilities that could not have even be dreamt of a few years ago. No one would have believed that there could one day be a machine which would replace the need to hand write additional copies of a book, but it happened when the first printing press was designed. No one would have believed that the huge pools of copy-typists which most large organisations employed would be replaced by a machine called a photocopier.

These products, whether they are replacing an existing one or not, have to either cater for a need or a want. In the case of replacement, there is an existing need. In the case of a want, this may have to be generated by an expensive advertising campaign which tries to convince the consumer that they really do want one!

Group activity

In pairs, consider your local area. Which of the organisations based in this locality have suffered in recent years from changes in customers' needs and wants? How have they adapted to the situation? Have there been any organisations forced out of business by changes in needs and wants? Begin your investigation by considering products and services which were popular when you were younger, but are no longer fashionable.

Present your findings to the rest of the group.

Element assignment

DESIGNING NEW PRODUCTS

In pairs, in the role of the Research and Development team of an organisation, create two new products, using the names Signet and Fable.

Any kind of product is acceptable, but you must choose something which would meet a market need.

In addition, you must cover the following aspects:

- Justify why you have chosen these particular products

- Explain how you believe the names match the products

- Give physical descriptions of the products

- Design short questionnaires with the aim of proving that there is a market for your products

- Produce an outline of a marketing plan for your products

- Investigate any potential competitors and their market share

- Assuming that the production of the products will take place in your local area, produce a list of resource considerations related to the products

- Present any statistical data in the form of pie or bar charts and line graphs.

Present your findings in the form of a report and be prepared to give a 15-minute presentation to the group, who will take the role of the Board of Directors. Your report should be produced by means of a word processor. Make full use of any illustrative material, including any diagrams or models you choose to produce.

UNIT TEST   Element 1.2

1 What do you understand by the term multiple?

2 What do you understand by the term multinational?

3 What do you understand by the term conglomerate?

4 Give three main resource requirements of a manufacturing business.

5 What is an enterprise agency?

6 Give three location criteria for a financial services organisation.

7 In your own words, explain the term 'market share'.

8 Which figures would you need to consider when determining market share?

9 How do the needs of a customer and the wants of a customer vary?

10 In terms of location, how do a manufacturing organisation and a service organisation differ?

11 What is the average size of an organisation in terms of employees?

12 For a food processing organisation, located in a remote area, list three transport considerations necessary.

13 What is the difference between a multinational and an international organisation?

14 Give two reasons for superstores being located in out-of-town sites.

15 Identify three areas currently receiving Government help and incentives to attract businesses.

16 What particular services would a ship building organisation require?

17 What particular services would a book printing organisation require?

18 Which do you think gives a better indication as to size of organisation? The number of employees, or their market share? Give two reasons for your answer.

19 How might a Local Authority attract businesses into an area?

20 What are the advantages of a business locating in an area which already houses organisations in a similar business activity?

Element 1.3
The UK employment market

PERFORMANCE CRITERIA

1 Types of employment are described
2 Features of employment are described
3 Levels of employment locally and in another region are identified and explained
4 Effects of technology on physical conditions and levels of employment are described
5 Employment findings are presented

RANGE

1 Types of employment: self-employed, employed, part time, permanent and temporary
2 Features of employment: physical working conditions, employment contracts, wages, taxation, national insurance, training and qualifications
3 Regional differences: investment, natural resources, labour and skills supply
4 Technology: robotics, telecommunications, computers

EVIDENCE INDICATORS

A presentation of findings comparing own region with another and giving examples of technology affecting the employment market. Evidence should demonstrate understanding of the implications of the range dimensions in relation to the element. The unit test will confirm the candidate's coverage of the range.

TYPES OF EMPLOYMENT

Nearly everyone at some stage considers starting their own business. However, this is not always practical. Equally, organisations do not necessarily employ people on a full-time basis, they may find it more useful to offer them various forms of employment.

The range of types of employment are very broad and include the following.

Self-employed

A self-employed person is usually an individual, or perhaps a group of individuals, responsible for finding and completing all their own work. Typical examples are plumbers, electricians, decorators, gardeners and bricklayers. Many professionals are also self-employed, such as accountants or solicitors. As a self-employed person's business grows, it may employ other people directly.

Employed

This is perhaps the most common form of employment but is not as straight forward as it may first appear. An individual may be employed on a full-time or part-time basis. The former refers to an individual employed for a full working week and a part-time employee would work for less hours a week than a full timer, and the hours worked would be set around busy times or perhaps weekend or evening work.

Permanent

Whether the employee works on a full-time or part-time basis, permanent refers to the fact that he or she has a commitment from the employer to continued employment. This gives the individual a certain level of job security and knowledge that he or she has a long-term future with the employer.

Temporary

This form of employment is on the basis of a short-term or perhaps seasonal contract with the employer. The contract usually states the duration of the employment period and may cover such things as maternity leave, exceptionally busy periods of the year, holiday periods, long-term sickness leave or any unusual work load. The employer may often use Job Centres, private employment agencies or direct recruitment to obtain staff.

FEATURES OF EMPLOYMENT

The variety of different types of job is as varied as the number of different organisations, perhaps more so. The overall working conditions within an organisation can be different depending upon which department, site or rank. The technology used may be different, the physical surroundings or the number of people worked with. Other factors may be an individual's qualifications and how they are used in the context of the job. Obviously, the way in which an employee is paid, and how much will differ, but the legal requirements governing pay will be similar. Training requirements and needs may be different, and also the opportunities for gaining additional qualifications and training. We need to consider all of these points in turn.

Working conditions

The basic working conditions are governed by health and safety rules (we will look at these in more detail later). It has long since been realised that employees work much better if the employer takes note of the following:

- *That the work place is well lit*
- *That the work place is kept at a constant temperature, regardless of the weather*

1.69

- *That the work place is pleasant and well-decorated*
- *That the workforce is kept fit and well, so as to reduce sickness*
- *That the hours worked are relatively flexible to take account of the employees' external commitments*
- *That the workforce receives regular training and the opportunity to gain additional qualifications*
- *That skills are rewarded financially in relation to their value to the organisation*
- *That, with age, additional payments are made so as to encourage experienced workers to stay with the organisation*
- *That Trade Unions are accepted, and that there is a regular dialogue with them*
- *That pay and conditions, overall should be attractive and competitive*

Having said all of this, there is a vast difference in how these points are adopted by individual employers. The physical working conditions of a person in an administra tive job are very different from someone working in industry. The former will enjoy relatively luxurious conditions, with carpets, curtains or blinds, comfortable seating, and above all a clean environment. For someone working in a factory, there will be a completely different set of conditions. The environment may be dirty and noisy, the employee may be on his or her feet all day, the job may be physically demanding and the hours longer.

By examining the nature of jobs in the different sectors of industry, you will find a wide spread of conditions. When we consider industrial working conditions we may have to further look at the following:

- *Where is the work? Is it outside or inside? Is the work in a hot or cold environment?*
- *Does the employee work on their own? Is there much opportunity for contact with others during the working day?*
- *Do the hours differ? Is there a requirement to start work early, finish late, or do regular shift work?*
- *Is the work carried out in a clean environment? Does the employee have to have regular health checks as a result of the environmental features of the workplace?*
- *How safe is the job? Putting health and safety aside, is the job itself dangerous? Is it physically demanding in the sense that it may result in injury?*
- *Does the employee have to wear protective clothing? Is the job sufficiently physical, dangerous, or unsafe to mean that the employee has to wear some kind of equipment or protection?*

The manufacturing industry is the section in which we will probably find the widest range of working conditions. Some organisations, although they may produce the same as another, only a few hundred yards away, may be radically different. The conditions may depend upon how much has been spent on updating old machinery and improving the overall environmental conditions.

The production process in the factory is obviously dependent upon what is being made. An organisation that produces fairly small numbers of products or components will be comparatively small in both its numbers of employees and space provided. In contrast, an organisation that makes cars on a production line will need enormous amounts of space, considerably more staff and larger premises. The size of the production process does not really have a bearing on how noisy and unsafe the conditions are, this is inevitably related to investment in new techniques and machinery.

Individual activity

Plan a visit to a local manufacturing organisation. Using the points made above, consider the general working conditions of the organisation. After your visit, write in the form of a memorandum a list of proposals or recommendations to improve the general working conditions of the employees. The memorandum would be for your own purposes only and should not of course, be sent to the organisation that you visited.

Administration jobs, despite the fact that they may be a part of the same organisation as the production process, will often have completely different working conditions. They may be housed on a separate site, or certainly away from the noise and demands of the 'shop-floor'. Dependent upon the nature of the administrative work carried out, and the demand placed upon it, we will find another spread of working conditions:

- *The administration section may be cramped, with severe lack of space and amenities. This may be due to the fact that the administrative unit is only seen as servicing the main operation of the organisation, namely making things*

- *The offices may be reasonably spacious but functional since no one will ever see them, such as customers*

- *The office space may be plush and well-appointed. This will be due to the use of the offices themselves. In other words, customers may regularly visit and need to be impressed by the furnishings and overall look of the place*

- *The offices may be relatively small and highly automated. In this case, the organisation may have invested heavily in computers and technological equipment, partly to ease the work load and partly to reduce the numbers of administrative staff*

- *Usually, the physical conditions of the administrative section will be a mixture of several of the above. It is the case, quite often, that administrative departments have grown and are not particularly well planned out. Having the right people to hand is not always possible since the administrative department may well be split up in a series of rooms, or even different sites*

- *The concept of a purpose-built administrative block has proved popular over the years, but ultimately it is the production process that often takes first place when considering investment.*

Individual activity

In the role of Administration Manager what aspects would you consider to be essential to ensure the ideal working conditions for office-based workers?

Compare your points with those of the group.

The service sector offers yet another broad range of working conditions. Since this sector includes many occupations from postmen to teachers and policemen to retail assistants, we can see a massive difference in conditions at work.

In these cases, the conditions will usually revolve around the nature of the job itself. If we take two contrasting examples, we can see the problems:

- *A teacher will have a room to use as an office. A retail worker may only have a small rest room, as no real administrative work needs to be undertaken*

- *The retail worker will carry out the bulk of the job on the shop-floor, the teacher may use a variety of different classrooms in the course of a day*

- *The teacher will deliver a predetermined course of study, and in some respects the day is mapped out ahead. The retail worker, on the other hand, will not know the demands to be faced until they happen*

- *The retail worker will have to cope with a variety of different customer problems. The teacher, meanwhile, will deal with the same customers (students), but may not be able to predict what they will demand.*

Individual activity

In order to compare the working conditions of the two groups given above, arrange to interview one of your teachers and a retail worker from a local establishment. Prepare your list of questions and give this to the interviewee before the interview takes place.

After the interview compare the two sets of answers. How do their working conditions vary? What working conditions do they have that they are happy with? What makes them unhappy? Can you think of any recommendations that would improve the general working conditions of either? Discuss these with the remainder of the group.

Contracts of Employment

Most of the conditions of work are laid down in the Contract of Employment (which we have dealt with in an earlier section), the main features include:

- *The name of the employer and the employee's name must be on the contract*
- *The date that the employee began working for the organisation*
- *The employee's pay (either the amount or the scale)*
- *When, in terms of frequency, the employee is paid*
- *The employee's hours of work*
- *The employee's holiday entitlements (if applicable)*
- *The employee's holiday pay entitlements*
- *The employee's right to sick pay due to injury*
- *The employee's right to sick pay due to illness*
- *The length of notice (both ways) required to terminate employment*
- *The employee's pension rights*
- *The employee's job title*

(*See* Fig 1.19)

CONTRACTS OF EMPLOYMENT STATEMENT

PARTICULARS OF MAIN TERMS OF EMPLOYMENT

This statement dated .... sets out certain particulars of the terms and conditions which, in conjunction with the Rules and Disciplinary Procedures, Working Arrangements and any other operating procedures, form part of the Contract of Employment on which   employs

1.   Your employment began on .... and employment with .... does count as part of your continuous period of employment.

2.   You are employed as:

3.   Your wage will be paid at 4 weekly intervals by cash or credit transfer in arrears. Details of your wage level have been notified to you. Any changes or amendments to this will be confirmed in writing within one month of them occurring.

4.   You will be required to work those hours necessary to fulfil the requirements of your job to the standards required by us and to the satisfaction of our clients.

5.   You are not entitled to any paid holidays. Conditions attaching to statutory/public holidays are shown in the Employee Information Binder.

6.   Payment for periods of absence due to authorised sickness will be made in accordance with the current Statutory Sick Pay Scheme.

7.   The Company does not operate a private Pension Scheme and there is no contracting out certificate in force in respect of your employment. Should you have made your own personal Pension arrangements where a contracting out certificate is in force, then you should inform the Company of this immediately.

8.   After 1 month's service you are required to give the Company 4 weeks notice to terminate your employment.

     You are entitled to receive the following periods of notice from the Company:

          Over 1 month but under 5 years continuous service - 4 weeks.
          Over 5 years continuous service - 1 week for each complete year
          of service to a maximum of 12 weeks after 12 years.

9.   The Company rules which form part of your conditions of employment are shown in the Employee Information Binder. It is your responsibility to familiarise yourself with these and observe them at all times.

10. If you are dissatisfied with any disciplinary decision taken against you, you should raise this in accordance with the Appeals Procedure shown in the Employee Information Binder.

11. If you wish to raise any grievance relating to your employment, you should do so in accordance with the Grievance Procedure shown in the Employee Information Binder.

Fig 1.19 A standard contract of employment

12.   In addition to the above rules, the following conditions shall form part of the Contract between the business and the employee and shall be rigorously observed. Each of these clauses and sub-clauses shall be construed as an entirely separate obligation and the enforceability of any one or more of the clauses or sub-clauses shall not in any way be affected by the unenforceability of any other clauses or sub-clause.

13.   You will not, either during the continuance of your employment with us, or at any time thereafter, divulge to any person, firm or company any confidential information which shall include (but without limitation) any information that we from time to time notify you as confidential and confidential documents, lists of customers, information concerning our internal and external affairs and business methods, and confidential information concerning the identity, location and requirements of our customers.

14.   Upon termination of your employment, howsoever occasioned, you will promptly return to us all documents, goods, samples, keys, memoranda, list of customers or other particulars and details which relate in any way to our business which you have received or prepared during your employment with us.

15.   You will not for a period of 6 months after the termination of your employment solicit custom from, deal with a supplier or any person, firm or corporation for the purposes of offering services similar to those provided by us where that person was one to whom you, on your own behalf, provided those services to or to whom to your knowledge services were provided by the business during your period of employment.

Signed by the employee ....

Date ....

Fig 1.19 Standard contract of employment — continued

Over and above the main contract, the employer is required to take note of a variety of different legislation, which we will deal with later. Essentially, they cover the following protection rights of employees:

- *The right to receive a contract of employment*
- *The right to receive a pay statement which details pay and deductions*
- *The right to have a period of notice when terminating employment*
- *The right to join a trade union if desired*
- *The right to have maternity leave*
- *The right to return to work after maternity leave*
- *The right not to be unfairly dismissed from employment*
- *The right to receive a redundancy payment*
- *The right to receive equal pay for equal work*
- *The right not to be discriminated against*

A good contract of employment would also cover such things as the disciplinary rules and grievance procedures in brief note detail.

Not all of the above rights come into force immediately. There may be a qualifying period. Equal pay, trade union membership and maternity leave are immediate. The employer must give a contract of employment within 13 weeks. The others, including maternity pay, the right to return after pregnancy and redundancy payments come into force after two years.

Group activity

In the role of a prospective employee, consider with a partner what you would expect to receive as a Contract of Employment. When would you want to know about your terms of employment? What would you consider to be fair terms of employment? What would you not accept?

Feed back your comments to the group.

Wages

Most people in work get paid in one way or another. The exception are those who are involved in some kind of voluntary work. Although most people are paid, they receive their reward in a variety of different ways:

- *Those paid strictly according to the hours worked*
- *Those paid according to working the number of hours required in a week*
- *Those paid according to working the number of hours required in a month*

These are the basic versions of being paid, but there are others (less common) which we will look at shortly.

It goes without saying that some people are paid more than others, this may be for a number of reasons, but may include:

- *The employee's period of service with the organisation*
- *The age of the employee*
- *The qualifications of the employee*
- *The training undertaken by the employee*
- *If the employee performs exceptionally (see later)*

Some employees receive a range of perks or benefits, such as company cars, health care, subsidised canteens or season ticket loans. These perks may be offered to keep valuable staff and to be more competitive with other organisations. In some cases, the existence of a perk is more valuable than actually receiving the cash alternative.

Despite the differences, two things remain the same. Everyone has to pay Income Tax and National Insurance. We will look at these in a little more detail later.

One more distinction exists between the ways in which people are paid. This is the difference between salaries and wages. Let us contrast the two:

- Salaries tend to be paid to clerical and managerial staff who are paid on a monthly basis, whereas wages tend to be paid to manual workers being paid on a weekly basis
- The salary is paid either every four weeks (i.e. 13 times per year), or at the end of each calendar month. The wage is paid, usually on a Friday, or at the end of the working week
- Salaries tend to be paid either as one-twelfth or one-thirteenth of the total quoted salary for the whole year. Wages, on the other hand, tend to be paid according to the quoted weekly pay rate, or the hourly rate times the number of hours worked
- Salaries are usually paid by bank credit transfer into the bank account of the employee. The wage is either paid in cash, or by cheque (which can often be cashed in a local bank by arrangement with the organisation)
- Salary-paid employees are not usually paid for any overtime that they may have to do. The overtime is considered to be a duty of the employee, this is particularly true of managerial staff. The wage earner is paid overtime according to the number of extra hours worked

- The salary-paid employee will always receive the same payment every month, since it is a proportion of the total yearly pay. A wage earner will earn money according to how many hours have been worked, and consequently they may earn different amounts each week

- Both salary and wage earners are often paid in arrears. This means that the employee has actually worked a period of time or hours before they are paid. The salary worker will have probably worked for a whole month before being paid, the wage earner will have only worked a week before receiving the pay packet.

These distinctions have become a little less obvious in recent years. Organisations have taken on many more part-time workers, both manual and clerical. Some of these individuals will be paid on a weekly basis or on a monthly basis.

Group activity

As we have said, it is not always easy to know whether someone in a particular occupation receives a salary or a wage. In pairs, consider the following groups of employees and try to agree whether they are wage or salary earners:

- A bricklayer
- An office cleaner
- A solicitor
- A switchboard operator
- A teacher
- A temporary secretary

Earlier, we mentioned that there are some less common ways of being paid. Some of these payment methods may be in addition to a basic salary. It is more likely to find these additional payments in the case of salespeople, or other employees which make a positive and visible contribution to the profits of the organisation.

- Commission is often paid to salespeople based on the income they generate for the organisation. They will often be on a relatively low basic salary, or none at all, and rely on the commission they earn for their income. In this way, the organisation positively encourages employees to work hard and make profits for them, but the obvious problem is that in cases where the salespeople have had a bad week or a bad month they will earn very little. This can mean that employees paid on this basis tend to leave the organisation if things are not going well

- Bonus payments are made in addition to a basic salary when specified sales targets are met. Employees may also receive bonus payments when the organisation is particularly busy, in holiday periods, for example. It is usual for an organisation to pay a bonus at Christmas, or after the annual accounts have been calculated and have shown exactly what profit has been made. In most respects, the bonus payment is then linked to the productivity of the employees over a given time period

- Profit sharing is another alternative source of extra income for the employee. This particular form of payment involves the organisation calculating its overall profit, then identifying a portion of it for distribution to the employees. Normally speaking the organisation will add up all of the years that all of the employees have worked, divide the total available funds by that figure and distribute accordingly. This means that the longer an employee has been working for the organisation, the bigger the share of the profit payout they will receive

■ Expenses form the final type of additional payment to the employee. Expenses are not really an additional payment at all, they are simply the repayment of monies already spent, or to be spent by the employee. These payments will include meals, petrol, hotel bills, travel and in some cases a clothing allowance. In many cases, the employee will not have to 'claim' these expenses and will be issued with a company credit card instead.

Individual activity

In the role of a Sales Representative, consider the advantages and disadvantages of being paid in two alternative ways:

■ Basic pay plus bonuses

■ Commission only

We will assume that any expenses are paid by the organisation. Which of the above payment systems would give you the following:

■ A guaranteed regular pay

■ A good incentive to work hard

■ Security

Present your findings in the form of a letter to a Sales Representative who has asked you, as a friend already working in this capacity, to offer him guidance.

Tax, National Insurance and other deductions

We have so far considered the pay of the individual employee. However, all employees do not actually receive this full amount at all. All salaries and wages are subject to a number of deductions from this gross pay (this means the total amount earned by the employee before deductions). What is left after the deductions is commonly known as net pay.

From the gross pay are deducted various forms of 'charges' against the employee. Some are required by law, such as tax and others are voluntary, such as pension contributions.

Tax is deducted by the employer on behalf of the Inland Revenue. They are required to do so, and promptly pass on the monies to the Government Department. The deduction process is complicated, but includes the following procedures:

Chancellor of the Exchequer's Budget Proposals: 1993

Income Tax 1993-94

Rates of Tax

The lower rate of income tax is to remain at 20%, the basic rate at 25% and the higher rate at 40%. But the lower rate will be payable on taxable income up to £2,500 instead of £2,000 as follows:-

		1992-93 Taxable Income £			1993-94 Taxable Income £		
Lower Rate	20%	1	-	2,000	1	-	2,500
Basic Rate	25%	2,001	-	23,700	2,501	-	23,700
Higher Rate	40%	Over		23,700	Over		23,700

Taxable income is the income remaining after deducting tax reliefs and allowances.

Main Income Tax Allowances

The main personal allowances are to remain unchanged as shown below.

Allowances	1993-94 £
Personal Allowance	3445
Married Couple's Allowance	1720
Personal Allowance (Age 65 - 74)	4200
Married Couple's Allowance (Age 65-74)	2465
Personal Allowance (Age 75 and over)	4370
Married Couple's Allowance (Age 75 and over)	2505
Additional Personal Allowance	1720
Widow's Bereavement Allowance	1720

Age-Related Allowances

The income limit for the age-related allowances is to remain at £14,200.
Above the income limit the age-related allowance will continue to be withdrawn at a rate of £1 for every £2 of income.

BP(1993)(T)

Fig 1.20 An Inland Revenue leaflet showing tax rates, thresholds and personal allowances   Crown copyright

- The Inland Revenue calculates the employee's eligibility for various personal allowances, in other words, how much an individual can earn before they must pay tax. These personal allowances are based on the marital status of the individual and other criteria (*see* Fig 1.20)

- An individual, once personal allowances have been calculated, will pay tax out of every pay packet or monthly pay cheque. This is known as PAYE (Pay As You Earn) and is the most common way to pay tax (*see* Fig 1.21)

- On the other hand, a self-employed person will pay their tax in a very different way. After having completed the end of year accounts, the self-employed person sends in the 'return' to the Inland Revenue and then

Inland Revenue
PAYE

Reference /

Coding claim

Please read these notes before you write anything

Your employer has given you this form because you have not given him a form P45. Without a P45 you may pay the wrong tax. If you can get a P45, you need not fill in this form. If you left a job recently and have not since then claimed unemployment benefit, ask your old employer for a P45. If you have been claiming unemployment benefit, sign off by returning card UB40. A P45 will then be sent to you.

You should however fill in this form
- if you cannot get a P45, or you have lost it or
- if this is your first paid job.

It will help you to get a correct PAYE code so that you pay the right tax. You may not have to fill in all of it. Please follow the instructions printed in blue and fill in those sections that apply to you, using CAPITAL letters.

A Everyone should fill in this section

Your surname ______ Mr/Mrs/Miss/Ms ______

Your first names ______

Your new employer's name and address ______

Postcode ______

The description or title of your new job ______ Your National Insurance number ______

Is this new job your **only** job? Please say YES or NO ☐

If you have a second job, or do part-time or evening work, any payments you receive are part of your income. They are liable to tax in just the same way as the earnings from your regular job.

If your answer is 'YES', please turn to page 2. If your answer is 'NO', please fill in section B below.

B Please give details of **any other work** for which you get paid

The description or title of the job ______ If you work for yourself please write 'self-employed' ______

Your employer's name and address ______

Your works/payroll number *if any* ______ The branch or site where you work ______

Your tax reference *if known* ______ Your total weekly earnings from the work before any stoppages £ ______

Which is your **main** job? Is it your new job, shown in section A? Or the job shown in section B?

Please write A or B ☐

If your answer is 'A', please turn to page 2.
If your answer is 'B', please turn straight to page 4: there is no need to fill in pages 2 and 3.

P15 1

G Please fill in this section if you are
- a married woman *not separated or divorced*
- a widow whose husband has died since 5 April last

These details are needed for reference purposes only.

Your husband's full name ______

The name of his Tax Office ______

His tax reference *if known* ______ His National Insurance number *if known* ______

Your husband's job ______

The name and address of his employer (or if he is unemployed, retired or deceased, his last employer and the date he stopped work).

______

His works/payroll number *if any* ______ His place of work ______

Your husband's business address if self-employed ______

A description of his business ______

If you were married after 5 April last, please give the date you were married ______ your surname before marriage ______

H **Please sign this declaration**

If you deliberately make false statements you can be prosecuted.

I declare that, to the best of my knowledge and belief, the particulars given on this form are correct and complete.

Signature ______ Date ______ 19 ______

Home address ______

Postcode ______

When you have filled in this form, please send it to the Tax Office in the envelope provided.

4

Printed in the UK for HMSO. D.8096595 5,000m 6/89. 36625.

Fig 1.21 Pages of an Inland Revenue PAYE form

they calculate how much tax should be paid. They will usually allow the tax to be paid in two instalments over the following year

The process as far as the wages department is concerned is based on the following procedure:

■ The deductions of each employee will be calculated on a form known as a P11. This will take account of any personal allowances that the individual is entitled to

■ They will then generate a pay slip for each employee which details the exact nature of the deductions made

■ Once a year they will generate another form known as a P60. This will detail all pay received, tax deducted, National Insurance contributions made and any statutory sick or maternity pay

■ If an employee changes their job in the course of the year, the wages department will issue a P45 which details the employee's tax code, total pay to date, any tax due and all tax paid to date. This must then be given to the employee's new employer to ensure that their tax is calculated correctly (*see* Fig 1.22)

Individual activity

Contact your local Tax Office. Find out the following information:

■ Standard rate of tax contributions

■ Rate of tax paid by people earning larger than average salaries

■ Personal allowance for a single person

■ Personal allowance for a married person

National Insurance is paid by all employees, and a contribution is made by the employer too. Self-employed individuals pay their NI on a quarterly or monthly basis direct to the Department of Social Security. The NI contributions are collected to provide a range of benefits and services which include the following:

■ *Unemployment Benefit*

■ *State Pensions*

■ *Statutory Sick Pay*

■ *Statutory Maternity Pay*

■ *Child Benefit*

■ *Industrial Disablement Benefit*

■ *Widow's Benefit*

■ *Death Grants*

The DSS is a large and complex Government organisation that has both central administration in London and a spread of regional offices throughout the country.

We have now looked at the two statutory (compulsory) forms of deduction from the employee's pay packet. These are not the only deductions made from the pay packet, however, there are a number of possible voluntary deductions.

The first, and possibly most common, is the pension. Essentially, there are four forms of pension. They are:

■ *SERPS (State Earnings Related Pension Scheme) which is a government-run pension scheme*

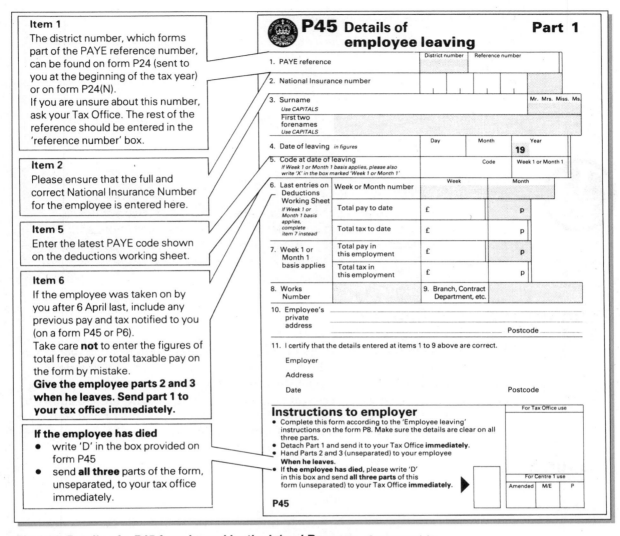

Item 1
The district number, which forms part of the PAYE reference number, can be found on form P24 (sent to you at the beginning of the tax year) or on form P24(N).
If you are unsure about this number, ask your Tax Office. The rest of the reference should be entered in the 'reference number' box.

Item 2
Please ensure that the full and correct National Insurance Number for the employee is entered here.

Item 5
Enter the latest PAYE code shown on the deductions working sheet.

Item 6
If the employee was taken on by you after 6 April last, include any previous pay and tax notified to you (on a form P45 or P6).
Take care **not** to enter the figures of total free pay or total taxable pay on the form by mistake.
Give the employee parts 2 and 3 when he leaves. Send part 1 to your tax office immediately.

If the employee has died
• write 'D' in the box provided on form P45
• send **all three** parts of the form, unseparated, to your tax office immediately.

Fig 1.22 Details of a P45 form issued by the Inland Revenue   Crown copyright

■ *Company pension schemes which are run and administered by the organisation on behalf of its employees*

■ *Personal pension schemes which have been set up by a pension or assurance company to cope with the individual demands of the employee*

■ *Occupational pension schemes (also known as superannuation) which are run and administered nationally for all members of an occupational group (such as teachers)*

Group activity

In pairs, discuss the following:

'Why would an individual wish to have a personal pension scheme, particularly if the company or organisation for which they work offers a company pension scheme?'

Other types of deduction include the following:

■ *Trade union subscriptions which are paid by an individual who belongs to a trade union*

■ *Social/leisure club subscriptions which are paid by the individual who uses the facilities offered by the organisation*

■ *Charitable donations which can be paid directly to the charity, before tax and National Insurance is deducted*

Group activity

In groups of four, contact as many trade unions, social and leisure clubs as possible and try to find out the subscription rates for membership of each. Do they offer good value for money? What alternative ways of paying subscriptions do they allow?

Training and qualifications

There is an incredibly wide variety of training and qualifications available to the employee. The exact nature of the training or the qualifications is dependent upon the nature of the job. Some jobs will require constant training or updating of qualifications, whereas others will not need anything beyond basic training to be carried out. Despite this wide variety of availability, upwards of one-third of the population still does not have any formal qualifications.

Training

Training basically falls into four separate categories:

■ *On-the-job training* – which refers to training carried out while at work and may be delivered by in-house training personnel or 'bought-in' specialists

■ *Off-the-job training* – which refers to training carried out at a location other than the work place and may require access to specialists or specialist equipment, not necessarily available in the work place

■ *Part-time training* – which refers to the 'mode' of training itself. This category includes day-release, evening classes and short courses. This type of training is usually paid, at least in part, by the employer and relates directly to required job skills

■ *Full-time training* – which refers to short- or long-term training courses which take the employee out of the work situation for an extended period. This may be because the employee needs to be trained in a complex area which would be unsuitable on a part time basis

Many organisations run special courses which may be either at the work place or in an alternative location. The nature of the training may involve specialist management skills, health and safety or supervisory skills. It is usually the case that key personnel are chosen to attend these courses who are then expected to pass on the knowledge they have acquired to the rest of the members of their work teams.

Reducing the "Paper Mountain"

"Where does all the paper come from?" "I am sinking under piles of paper!" We have probably uttered this sort of thing from time to time. We all complain about the volume of paper which flows across our desks, has to be stored and retrieved. It is a problem which affects the whole of DTI and the Civil Service because:

❑ we have a lot of work to do;

❑ we have a culture flowing from the Public Records Act which is based very strongly on working on paper;

❑ it's part of our culture, and arguably necessary for our work, to consult widely and this means a lot of drafting, redrafting and copying.

We cannot hope to change our culture easily and in some respects we wouldn't want to. The paper which flows across our desks helps us to keep informed and to do our jobs effectively. But there are times when the volume of paper does just the reverse - taking up our time and preventing us from getting on with the most important tasks.

The mountains of paper don't just happen and many of the causes can be controlled by avoiding unnecessary:

❑ working on paper;

❑ photocopying of papers to other people;

❑ photocopying of papers to us by other people;

❑ personal filing systems for personal copies.

All we need to do is think a bit harder and to follow the guidance set out below.

Photocopying
Before copying papers think hard about the number you really need and keep them to the minimum.

❑ Do you need to copy the whole document? Would an extract do?

❑ Does everyone on the circulation list need to see the attachments?

❑ Float copies of minutes and letters don't need to include copies of attachments and some file copies may not need attachments either.

❑ Whenever you can, use both sides of the paper when copying.

Is it really necessary?
Always think twice before originating any piece of paper. Would a phone call do with a brief manuscript record on the file? If you must put it on paper;

❑ keep it short;

❑ emphasise that telephone responses are acceptable whenever you can and consider using the "unless I hear from you by… I shall assume that you are content" formula. This saves all those pieces of paper that say no more than "nil return".

Circulation Lists
Just because the original had a long circulation list, this does not mean that you have to slavishly follow it with the response. Be very selective. In particular don't copy advice and draft replies to routine Ministers' cases to everyone on the Private Office's original list. Sometimes it is only necessary for the actual reply to be copied to the action officer on the case file when it is returned. Always try to help correspondence staff in the Private Offices to improve their distribution. They try hard to keep the circulation lists short but they need your help and guidance from time to time.

Encourage others to tell you if they are not interested in seeing further papers on a subject and tell others yourself, when you are no longer interested in receiving copies. Share copies by circulating them on a sequential 1,2 basis wherever possible. Don't make individual copies unless the paper will need to be kept for frequent reference by those concerned.

Filing Systems
If your section has been an efficient filing system, it should not be necessary for you to keep a parallel system of personal copies.

Weeding and Destruction
If you have had separate copies for information only, weed them out and destroy them once the need has passed. Do be careful however, not to destroy originals needed for the public record. If in doubt consult the Departmental Records Officer (Stella Wood on 081-874 3345 or GTN 3502 175).

Fig 1.23 As part of the DTI's 'Help for Managers' series of leaflets and booklets, 'Reducing the Paper Mountain' attempts to tackle over-production of documents

The types of skills required for business can range from knowledge of new software packages to more general managerial skills. Depending on the area of work which the individual is involved with, this will dictate the type of training needs for that individual. Personal skills development has become a very popular area of training in recent years and will attempt to offer guidance in the following areas:

- *Time management*
- *Supervisory skills*
- *Assertiveness*
- *Counselling skills*
- *Coping with meetings*

- *Stress management*
- *Management skills*
- *Communication skills*
- *Negotiating skills*
- *Leadership skills*

Individual activity

In the role of Personnel Manager, investigate locally available training courses which would be relevant for Supervisors in an office environment. Your organisation is looking for good value for money and the minimum disruption to the working week of its employees placed on such courses.

Begin by looking at local colleges, then extend your search to private providers of training. Many local Chambers of Commerce and Trade Associations offer training courses to their members' employees.

In the form of a memo from the Personnel Manager, offer a menu of training programmes from which the Supervisors may choose.

Qualifications

Most people will start their careers with little or no qualifications. Most individuals will have at least some basic understanding of English or Mathematics but it is only when they begin to consider what their career goal may be, that they should start to gain qualifications which will help them achieve their goal. Depending on the time and effort put in, individuals can slowly progress in their collection of qualifications. At the same time, particularly if the individual is in work, they will be gaining additional responsibilities in relation to the qualifications they have achieved.

Whether we are considering training or qualifications, there are two more important distinctions to be made in the nature of the course of study. These are vocational and non-vocational.

Vocational

Vocational training or qualifications are those which relate directly to a job or job area. It does not necessarily matter whether the individual is in work or not, since the programme is designed to offer the learner the opportunity to practice the type of skills required for a particular job. This has become a very popular area, much supported by employers, who see this as the only useful and relevant way of preparing individuals for work within industry or technology.

Non-vocational

In some respects, a non-vocational course may be seen to be the opposite to a vocational course. This may not necessarily be the case. Typically, a course which falls into this category will not have a direct relevance to a particular job and may be more general in nature. Alternatively, non-vocational courses may be academic and provide a wide range of knowledge which is not necessarily applied. In cases like this, the individual would need to undertake further training to learn how to put into practice the extensive knowledge which they have gained.

Individual activity

Thinking about the qualifications you personally hold at the moment, place them in the two categories given below:

- Vocational
- Non-vocational

Did the learning differ in any way? If so, how did it differ? Do you think that some of the qualifications you have are more important than others?

Now write a list of the qualifications you think you would like to achieve in the future. How do you think they will improve your job prospects? Are these qualifications vocational or non-vocational?

Discuss your opinions in groups of four, then feed back your discussion to the rest of the group.

REGIONAL VARIATIONS IN EMPLOYMENT

The type and nature of employment obviously differs from one region to another. There are many reasons for this, which we will look at shortly, and also many reasons why economic conditions affect regions in different ways.

Regional investment

Some areas of the country are more successful than others. Just how prosperous an area is will directly affect how easy it is to get a job. Obviously, some areas which have large populations and thousands of organisations sited there offer better job prospects than more remote, sparsely populated rural areas. With prosperity comes the ability to provide an extensive transport and communications network, which, in turn, generates more jobs. Some areas with low employment

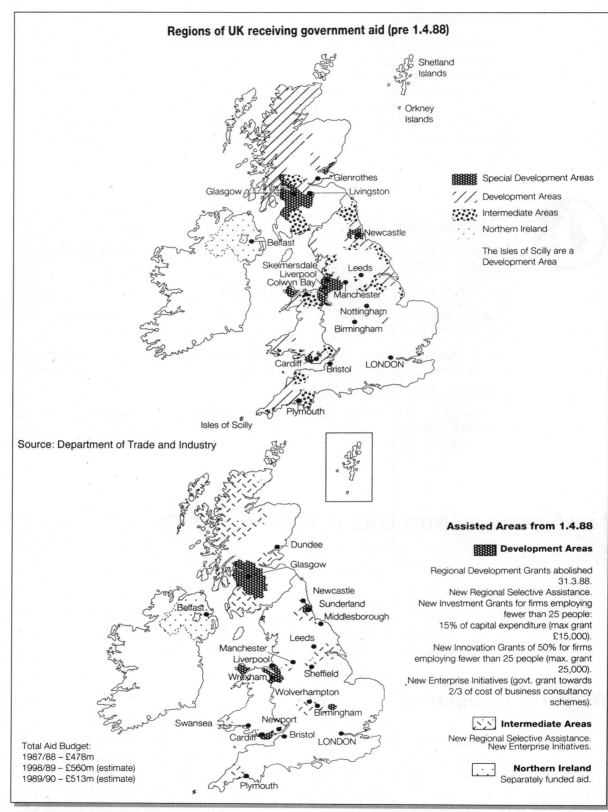

Regions of UK receiving government aid (pre 1.4.88)

Shetland Islands

Orkney Islands

Glenrothes
Glasgow
Livingston

Newcastle

Belfast

Skelmersdale
Liverpool
Colwyn Bay
Manchester
Leeds
Nottingham
Birmingham

Cardiff
Bristol
LONDON

Plymouth

Isles of Scilly

Special Development Areas
Development Areas
Intermediate Areas
Northern Ireland

The Isles of Scilly are a
Development Area

Source: Department of Trade and Industry

Dundee
Glasgow
Newcastle
Sunderland
Middlesborough
Belfast
Leeds
Manchester
Liverpool
Wrexham
Sheffield
Wolverhampton
Swansea
Newport
Birmingham
Cardiff
Bristol
LONDON

Plymouth

Assisted Areas from 1.4.88

Development Areas

Regional Development Grants abolished
31.3.88.
New Regional Selective Assistance.
New Investment Grants for firms employing
fewer than 25 people:
15% of capital expenditure (max grant
£15,000).
New Innovation Grants of 50% for firms
employing fewer than 25 people (max. grant
25,000).
New Enterprise Initiatives (govt. grant towards
2/3 of cost of business consultancy
schemes).

Intermediate Areas

New Regional Selective Assistance.
New Enterprise Initiatives.

Northern Ireland
Separately funded aid.

Total Aid Budget:
1987/88 – £478m
1998/89 – £560m (estimate)
1989/90 – £513m (estimate)

Fig 1.24 Map of UK assisted areas
(Source: *Business: A Student's Guide*, Desmond W Evans, Pitman Publishing, 1993)

find themselves in a downward spiral, from which they cannot escape. If only a few organisations have located in a particular area, there may not be a great deal of investment in transport and communications. This, in turn, means the area is less likely to attract new businesses. Unemployment will stay high and perhaps increase as existing businesses find it impossible to compete with organisations in better located areas.

The Government recognises the unfair advantages related to location. It does not want whole areas to be centres of unemployment. Consequently, it has developed a series of programmes and schemes to encourage 'under-developed' areas to grow. These include the following.

Assisted areas

The Department of Trade and Industry offers a range of grants to companies wishing to set up in a particular area which has been identified as having particular problems. The grant will help them finance the move or setting up of new premises, assist in the recruitment and training of personnel and may offer reduced accommodation costs.

Urban programme

This is a similar set of grants to assisted area programmes, but relate to city-centre locations.

Department of Environment grants

This Government department offers specific grants particularly to inner-city developments, where previous business activity has reduced to a point where there are many empty premises which could be filled by new businesses. These new businesses are encouraged financially to relocate or set up premises in the run-down areas.

Urban and Non-Urban Development Agencies

To help with the allocation of Department of Environment grants, the Government has set up these agencies to concentrate on the handing out of funds to increase local employment levels.

Training and Enterprise Councils (TECs)

This is a network of organisations which assist local training needs, offer help to employers to identify training needs and encourage closer links with educational establishments and businesses.

Rural Development Commission

To discourage, particularly the young, from moving away from rural areas to cities, the Government has set up this commission. It aims to support rural areas in the following ways:

- *Identify training needs of businesses in rural locations and help them to get funding from the Training and Enterprise Council*

- *Encourage collaboration between organisations within rural locations to exchange ideas and training experiences*

1.87

- *Identify particular dangers in terms of job losses within rural areas, such as the decline of the agricultural businesses*

- *Offer a range of additional grants, such as the Training and Enterprise Fund, which is available to help promote employment in the rural areas*

Since joining the EC, Great Britain is now eligible for a series of EC grants, which are aimed at reducing unemployment throughout the whole of the European Community. The main grants available are:

- *European Regional Development fund* – which is designed to target areas blighted by high unemployment and offers extensive financial assistance to encourage businesses to locate within the region

- *European Social fund* – again, this is aimed at areas of high unemployment, but concentrates on the problems and training of the young within the region

Individual activity

In the role of Assistant to a Managing Director who is looking to locate a new site within the UK for a major manufacturing organisation, and hoping to employ at least 500 people. Decide what steps this Managing Director would need to take to find out whether or not this organisation is eligible for a grant from one of the various funds available. The Managing Director is prepared to locate these new premises in almost any part of the UK, provided that the communication and transport systems are at least of an acceptable standard.

Having completed your research, write a memorandum to your Managing Director, outlining the main grants available, the conditions required to be accepted for funding and the addresses to which any applications must be made.

Natural resources

Exactly why an organisation may choose to locate in a particular region may be dependent upon the natural resources available. As you will remember, there are three main sectors of any economy. These are the primary, secondary and tertiary sectors. The primary sector, since it involves the use of natural resources directly, means that certain industries have traditionally been located in specific regions. The other two sectors, to varying levels, rely on the natural resources, but not to such a great extent. Let us take a brief look at the natural resources of the UK and the way they influence the location of industry:

Coal

Although the coal industry is in decline, with less than 50 mines still in operation, we will still find that coal fields dictate the location of the mines. Essentially, they are located in the Midlands, South Wales, the North East of England and southern Scotland. The prosperity of these areas is heavily dependent upon the success of the coal mines and many areas which have suffered the loss of this industry have subsequently declined to such an extent that they have become assisted areas.

Fig 1.25 Coal mining – a primary sector industry

Minerals

This industry involves the extraction of various materials from the earth, such as chalk, limestone, clay, salt, sand, gravel and shale. The success or failure of these industries may be related to such things as road building, construction and house building.

Water

Recently, the 10 Water Authorities have been privatised. These new industries are responsible for providing a plentiful water supply and the treatment of sewerage. This means they are involved in the management of rivers, canals, streams, lakes, reservoirs, wells, springs and underground waterways. Not only do they provide water to homes but also to industry. Depending on the type of industry located within a region, the amount of water required will differ greatly. In agricultural areas, water demands will be related to the rainfall, in other industries, such as the electricity generating sector, vast amounts of water are used daily.

Gas

The gas industry was privatised in the 1980s and is required to supply gas throughout the UK, either directly or in the form of gas containers. While this industry does offer many jobs offshore, it does employ quite large numbers of people at the terminals located on land. Primarily, these terminals will be found in coastal areas.

Oil

The UK is fortunate in the sense that vast oil deposits have been discovered offshore around the coast. Like gas, the oil industry is highly dependent on machinery and so does not employ large numbers of people. It does, however,

Fig 1.26 The North Sea has proved to be a vital provider of natural resources such as oil and gas

require additional employees in the processing, refining, storage and transportation of oil. In addition to the offshore deposits, substantial finds have been made on the South Coast, in southern East Anglia, Wales, the North East of England and Southern Scotland.

Forestry

The production of wood has become an increasingly profitable industry in recent years. Indeed, in the past 20 years, production has doubled. Nearly half of all wood production is controlled by the Forestry Commission, which is a government organisation.

Farming

Certain rural areas have traditionally concentrated on particular types of farming. Here is a by no means comprehensive list of farming regions:

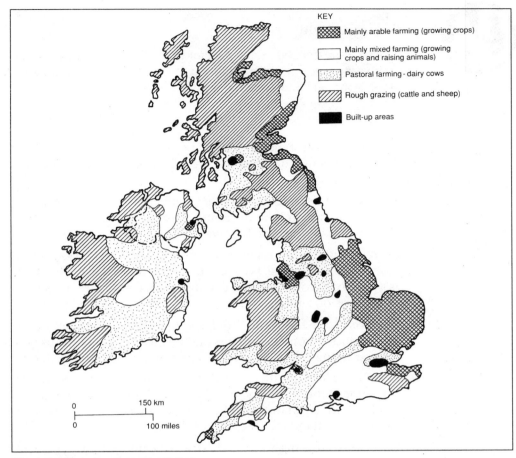

Fig 1.27 Farming types in Britain

- *South West of England* – Sheep and cattle, potatoes and arable
- *South East of England* – Vegetables, potatoes and arable
- *Eastern England* – Pigs, poultry, vegetables and arable
- *Midlands* – Mainly arable
- *Wales* – Sheep and cattle
- *North Midlands* – Pig, poultry and arable
- *Borders* – Sheep and cattle and vegetables
- *Scotland* – Sheep and cattle, arable and potatoes
- *Northern Ireland* – Sheep and cattle and potatoes

Fishing

Fishing is vitally important to the UK economy. The fishing fleets operate from many locations in Scotland, the East Coast and the South West Coast of England and Northern Ireland. In addition, there are an increasing number of fish farms which are largely located in the Highlands of Scotland. The UK fishing industry provides nearly two-thirds of all the UK's requirements.

The secondary sector includes all manufacturing industries. There is a bewildering variety of different industries, but we will attempt to cover the more important ones:

- *Aerospace* – this industry includes both civil and military aircraft and is concentrated mainly in the South West, South East and North West of England, and Northern Ireland

- *Ceramics* – the ceramics industry includes pottery, pipes, earthenware, stoneware, tableware, bone china and sanitary ware. The ceramics industry is scattered throughout the UK, although certain areas specialise in particular forms of ceramics

- *Chemicals* – the UK is the fifth largest chemical manufacturer in the world, and includes cosmetics, drugs and pesticides. These industries are mainly located in the North, North West and South East of England

- *Clothing* – although this manufacturing sector is widely scattered throughout the UK, principle concentrations will be found in the North of England, the Midlands and London. Knitwear, on the other hand, will be found in Scotland and the East Midlands

- *Computers* – this high-tech industry is located primarily in Scotland and the South East of England

- *Drinks* – this industry covers a wide variety of different beverages. Obviously whisky is produced in Scotland, however, the North and North East of England specialise in cocoa

- *Food processing* – this industry centres on the production of convenience foods and is mainly located in East Anglia, and the North West and South East of England

- *Glass* – although there are several businesses which produce glass, the main manufacturer is based in Liverpool

- *Linen* – this industry's principle area of operation is Northern Ireland

- *Mechanical machinery* – this area includes the production of tractors and machine tools. It is located in Yorkshire, Humberside and the West Midlands

- *Metals* – this includes all forms of specialist metal manufacturing, and is mainly located in Wales and the Midlands

- *Paint* – the UK is one of the largest manufacturers of paint and the main centres of production are in the North, North West and South East of England

- *Printing* – this is another industry which is widely dispersed throughout England, although the main concentrations are in the South East

- *Steel* – this is located in Wales, and the North and East of England

- *Textiles* – this industry involves the processing of raw materials for the clothes industry, and is located in the North and North West of England, the East Midlands, Scotland and Northern Ireland

- *Wool* – this industry is centred in West Yorkshire and Scotland

Individual activity

Investigate your local area in terms of secondary sector business activity. Choosing two organisations which are part of this sector, but are involved in different business activities, describe by means of a list, at least four reasons why they have decided to locate there.

Compare your findings in groups of four.

The tertiary or service sector can be found in nearly all areas of the UK. The exact nature of the service is dependent upon the region. In some cases, the service industry will be restricted to tourism, whereas others will be involved in television, advertising and newspapers. As far as the tourism industry is concerned, this is supported by the British Tourist Authority, whose job it is to promote various regions and support local businesses involved in servicing the tourist sector.

Group activity

In pairs, investigate the tertiary sector within your local area. Since the tertiary sector has suffered quite badly in recent years, after a period of rapid growth, discuss how this has affected the local labour market.

Labour and skills supply

Despite the availability of all of the funds offered by the various agencies, the key issue as far as businesses are concerned is the availability of labour, and the skills that the workforce has to offer. Just as the number of people who are employed or unemployed in an area is different, so are the skills which they offer. As traditional industries have disappeared, there is the problem of retraining individuals in such a way that their existing skills can be used in new situations. Many of the training grants try to address this issue.

The other concern for businesses, is whether the area itself is declining, or one which has few young people, since they have already moved away. An organisation which is considering locating or relocating in a new area, would be well advised to look at the available government statistics before making a decision.

The rates of pay will differ greatly from area to area. Obviously, those who work in and around large cities, particularly London, will expect and receive higher rates of pay. Indeed, those working in London are likely to earn as much as 15 per cent more than those in rural areas.

Group activity

Continuing from the previous activity, in the same pairs, draw up a list of available training grants and organisations which offer retraining facilities. If possible, try to find out how successful these retraining programmes have been and how it has had a positive effect on unemployment levels in your particular area.

TECHNOLOGY

Technology has had massive and drastic impacts on jobs, particularly in recent years. Since technology is always developing, we may not know exactly the end effects it will have on the job market. Technology may affect jobs in the following ways:

- *It may permanently destroy them*
- *It may create new types of jobs*
- *t may change the nature of the job*
- *It may require the job to be carried out in an alternative location*

Robotics

Robots have been increasingly used in various industries to perform a variety of tasks which were previously carried out by humans. Specific examples are:

- *Tasks which were hazardous to the employees by virtue of them being dangerous*
- *Tasks which were hazardous to the employees by virtue of them being dirty or toxic*
- *Tasks which were monotonous and boring to the employees and did not give much job satisfaction*
- *Tasks which require a high level of dexterity skills and would therefore require substantial training of employees*

The major problem with using robots in place of human beings is their initially high cost to purchase. A complex production line may need to employ a large number of robotic machines and may not be, as yet, cost-effective to install, since the investment would not show a good return for many years. It is mainly for this reason that many employees are subjected to dangerous, dirty and monotonous work when perfectly adequate machines exist to carry out the task.

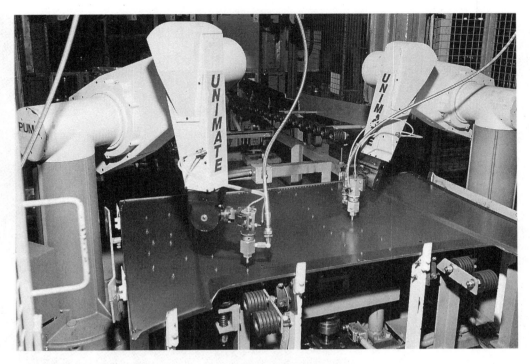

Fig 1.28 Robots applying spots of adhesive to a car bonnet

Group activity

As a group, visit a local organisation which makes substantial use of robotics or machines to replace human beings in the manufacturing or production process.

Compare this visit with your previous one to a standard manufacturing organisation. How do conditions differ between the two organisations? Has production been increased since the introduction of robotics? Could the first organisation benefit from introducing robotics or automated production?

After the visit discuss your findings within your group and identify the implications of the introduction of machinery.

Telecommunications

Every day we all use various forms of telecommunication equipment. In the home we may use telephones, radio, television and computers. It is, however, in businesses that we have seen an explosion of telecommunications equipment to aid industry. Here is a list of some of the more common forms of telecommunication:

■ *Switchboards* – these machines now operate digitally and the operator is kept updated as far as calls are concerned through a VDU system

Fig 1.29 A digital telephone switchboard   (Photo: Roger Stanton Associates Limited)

■ *Pagers and bleepers* – these relatively simple devices enable employees to keep in touch with the office. A simple message is relayed to the device giving them basic information to act upon

Fig 1.30 A radiopager

■ *Mobile and car phones* – the popularity of this type of equipment now allows managers and members of the sales force to keep in constant contact with the office, and allows many of the communications responsibilities to be carried out in alternative locations, or while travelling

Fig 1.31 A mobile phone   (Photo: Courtesy of British Telecomm)

■ *Answering machines* – these have been available for some years and recent developments include the ability to listen to messages from a remote location

■ *Facsimile machines* – this equipment is capable of relaying documents and graphics via the telephone network to another location in a few seconds. These machines have become invaluable to most businesses, particularly if they have a number of sites within the group, or need to contact establishments abroad easily

■ *Telex machines* – although these machines have been largely replaced by the facsimile machine, they still provide a useful service to businesses in terms of offering the facility to transmit larger documents. Their major downfall is their inability to transmit anything other than text. Commonly, telex machines now look like computers and not our popular image of a large and noisy typewriter

■ *Video phones* – although these are a relatively new development, they offer the potential to communicate 'face to face' from remote locations. Despite the fact that they are relatively expensive at the time of writing, it is inevitable that the cost will reduce and they will become a more popular and vital part of business life

• *Video conferencing* – the central service which provides this facility is run by British Telecom and known as Confravision. Essentially, it links a number of

1.97

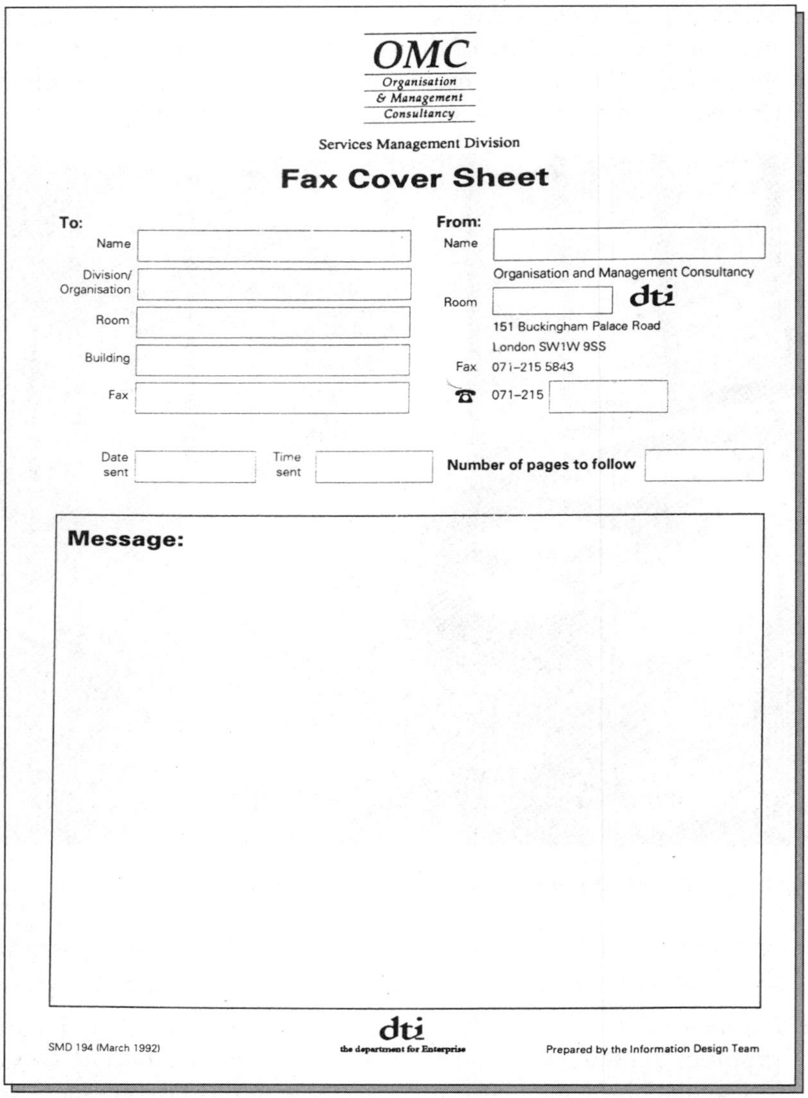

OMC
Organisation
& Management
Consultancy

Services Management Division

Fax Cover Sheet

To:

Name

Division/
Organisation

Room

Building

Fax

From:

Name

Organisation and Management Consultancy

Room   **dti**

151 Buckingham Palace Road

London SW1W 9SS

Fax   07i-215 5843

☎   071-215

Date
sent

Time
sent

Number of pages to follow

Message:

dti

SMD 194 (March 1992)   the department for Enterprise   Prepared by the Information Design Team

Fig 1.32 DTI's version of a fax cover sheet

studios located in major cities throughout the country, so that organisations may hold meetings without the need and expense of travel

■ *Electronic mail* – rather than rely on the traditional methods of sending information on hard copy through the post, electronic mail offers the opportunity to instantaneously transmit information to remote but linked computers. Further advantages of this system include an alarm device which informs the recipient that there are message(s) awaiting them

■ *Electronic libraries* – essentially, these are databases which may be accessed in a variety of ways. They range from Prestel and Oracle to complex research databases situated on remote continents

Fig 1.33 A facsimile machine   (Photo: Penn Communications Ltd)

As we have mentioned, what has made a lot of these facilities possible is the change from analogue signals, which were required to be transmitted at different frequencies, to a more flexible system called Digital. Digital signals are pulses which can be understood by computers. These pulses are sent from one computer to another via a modem or similar device and may be accessed instantly.

Fig 1.34 A telex terminal   (Photo: Manners, Borkett & Partners Limited)

1.99

Fig 1.35 Videoconferencing

Fig 1.36 An electronic mail workstation

Group activity

In groups of four, in the role of Directors of an organisation wishing to introduce new telecommunications technology, investigate sources and costs of as many of the above telecommunications devices as possible.

If the organisation was working to a limited budget, which of the devices would be purchased as a priority?

Present your recommendations in the form of a report to the Chairperson of the Board of Directors.

Computers

When we are considering computers and their effects on business, we must first realise that there are, in fact, two main types of computer. These are main frames and micros.

Mainframes

In varying forms, complexity, speed and ability, mainframe computers have been available since just after the Second World War. They are, in essence, machines with large memories and data processing abilities which can be used to store a mass of information for immediate access and amendment. It is normally the case that mainframes operate 24 hours a day, 365 days of the

Fig 1.37 A personal computer with a touch-sensitive screen

year. The advantage with running these machines continuously is that routine data processing work can be undertaken when demands on the machine are at their lowest, i.e. at night. Mainframes are used as the work horses for networked computers, providing such services as word processing, database storage, spreadsheet calculations, graphics production, stock control, accounts and electronic mail.

Micros

Microcomputers have changed beyond all recognition since their initial development only 30 years ago. Modern microcomputers are more powerful than mainframes of the past. It is the common trend for computers to become more powerful, faster, cheaper, smaller and have the ability to be used for a number of different applications. Recent developments have seen computers which can understand handwritten instructions on a touch-sensitive screen and machines which do not require a keyboard, but respond to voice activation.

Group activity

As a group, investigate the available computer technology within the institution at which you are studying. You should consider the use of computer technology within the following areas:

- Computers available for student use

- Computers available for teaching staff only

- Computers used by administrative or technical personnel

- Software packages available

- The type of information stored on a permanent basis

Discuss the current availability of computer technology to the various parts of the organisation and whether the availability should be widened to include groups presently excluded. Are there any forms of computer technology which are absent from the organisation but would be of benefit if purchased?

Technology and employment

As we said earlier, developments in technology have drastically affected the job market. Jobs have been lost, but at the same time, many jobs have been created. In the past, some of the following jobs would not have existed if it were not for developments in technology:

- *Research and development personnel*

- *Computer marketing specialists*

- *Distribution specialists*
- *Specialist retail outlets*
- *Manufacturers and assemblers of new technology*
- *Computer operators*
- *Computer programmers*
- *Computer service engineers*
- *Software engineers*
- *Data processing staff*
- *Computer analysts*

Aside from the creation of jobs, there have been a number of positive benefits which may be attributed to new technology.

Increased productivity

One of the main reasons for using new technology is to improve the flow and extent of work carried out. There have been a number of direct benefits which we can all see, a good example is a supermarket which now uses bar codes instead of price labels. By simply passing the bar-coded item over the sensor, the computer recognises the code, item and price, automatically adding this to the customer's bill. Additionally, the computer will then pass this information on to a stock control management system, which will generate reorders for the goods to ensure that stock levels are maintained. Even when it comes to paying the bill, by simply swiping a charge, debit or credit card through the till, only the customer's signature us needed.

Job changes

Although many people may think that new technology has led to many jobs being replaced or simplified, known as de-skilling, it is also the case that new technology has offered other employees the ability to upgrade their skills from, for example, the ability to only use a typewriter to becoming competent using a word processor. This is known as up-skilling. Equally, other individuals may have had the range of their skills enhanced and expanded by the use of new technology, making them more desirable as employees. This is known as multi-skilling.

The other major change which new technology has made on the employment market is regarding the location of work itself. It is no longer necessary, through such systems as tele-working to actually have to work at the office. They may well be able to work at home, or at a remote location from the main organisation. In turn, such facilities as tele-working have given individuals the opportunity to work on a flexible, part-time basis, to fit in with their other commitments. It is predicted that several million people may be able to work at home by the turn of the century and thus, for an initial investment, organisations may reduce costs and dispense with the need for expensive office premises. It should also have a positive affect on such things as sickness, lateness, travel delays and the expense of providing temporary cover for holidays.

Group activity

In groups of three, discuss the following statement:

'Computer technology in particular has had a drastically bad impact upon employment levels and job prospects.'

List your reactions to this statement and decide, as a group, whether you agree with the statement or not.

Element assignment

IMPROVING BUSINESS PERFORMANCE

Organisations can now purchase a variety of systems which are designed to improve and monitor business performance. In a great many cases, this has had a massive impact on the number of employees, their job prospects and the conditions under which they must work.

Working in pairs, compiling the information that you have gathered from the other student activities in this element, you must now produce a comprehensive report detailing the impact of technology on employment. In addition, you must compare the impact locally with that of another area.

In order to carry out this task, you might find it useful to consider the following:

■ Has unemployment in your local area increased in recent years? Could this increase be blamed on technology? If so, why?

■ When you visited the two different organisations, do you think they had been affected by the introduction of technology? If so, why?

Potential sources of information may include the following:

■ Local trade unions (who will be able to positively identify areas of business activity which have introduced technology at the expense of jobs).

■ Local Chambers of Commerce or Trade Associations

■ Local libraries (who will hold copies of local newspapers which may detail organisations who have introduced technology)

■ Your family and friends may work in organisations which have introduced technology. Ask them what effects the technology has had upon the number of people employed.

When you are considering another area to compare your local area with, you may well have to contact a Central Government Department, such as the Department of Trade and Industry for useful information and statistics.

You will find the correct format for a report in Unit 4 of this book.

UNIT TEST Element 1.3

1 What are the major differences between part-time and temporary employment?

2 What is the average working week in terms of hours for a full-time employee?

3 Identify six physical working condition in a manufacturing organisation?

4 Identify six physical working conditions in an administrative organisation?

5 List three items appearing on a typical Contract of Employment?

6 How soon does a Contract of Employment have to be issued to a new employee?

7 Who is responsible for calculating deductions from the wage or salary of an employee?

8 What is a P45?

9 What is a P11?

10 In percentage terms, how much does the employee contribute to National Insurance?

11 What is meant by vocational training?

12 What is meant by non-vocational training?

13 List four available sources of incentives for organisations to locate in particular areas?

14 List three natural resources commonly found in the North of England?

15 Idenfify two manufacturing industries commonly found in the South West of England?

16 List three portable telecommunications devices?

17 In terms of computers, what is meant by 'industry standard'?

18 What is meant by the term 'de-skilling'?

19 What is EPOS?

20 What are the major differences between a mainframe and a micro?

UNIT 1   End Test

1 Identify which one of the following organisations is not in the private sector
   (a)   Sainsbury
   (b)   British Telecom
   (c)   Dixons
   (d)   British Coal

2 How many of the following are primary sector industries? Coal-mining, gold-mining, waste disposal and forestry
   (a)   One
   (b)   Two
   (c)   Three
   (d)   Four

3 What are the minimum and maximum numbers of partners allowed in a partnership?
- (a)   2–3
- (b)   2–30
- (c)   2–10
- (d)   2–5

4 What does 'market share' mean?
- (a)   The fact that several organisations have the whole market
- (b)   A shop contains several smaller businesses
- (c)   The percentage of a total market controlled by an organisation
- (d)   Two or more businesses agreeing to help one another

5 What is the difference between a multinational and an international business?
- (a)   One is a group of foreign businesses, the other is not
- (b)   One has foreign directors, the other does not
- (c)   There is no difference
- (d)   One produces and sells in many countries, the other just sells

6 Which of the following organisations do not involve themselves in attracting business into depressed areas?
- (a)   United Nations
- (b)   European Community
- (c)   Local authorities
- (d)   The UK Government

7 Which of the following could best describe seasonal employment?
- (a)   Full-time
- (b)   Part-time
- (c)   Temporary
- (d)   Occasional

8 What is a P45?
- (a)   A VAT document
- (b)   A feature of a contract of employment
- (c)   A tax document
- (d)   A code for a training programme

9 What does EPOS mean?
- (a)   Efficiency Programme for Organisational Structure
- (b)   Ethics, Policy, Ordinary Strategies
- (c)   Educational Portions of Student
- (d)   Electronic Point of Sale

10 What does the term 'de-skilling' mean?
- (a)   Teaching an employee to undertake another task
- (b)   The changes in a job, brought about by technology
- (c)   The gradual increase in skill needs
- (d)   Not needing skills, as they may be 'bought-in' from outside the business

Unit 2
PEOPLE IN BUSINESS ORGANISATIONS
Intermediate Level

Element 2.1
Examine and compare structures and functions in business organisations

Element 2.2
Explain rights and responsibilities of employees and employers

Element 2.3
Investigate job roles

Element 2.1
Structures and functions in business organisations

PERFORMANCE CRITERIA

1 **Organisational structures are described**
2 **Influence of different structures on decision making is decribed**
3 **Functions within organisations are described and explained**
4 **Different structures and functions within business organisations are identified**

RANGE

1 **Organisational structures: hierachical and flat**
2 **Functions: design and production, personnel, finance, administration, sales and marketing, and distribution**

EVIDENCE INDICATORS

Organisational charts showing structures and functions for two business organisations. The candidate should give examples to show how decision making differs between organisations (e.g. the sole trader, flat structure, takes all decisions for planning, quality, delivery, etc., while larger organisations spread decision making). Evidence should demonstrate understanding of the implications of the range dimensions in relation to the element. The unit test will confirm the candidate's coverage of the range.

FACTORS AFFECTING ORGANISATIONAL STRUCTURES

There are many factors which influence the organisational structure of a business or enterprise. In order to appreciate the important demands which an organisation must fulfil, we must look at private and public sector organisations separately.

Private Sector organisations

Factors which affect private sector organisations include:

1 **The number of employees,** in effect the actual size of the organisation

2 **Type of premises used.** A multi- or split-site organisation with a number of different branches would need to be organised in a radically different manner from an organisation which is based in a single building

   An organisation which is regional, national or international will base its organisational structure around logical groups of employees

3 **Type of business.** If the organisation is in the primary sector, it is likely to be organised in such a way as to allow the efficient processing of the raw materials as possible, and may be based around a single mine, forest or quarry

   A manufacturing organisation may either carry out all its processing procedures on a single site, or may need to transport partly finished goods to other specialist sites. Organisations in this case may be based on the single factory unit, or a cluster of factories which contribute towards the finishing of a product

   Distribution organisations tend to be organised around a regional, national or international framework. Depending on the bulk of goods being distributed, the organisational structure will be complex in certain geographical areas and more simple in others. In other words if the organisation is busy in one area, its size and complexity will reflect this. As with many organisations, good communications between the regions is vital and a separate part of the organisational structure may concentrate on dealing with this area

   In the retailing sector the obvious organisational structure is that of the branch. However, many functions of the business are carried out centrally. These services tend to be of a managerial, financial or buying nature, which allows the individual branches to concentrate on the selling process

   Professional services tend to operate on the basis of a number of specialist individuals who are assisted by a variety of support staff. Often these support staff are drawn from a 'pool' of clerical and secretarial employees

4 **The number, type and size of the clients may have a bearing on the organisational structure.** If the organisation deals with only a handful of clients, then the structure need not be overly complex. On the other hand, if it is dealing with literally millions of retail customers, then the demands on the structure may be much greater

5   **The past structure of the organisation and its history may be a good or bad influence on how it is structured.** An old-fashioned organisation which has successfully managed to survive for many years may not see the need to change its structure. It may not appreciate the benefits of reorganisation and may be structured in such a way as to prevent the possibility of growth or adaptation to new demands

6   **The current structure of an organisation can again be a positive or negative influence on the day-to-day running of the business.** If the organisation has recently undergone changes, it will be unlikely to adapt to further changes without encountering considerable problems.

7   **Future needs of an organisation should directly influence its structure.** The need to constantly react to changing demands, diversify into new areas and respond to changes in legislation are all strong reasons to consider how the organisation is structured

Group activity

In pairs, research a local organisation belonging to the private sector. Your main aim is to look at the organisational structure and try to draw up an organisation chart. You may also wish to look at the student activity on page **2.6**, as you may be required to look at the job functions of various employees in that activity.

It may be useful for you and your partner to consider any work experience, Saturday work or vacation work you have undertaken in the past.

Your chart should include as many individual employees as possible. It would also be useful to indicate on the chart the hierarchy of the organisation, showing where decisions are made and who implements them.

When you have completed your chart, compare this with other charts drawn up by other members of the group.

Public Sector organisations

1   The duties and responsibilities of the organisation will directly affect the way in which it is structured. The more diverse and complex its operations, the more complicated the structure will be. It may also be required by law to provide certain additional services (e.g. an information office) and monitoring services to keep a constant check on spending and budget control

2   The geographical extent of the organisation's responsibility will not only affect the size of the organisation, but also its structure. From the smallest parish to the organisation responsible nationally for delivering a range of services we can see some basic similarities, but obviously the former is far less complex than the latter. Other types of organisation which can be identified by their size are borough, district, town, city, county and region

3   The ever-changing Government policies that impact upon the running of public sector organisations may well influence the structure of the

organisation. In recent years Rate Departments transformed into
Community Charge Departments, then into Council Tax Departments,
meaning rapid reorganisation, retraining and redeployment of staff

4 The amount of income the organisation has, which may come directly from
Central Government or from payments made by the public, will determine the
complexity of the structure. In cases when much of the finance is collected by
the organisation itself, large departments may be solely responsible for
collection of money. In addition, the organisation must have other departments
which oversee the services provided to the public

5 Technological change has had a general impact on all types of organisation.
Many have developed complex and sophisticated computer systems in order to
handle as many of the routine tasks as possible. The availability of computers
and their relative fall in price has made them accessible to even the smallest
types of public sector organisation

6 The public makes many more demands on public sector organisations than in
the past. One of the most significant is its interest in how and why decisions are
made on its behalf. Public sector organisations must therefore be ready, willing
and able to provide a wide variety of information instantly and on demand.
Public Relations Departments and Liaison Officers have become common in
nearly all public sector organisations. Meetings are nearly always open to the
public with information packs available on request

7 As in the private sector, public sector organisations are finding it increasingly
difficult to operate in isolation. Many factors which influence the decision
making in a private organisation also apply to them. Important decisions may
have been made nationally or internationally that public sector organisations
cannot ignore, therefore the structure needs to be flexible enough to cope

8 Some public sector organisations may have direct contact with the public.
Those which provide goods, services or advisory assistance will need to devote
part of their activity to this area. Those which do provide these types of services
are similar in many ways to either private sector manufacturing or retailing
organisations. A great many public sector organisations, however, only have
minimal direct contact with the public

Group activity

This is a similar task to the previous one. Remaining in the same pairs, first
identify a public sector organisation in your local area. Second, try to draw up an
organisational chart along the same lines as the one which you completed for the
private sector organisation. In all probability this chart for the public sector organisation will be more difficult to complete. There may well be many more employees, departments and functions to consider. If necessary you may have to draw
up additional charts to show the structure of particular departments and how they
inter-relate with other departments.

Again, try to show where decisions are made and who must implement them.
Once you have done this, compare your private sector chart with this public sector
one. You will notice that there are many more layers of decision making in the
public sector chart than in the private sector chart. Why do you think this is so?

TYPES OF ORGANISATIONAL STRUCTURE

As we have seen, the structure of an organisation will vary depending on the nature of a number of factors:

1 *The size and nature of the market in which it operates*
2 *The type of business it is involved in*
3 *The maintenance of good communications*
4 *The size of the organisation*
5 *The number of branches/outlets/sites*
6 *The type and number of clients*
7 *How much it is affected by Government legislation*
8 *Impact of new technologies*
9 *Nature and extent of responsibilities and obligations*
10 *Past and current structure*
11 *Future plans*
12 *Complexity of business activity*

Before we concentrate on the activities of each individual department, division or unit of an organisation, we must first look at the overall nature of the structure.

Individual activity

Individually, try to put in ranking order the 12 points made above. Give yourself 10 minutes to think about this. When you have completed this task, compare your list with those of the rest of the group. Try to agree a common ranking order.

Hierarchical structures

The best way to understand what a hierarchical structure looks like is to imagine a pyramid. At the top of the pyramid are the owners or major decision makers of the organisation. As we look further down the pyramid the shape of the organisation broadens as more employees are involved at that level. At the base of the pyramid are the majority of the employees and below them are the customers.

Responsibility, power and authority are all much greater at the top of the pyramid than at the bottom. Decisions flow down the pyramid affecting a succession of layers of employees.

This form of structure can be also referred to as 'a pecking order' as the higher up the pyramid you are as an employee, the more power and

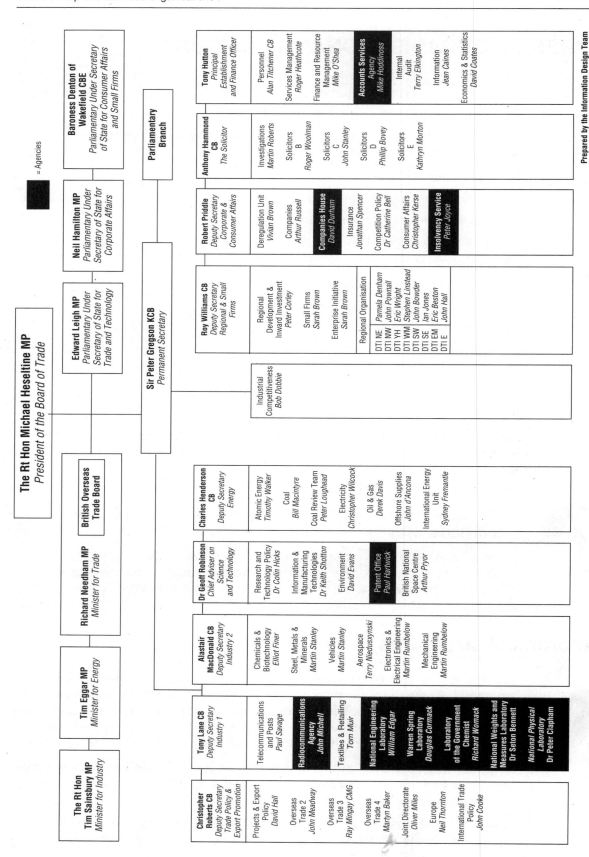

Fig 2.1 The DTI's organisation chart

Prepared by the Information Design Team

= Agencies

The Rt Hon Michael Heseltine MP
President of the Board of Trade

The Rt Hon Tim Sainsbury MP
Minister for Industry

Tim Eggar MP
Minister for Energy

Richard Needham MP
Minister for Trade

British Overseas Trade Board

Edward Leigh MP
Parliamentary Under Secretary of State for Trade and Technology

Neil Hamilton MP
Parliamentary Under Secretary of State for Corporate Affairs

Baroness Denton of Wakefield CBE
Parliamentary Under Secretary of State for Consumer Affairs and Small Firms

Parliamentary Branch

Sir Peter Gregson KCB
Permanent Secretary

Industrial Competitiveness
Bob Dobbie

Christopher Roberts CB
Deputy Secretary Trade Policy & Export Promotion

Projects & Export Policy
David Hall

Overseas Trade 2
John Meadway

Overseas Trade 3
Ray Mingay CMG

Overseas Trade 4
Martyn Baker

Joint Directorate
Oliver Miles

Europe
Neil Thornton

International Trade Policy
John Cooke

Tony Lane CB
Deputy Secretary Industry 1

Telecommunications and Posts
Paul Savage

Radiocommunications Agency
John Michell

Textiles & Retailing
Tom Muir

National Engineering Laboratory
William Edgar

Warren Spring Laboratory
Douglas Cormack

Laboratory of the Government Chemist
Richard Womack

National Weights and Measures Laboratory
Dr Seton Bennett

National Physical Laboratory
Dr Peter Clapham

Alastair MacDonald CB
Deputy Secretary Industry 2

Chemicals & Biotechnology
Elliot Finer

Steel, Metals & Minerals
Martin Stanley

Vehicles
Martin Stanley

Aerospace
Terry Nieduszynski

Electronics & Electrical Engineering
Martin Rumbelow

Mechanical Engineering
Martin Rumbelow

Dr Geoff Robinson
Chief Adviser on Science and Technology

Research and Technology Policy
Dr Colin Hicks

Information & Manufacturing Technologies
Dr Keith Shotton

Environment
David Evans

Patent Office
Paul Hartwick

British National Space Centre
Arthur Pryor

Charles Henderson CB
Deputy Secretary Energy

Atomic Energy
Timothy Walker

Coal
Bill Macintyre

Coal Review Team
Peter Loughead

Electricity
Christopher Wilcock

Oil & Gas
Derek Davis

Offshore Supplies
John d'Ancona

International Energy Unit
Sydney Fremantle

Roy Williams CB
Deputy Secretary Regional & Small Firms

Regional Development & Inward Investment
Peter Corley

Small Firms
Sarah Brown

Enterprise Initiative
Sarah Brown

Regional Organisation

DTI NE	*Pamela Denham*
DTI NW	*John Pownall*
DTI YH	*Eric Wright*
DTI WM	*Stephen Linstead*
DTI SW	*John Bowder*
DTI SE	*Ian Jones*
DTI EM	*Eric Beston*
DTI E	*John Hall*

Robert Priddle
Deputy Secretary Corporate & Consumer Affairs

Deregulation Unit
Vivian Brown

Companies
Arthur Russell

Companies House
David Durham

Insurance
Jonathan Spencer

Competition Policy
Dr Catherine Bell

Consumer Affairs
Christopher Kerse

Insolvency Service
Peter Joyce

Anthony Hammond CB
The Solicitor

Investigations
Martin Roberts

Solicitors B
Roger Woolman

Solicitors C
John Stanley

Solicitors D
Philip Bovey

Solicitors E
Kathryn Morton

Tony Hutton
Principal Establishment and Finance Officer

Personnel
Alan Titchener CB

Services Management
Roger Heathcote

Finance and Resource Management
Mike O'Shea

Accounts Services Agency
Mike Hoddinoss

Internal Audit
Terry Elkington

Information
Jean Caines

Economics & Statistics
David Coates

authority you have. Equally, we can see that the lower down the pyramid you are, the less influence you have on the organisation as a whole.

The reason for this hierarchical structure is that important decisions need to be made by those who have expertise and experience along with enough authority to make sure that a decision is implemented. Those at the top of the pyramid take all the credit for success, but also bear the consequences of failure.

Typically, a structure would begin with Directors at the top of the pyramid making decisions for Heads of Departments below to pass on to Middle Managers who would then tell the junior members of staff to implement them. The higher an individual is in the pyramid, the less likely they are to understand how things are implemented. They may just have an idea of overall strategy and base their decisions on information received via the various layers below them. Each time information passes from layer to layer, the relative importance of what has been said may change. It is therefore likely that those at the top of the pyramid will have a distorted view of the organisation and how it really works.

For those at the bottom of the pyramid, the Directors will seem remote, unable to understand the organisation's needs and unwilling to change decisions which may adversely affect the day-to-day running of the business.

The main advantage of this structure is that each layer sees the organisation in its own peculiar way. Each layer will have different opinions, priorities and interpretation of overall organisational policy.

There are two main versions of hierarchical structure:

The Steep Pyramid

In this version of the hierarchical structure, there are many layers of management. The reason for this may be that the organisation operates in several different locations and needs to duplicate the administration in order to function efficiently. Alternatively, the nature of the business may be very complex, requiring the processing of many orders, messages, pieces of information or complaints.

Because the structure is multilayered and complicated, those further down the pyramid find it difficult to understand how and why decisions are made and the organisation may find it impossible to make sure that the employees follow through 'corporate decisions' (general statements of policy and procedures). The organisation may also suffer from being 'bureaucratic'. This means that decisions must pass through so many layers that they take a very long time to put into operation, and the systems designed to help implement them become more complicated than they need to be.

The Flat Pyramid

The theory behind having less layers in the pyramid is that decisions can be made quickly and efficiently. Each layer is able to communicate easily with other layers and avoids the danger of becoming 'bureaucratic'. This simpler structure is generally found in organisations operating from a single site where Directors and other decision makers are readily available for consultation and guidance.

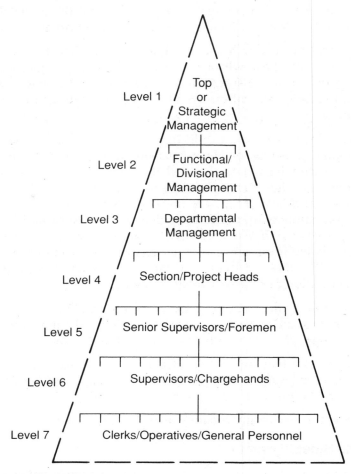

Fig 2.2 The steep pyramid

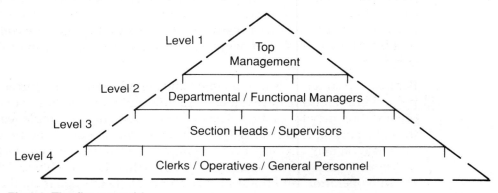

Fig 2.3 The flat pyramid

Employees find it easier to understand the Directors' reasoning behind decisions and therefore feel more a part of the organisation and less isolated.

Cone structures

In recent years, some major organisations have recognised that relying on a pyramid structure has prevented quick and necessary decisions and change from taking place. This new form of structure is known commonly as 'decentralisation'. This is the exact opposite to having centralised services which assist individual branches or sites. Each part of the organisation which carries out a distinctly different function in the organisation is given a level of autonomy. This means that they are allowed, up to a point, to make decisions for themselves without the permission or consent of the Directors or the central office. This allows each sub-organisation to be more flexible to its own needs and customers without waiting for central office to consider any points of concern which have been passed on to it. Most typically the structure consists of a central 'holding' company (these are the owners of several companies who, while interested in the profits and decisions made by their companies, do not meddle in the day-to-day business) which has devolved (passed down power and authority) responsibility to each company forming part of the group.

Line Management structure

As we have seen, a typical hierarchy in an organisation consists of a number of layers, through which power, responsibility and authority are delegated. This process is known as Line Management. In other words, each person knows to whom they are responsible and from whom they should take instructions. A typical example of this would be the Sales Director who is responsible for supervising the Sales Manager, who, in turn, directs the operations of the Regional Sales Managers. They have authority over their own Sales personnel.

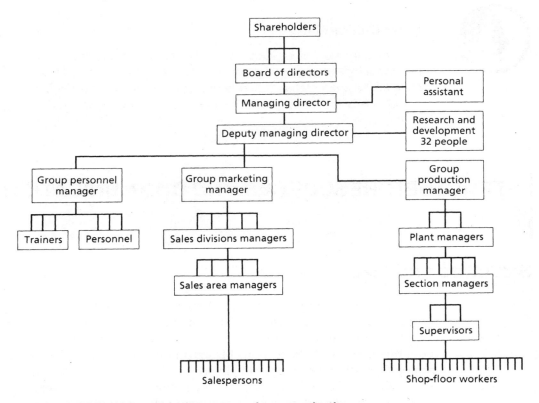

Fig 2.4 Typical hierarchical structure of an organisation
(Adapted from *Understanding Business*, A Norman, P Norman and P Shortt, Pitman Publishing, 1993)

Staff Management structure

This type of structure refers to individuals who carry out a specialised function within the organisation. In a typical retail outlet there will be a Line Management structure which can trace authority from the Directors at Central Office right down to the sales assistants. However, certain members of staff are not directly part of this line. The Personnel Department, for example, does not have day-to-day authority over the branches, but does get involved in matters relating to personnel when needed. Equally, the Marketing Department, which again may be based centrally, will be carrying out functions which do not require reference to the branches. Generally speaking a staff relationship describes the liaison between other employees in the organisation that are not part of the direct line of authority.

Line and Staff Management structure

In reality, most organisations have a mixture of both Line and Staff structures. This can also be described as a Matrix Structure. This particularly suits larger organisations with a number of different sites and complex production/sales operations. The departments which make up the staff side of the organisation tend to service the various lines of authority. In other words, they have respons-ibilities and authorities which span across a number of lines of authority and provide a specialist service. Good examples of this are the warehouse, the Buying Department and the Personnel Department.

Individual activity

Returning to your two organisational charts, try to match them against the struc-tures which have just been covered. You may find that they do not necessarily have all the characteristics of one of them. In fact, they may be a mixture of two or more. Now try to reorganise your charts to fit one of the structures above of your choice.

STRUCTURE, RESOURCES AND COMMUNICATION

Structure and size

If we start with the most simple structure of an organisation we begin with the person who works on their own. This person would obviously be responsible for everything that the organisation does. Someone, for example, who set up a mail order business would be responsible for buying in products, designing the catalogue, getting it printed, carrying out market research to find the kind of person that would buy its products, researching a mailing list, sending out catalogues, taking orders, despatching them, dealing with any correspondence, paying bills, banking cheques, doing the accounts and a hundred other things.

In this situation the individual who is running the business is at the centre of everything.

The larger the organisation, the more need there is for people to specialise in a particular area. Good examples are bank managers, solicitors and accountants. All of these people have specialist skills. All of these people can take some of the responsibility off an individual business person's shoulders.

As a business expands it needs to employ people, some part time, some full time. As it expands, the person who set the company up, has to think about what they need to do. The business needs to be organised in the best possible way in order to meet the objectives that have been set for it. A definition is needed for what individuals do, and precisely what departments are responsible for. Who will supervise the employees? Who should tell them what to do? Where does everyone fit into the organisation? And who is ultimately responsible? This is known as the division of labour and specialisation.

The division of labour involves breaking down the process of producing things or providing services into clearly defined specialist tasks. The fact is that if the process is broken down into these separate tasks then production can actually be increased. Instead of one person trying to do everything, everybody who works as part of the production of goods or services specialises. Specialism means being more efficient.

Advantages and disadvantages of specialisation

Advantages	Disadvantages
■ Resources can actually be concentrated where they are needed the most	■ Specialisation can often lead to doing a very boring job. Simple repetition of the same task day in day out demoralises people and they can become less efficient
■ If the worker becomes more efficient at doing a particular job they become more skilled	
■ Specialisation allows greater output. This means that each item produced is produced cheaper because the labour involved in producing it is less for each unit	■ Specialisation is always dependent on how good or efficient the specialists in the previous task were. If they are not as efficient or as fast at every stage of the production this can cause bottlenecks
■ If people specialise then they can pass on their skills and experience to others and help them become more efficient	■ There is a tendency in specialisation for workers to become little more than machines. This in turn could lead to loss of skill
■ Specialising will hopefully bring a better standard of living. By specialising, talents can be developed and traded with other people	■ Specialising actually reduces a worker's ability to adapt to change
■ A specialist can do a job well rather than lots of jobs badly	■ Those that specialise have only got a narrow view of the product or service which they are actually producing. If someone makes something from start to finish they have got a greater overview and can help make things more efficient in the long run

Group activity

Considering the establishment in which you are studying, work in pairs in an attempt to discover the level of specialisation of the teaching staff. You will find that some of them concentrate on particular subject areas, while others are involved in a range of different topics.

Construct a series of pie charts which illustrate the amount of time each of the teachers spend on particular subject areas. Colour code the pie charts so that you can easily see who is involved in which area. When you have done this, show the pie chart to the teacher(s) involved and obtain feedback from them as to whether they consider themselves to be a specialist or not.

THE DESIGN OF ORGANISATIONAL STRUCTURES

Many organisations are constructed in a formal way. The organisation needs to reflect the kind of activities for which each worker is going to be responsible, and it also needs to see exactly what they are responsible for.

Departmental structures

Departmentalisation is the process by which an organisation has certain functions which it carries out grouped logically under a particular manager. There are usually four ways of grouping employees or things which an organisation does:

1 What they produce, known as the product
2 By their function, or what they do for the organisation
3 By process, which means how they do it by geographical area and maybe various regional offices to a company
4 By type of customer, for example they may deal with other business organisations, or they may deal with retail

This leads us to look at another form of organisational structure and that is the Division by Function. As we saw above, one of the most common ways of organising the structure of the business is to look at exactly what employees do. Every organisation has its own way of structuring the functions that it carries out and some of the more common ones follow. (*See* Figs 2.5 to 2.12.)

The Administration Department

Most organisations have a central administration. The main function of an Administration Department is to control paperwork and to support all the other departments by servicing their needs for secretarial work – filing, mailing, handling data, etc.

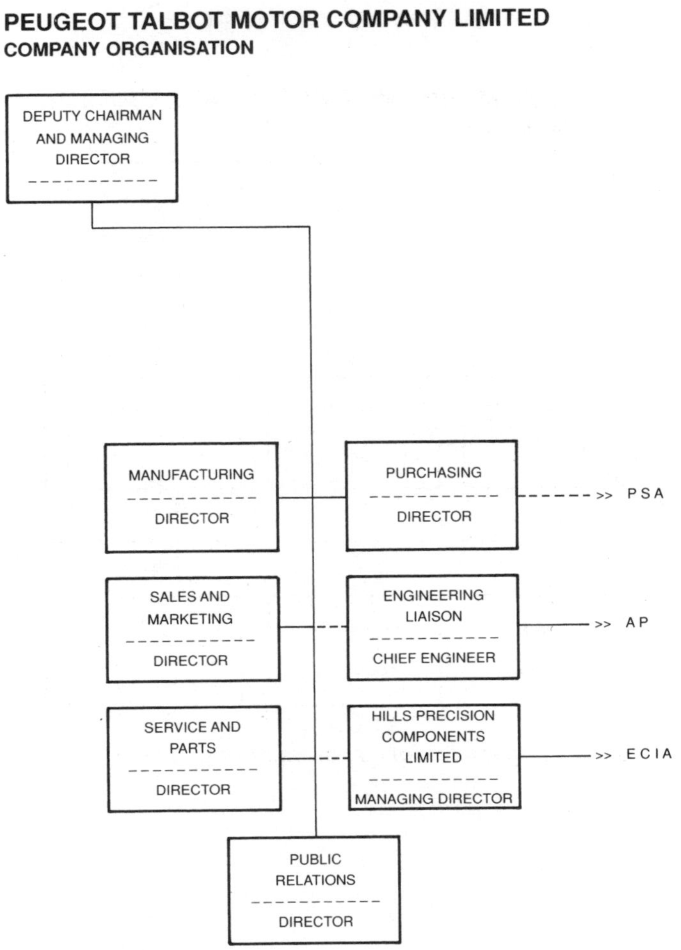

PEUGEOT TALBOT MOTOR COMPANY LIMITED
COMPANY ORGANISATION

```
                    ┌─────────────────┐
                    │ DEPUTY CHAIRMAN │
                    │  AND MANAGING   │
                    │    DIRECTOR     │
                    │  ──────────     │
                    └─────────────────┘
```

| MANUFACTURING | PURCHASING |
| ─────────── | ─────────── |
| DIRECTOR | DIRECTOR | ----->> P S A

| SALES AND MARKETING | ENGINEERING LIAISON |
| ─────────── | ─────────── |
| DIRECTOR | CHIEF ENGINEER | >> A P

| SERVICE AND PARTS | HILLS PRECISION COMPONENTS LIMITED |
| ─────────── | ─────────── |
| DIRECTOR | MANAGING DIRECTOR | >> E C I A

| PUBLIC RELATIONS |
| ─────────── |
| DIRECTOR |

Fig 2.5 Peugeot Talbot's company organisation charts illustrate the value of departmentalisation and specialisation

As offices have become more used to using computers, Administration Departments have shrunk in size because many of the tasks carried out by them can now be carried out simply at the desktop with a networked computer. We will look at this in more detail later.

One of the more common features that is still carried out by an Administration Department is that of organising office services. The manager in charge of office services is responsible for training, advising departments about how their space should be organised, supplying equipment, stationery and setting up an effective communication system within the organisation, which obviously includes the telephones and the mailing.

The Administration Department will also provide a centralised purchasing service for office supplies and storage. It also operates as a 'pool' of business stationery and corporate materials, e.g. memoranda and letterhead paper, and will co-ordinate the mass printing of the stationery. Allied to this it will control the large central photocopying facilities, providing a fast and efficient reprographic facility, which may include photocopying, collating and binding of documents.

PEUGEOT TALBOT MOTOR COMPANY LIMITED
MANUFACTURING

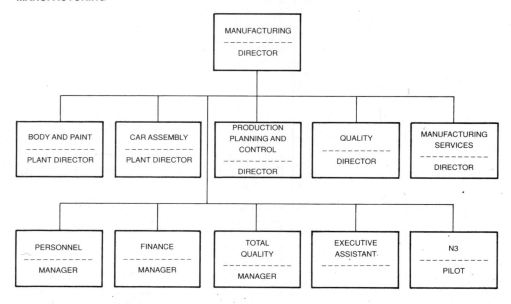

Fig 2.6 Peugeot Talbot – manufacturing division

PEUGEOT TALBOT MOTOR COMPANY LIMITED
SALES AND MARKETING

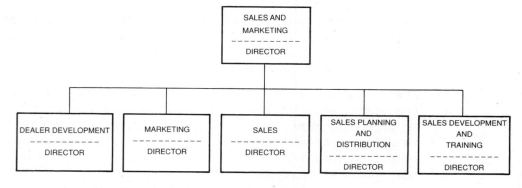

Fig 2.7 Peugeot Talbot – sales and marketing division

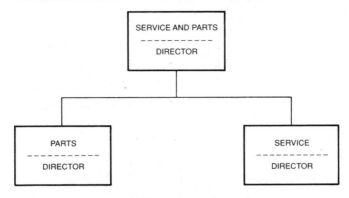

PEUGEOT TALBOT MOTOR COMPANY LIMITED
SERVICE AND PARTS

Fig 2.8 Peugeot Talbot – service and parts division

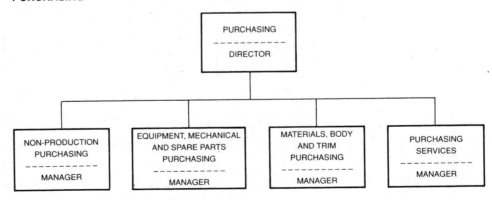

PEUGEOT TALBOT MOTOR COMPANY LIMITED
PURCHASING

Fig 2.9 Peugeot Talbot – purchasing division

2.17

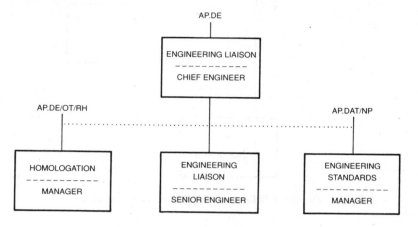

PEUGEOT TALBOT MOTOR COMPANY LIMITED
ENGINEERING LIAISON

Fig 2.10 Peugeot Talbot – engineering liaison division

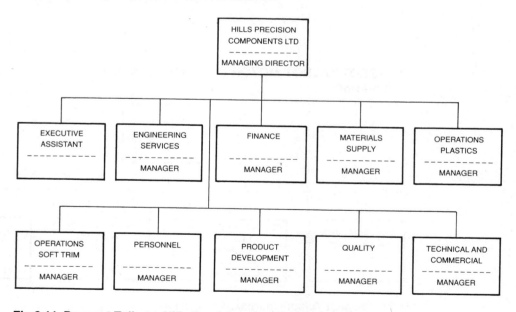

HILLS PRECISION COMPONENTS LIMITED

Fig 2.11 Peugeot Talbot – Hills Precision Components Limited

PEUGEOT TALBOT MOTOR COMPANY LIMITED
PUBLIC RELATIONS

```
                    ┌─────────────────────┐
                    │   PUBLIC RELATIONS  │
                    │   - - - - - - - - - │
                    │      DIRECTOR       │
                    └─────────────────────┘
                              │
        ┌─────────────────────┼─────────────────────┐
┌─────────────────┐ ┌─────────────────┐ ┌─────────────────┐
│ PUBLIC RELATIONS│ │ PUBLIC RELATIONS│ │   MOTOR SPORT   │
│ - - - - - - - - │ │ - - - - - - - - │ │ - - - - - - - - │
│     MANAGER     │ │     MANAGER     │ │     MANAGER     │
└─────────────────┘ └─────────────────┘ └─────────────────┘
```

Fig 2.12 Peugeot Talbot – public relations division

Traditionally, Administration Departments are responsible for arranging insurance for the organisation and the monitoring of leasing agreements (cars, equipment and premises).

Individual activity

Using the information that you have gathered from the organisations in the previous activities, try to work out in percentage terms how many employees work in the Administration Department of the organisation.

The Accounts/Finance Department

The Accounts Department supervises all matters involving finance. Again computers and calculators are used extensively. It is often the case that an Accounts Department is split up into two further sections.

The day-to-day accounting procedures are handled by the Financial Accounting Section. Essentially this keeps track of all incoming and outgoing cash or credits.

On the other hand, the Management Accounting Section concentrates on analysing the figures and trying to predict possible income and outgoings into the future.

In detail, the Accounts/Finance Department will record and monitor the following: sales, purchasing, manufacturing costs, running costs (lighting, heating, etc.), dividends to shareholders, payment of salaries and wages and departmental and organisational budgets.

At all times, the Accounts/Finance Department must know whether the organisation is operating at a profit. This is achieved by checking that revenue from sales is greater than costs. The Directors, shareholders and senior managers will need to have access to this information instantly. This is presented in various forms, such as Balance Sheets and Profit and Loss Accounts. We will look at this in much more detail later in the book.

The department is also responsible for maintaining records of financial transactions required by law, e.g. the payment of tax, National Insurance and pension fund arrangements.

Individual activity

Following on from the work carried out regarding the Administration Department, calculate a similar percentage for this area of work. Also try to find out whether the organisations carry out all of the accounts and finance functions themselves, or whether some tasks are undertaken elsewhere by other organisations.

The Sales Department

The Sales Department's main responsibility is to create orders for goods and services. Many organisations employ a large sales force which can be based either, in the case of retail stores, on a local level, or, in the case of organisations which supply to other organisations, on a regional basis.

The greater the emphasis on selling to individual customers, the larger the sales force, and those organisations which rely on heavy advertising to stimulate interest in their goods or services can have a relatively small sales team.

In terms of organising the efforts of the sales employees, the Sales Department will draw up a detailed Sales Plan which will include targets to be met by each area or region of the sales force. It will also include in this the level of profit that can be expected from each and every product.

Working closely with the Marketing Department, the Sales Department will regularly supply sales information regarding sales levels, activities of competitors and requests from customers for new or improved products. The sales force compiles the raw data about its sales figures on a weekly basis, this will be interpreted by the Sales Manager, who will then pass it on for analysis by the Marketing Department.

In order to stimulate sales, the Sales Department will develop a range of 'point of sale' (this will include posters, leaflets and boxes with the company logo) and other promotional materials.

Individual activity

Again, work out the percentage of employees engaged in this area of activity from the organisations you researched.

In the role of a Sales Representative, try to map out a typical working week, assuming the following:

■ You are only required to be present on the organisation's premises for two hours per week

■ Your customer list extends to over 200 organisations

■ The sales area for which you are responsible is roughly one-tenth of the UK

■ Your normal travelling time (i.e. time spent driving from customer to customer) is around 20 hours per week

■ Your normal visiting time per customer is approximately 20 minutes

■ You are required to spend around one and a half hours per day on paper work

■ You are usually on the telephone (you have a car phone – but remember you are not supposed to use the phone whilst driving) for approximately an hour each day

Compare your weekly timetable with those in the rest of the group.

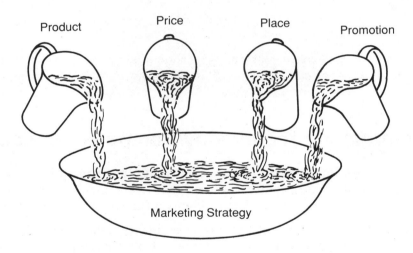

Product   Price   Place   Promotion

Marketing Strategy

Fig 2.13 The marketing mix

The Marketing Department

The main function of the Marketing Department is to try to identify customer requirements. There is also an element here of trying to predict customer needs into the future.

The Marketing Department works very closely with the Sales Department, and it is important that the two communicate well.

The starting point for most marketing functions is to carry out extensive research on a particular market to try to discover exactly what consumers want, where they want it, how much they want to pay for it, and the most effective way of getting the message across. This is known as the Marketing Mix. We will look at this again in more detail later (*see* Fig 2.13).

The Marketing Department needs to work closely with the R&D Department and the Production Department in developing attractive and sellable products. This will also include the constant updating of existing products to cater for changes in taste and demand.

One of the more obvious responsibilities of the Marketing Department is the design and development of advertising ideas and marketing campaigns. This design and development process will take account of the needs of the Sales Department and any other interested area of the organisation.

As a part of the regular market research procedures, the Marketing Department will monitor changes in trends and fashions related to its customers. Some information is readily available as statistical tables published by the Government, but much information must be researched as required by the organisation itself.

Individual activity

As carried out in the tasks related to other departments of an organisation, we would like you to calculate the percentage of employees engaged in this area of the organisation's activity.

In the role of Marketing Manager, where would you look for changes in customer trends and fashions? What use do you think you could make of this information?

The Information Technology/Computer Services Department

The Information Technology/Computer Services Department's responsibility will include computing (both hardware and software), maintenance of databases, telecommunications, and other technological office developments.

As most organisations are now incorporating computers into almost everything that they do, the number of Information Technology/Computer Services Departments that can be considered to be truly separate are diminishing.

The Information Technology/Computer Services Manager must not only be aware of new developments in technology, but must also know how to use them. They will also supply all support and guidance to help others accomplish this too.

Individual activity

Referring back to your review concerning the computers and software available in your institution, draw up a chart which shows the responsibility for the purchasing, maintenance and training related to information technology.

Do not forget to also calculate the percentage number of employees engaged in activities related to information technology in your two organisational charts.

The Research and Development Department

Working closely with the Marketing Department, which is keeping a constant check on competitors' products and services, the R&D Department may be informed of the need for a new product. Equally, it may be developing new products or ranges of products in its own right.

The main function of the R&D Department is not only to design new products, but work out the most efficient and logical method of producing them. It will, after a number of exhaustive tests, pass on its designs and proposed methods of production to the Production Department itself, which will then be responsible for putting it into production.

Routinely, the R&D Department will test random samples of products being manufactured to ensure that they comply with the quality standards set by the organisation, as well as Government legislation. In some organisations this function is separated from the R&D Department and called the Quality Assurance/Control Department.

The R&D Department will also test competitors' products to see how they have been manufactured and whether the organisation's products compare favourably to them. Additionally, it will keep a close eye on the technological advances made within its area to see if the design and production processes used can be improved.

Individual activity

With reference to your organisational charts, you may have discovered that neither organisation has a Research and Development Department. If they have, calculate the percentage number of employees engaged in the organisation's business activities. What kind of research and development is carried out in this department?

If you have discovered that they do not have a Research and Development Department, what benefits could the organisation obtain from the setting up of a department to deal with research and development?

The Production Department

The Production Department is involved in all functions which revolve around producing the goods or services for the customer.

This department will also monitor levels of wastage to ensure the most efficient use of resources, it will check the costs of raw materials and parts purchased to make sure that profit margins are maintained.

As new products are developed, and technology changes, the Production Department will be responsible for purchasing all the necessary plant and equipment required, as well as organising the production process.

In consultation with the Sales Department, the Production Department must make sure that it can manufacture or supply customers with the quantity required at the time they have been requested. The tight monitoring of production levels means that the Production Department should know how long it would take to produce enough products to fill a particular order. Advanced planning and close liaison with the Sales Department is vital as deadlines must be met.

Regardless of how many units of products are being produced, the Production Department is also responsible for the maintenance of quality. Each product must meet a number of strict quality standards and must to all intents and purposes be exactly the same every time. Periodically, products will be randomly selected from the production line and tested by either the R&D Department or the Quality Assurance/Control Department.

A good Production Department will monitor methods of production used by all major competitors and allied industries and be taking steps to implement any useful methods of production used elsewhere.

Increasingly, as production becomes steadily more automated, the Production Department will also have to design computer programs which can handle the new processes.

Individual activity

Again, your organisations may not necessarily produce physical goods. If they do, calculate the percentage of employees engaged in this activity. Looking at the turnover of the organisation involved, divide this number by the total number of employees in the Production Department. This will give a very crude idea of how productive each employee is. Compare your total with those of other members of your group and see whose organisation is the most productive.

If your organisations do not have a Production Department, then try to identify another department which fulfils a similar function. It may not necessarily be called a Production Department, but may produce something which the company then sells. Why do you think this department is not called a Production Department?

The stores/warehouse

This department has the responsibility for safely housing a variety of the organisation's property. This may take the form of products ready to be sold, various packaging materials, part-finished goods or raw materials, presently unused or unwanted equipment and machinery and bulk amounts of stationery and corporate materials.

This Service Department must keep a careful check on the stock levels of all items for which it has overall responsibility, and should inform the relevant department should stocks begin to approach their minimum stock level.

Fig 2.14 Mobil's automated warehousing at Birkenhead
(Photos by courtesy of Mobil Oil Company Limited)

Individual activity

Carrying on from the previous tasks, again calculate the percentage of the employees engaged in this area of the organisation's activities.

In the role of Warehousing Manager, draw up a list of essential equipment which you would expect to find in a warehouse. In order to help you consider this role, assume that the warehouse receives at least two lorries full of goods inwards per day and distributes via the Royal Mail at least 100 packages per day. You may also like to consider how many employees you would need to carry out all of the tasks involved.

The Distribution/Transport Department

The main function of this department is to co-ordinate the organisation's transport needs. This will include the purchasing or leasing of vehicles (company cars, etc.) and servicing and maintaining delivery vehicles.

As an integral part of this transport service, the department will have to maintain records such as insurance, vehicle registration, road tax, service records and leasing and purchasing agreements.

In situations where an organisation provides a delivery service to the customer, it is essential that the most efficient and cost-effective delivery routes are used. This is increasingly done with the aid of computer packages, specifically designed for this purpose.

As with most departments, when training or retraining needs are identified, the Distribution/Transport Department will liaise with the Personnel Department to organise training programmes.

Group activity

Carrying on from the previous tasks, again calculate the percentage of the employees engaged in this area of the organisation's activities.

As we have mentioned, Distribution Departments are increasingly using computer packages. What type of software package do you think would be of assistance? How could they make use of such software packages as part of their day-to-day operations?

You should consider this question in groups of three.

The Personnel Department

The main function of the Personnel Department is the recruitment and organisation of individuals required for the various functions required to run the organisation.

This primary responsibility is achieved through a close monitoring process which begins with the selection of potential employees through promotion and training of existing members of staff to the termination of employment (either retirement, redundancy, those who leave to go elsewhere and those who are asked to leave).

Close liaison is maintained with all other departments to identify the various training needs of staff. This may include the induction of new employees, additional training (perhaps to cope with new technology) and retraining (e.g. when a job has been replaced by a new process and the employees have been redeployed to a new area).

The Personnel Department maintains all records relating to employees, including holiday entitlements, sickness records, qualifications and experience, salary, pension contributions and entitlements and confidential reports from line managers. Some of this information is very useful in identifying training needs, as well as matching existing staff to new vacancies within the organisation. Much of this information is of a confidential nature, and is restricted by the Data Protection Act, which we will look at later in the book.

A further useful function of this information is to provide background for confidential counselling of employees. This will take account of any welfare or social difficulties employees may be experiencing.

The Personnel Department is the main negotiator for the organisation in matters relating to trade unions and associations and general problems regarding pay and conditions of employees.

In many medium to large organisations a wide range of social activities and facilities are provided. The Personnel Department is responsible for running these, which may include such things as subsidised catering, sports and social clubs, non-trade union employee associations and season ticket loans.

Any organisation which truly values its key personnel will take all the steps necessary to ensure that they are happy and contented in their work. If these key employees feel that they could achieve a higher salary, better working conditions or a wider range of fringe benefits (e.g. company cars, better pension schemes or reduced rate mortgages), then they will be seriously considering leaving the organisation. The Personnel Department is responsible for monitoring and expanding the total package offered to employees and ensuring that it is better than competitors.

Individual activity

Carrying on from the previous tasks, again calculate the percentage of the employees engaged in this area of the organisation's activities. In the role of Assistant Personnel Manager, you are responsible for organising the induction schedule for new employees. What do you think would need to be included in such a schedule? Imagine that you have four new employees starting work in one month. Each of these employees will be working in different departments of the organisation and will receive specific training from these sections.

Draw up a general organisational training schedule, ensuring that it covers all aspects required. Word process your document and take copies using the photocopier.

The Customer/Public Relations Department

Increasingly, organisations have recognised the value of not only responding to customer needs by adapting or expanding product ranges, but also in providing particular employees whose sole responsibility it is to liaise with the public and the media.

The Customer Relations Department is the main point of contact for customers who have complaints about the product or service supplied by the organisation. The smooth, efficient and courteous response to customer complaints is a key feature in making sure that the organisation's reputation is maintained. You will often see a short sentence on many products which states that if you have any problem with the product, to simply return it to the manufacturer. This is an offer in addition to the legal requirements that a product must be fit for the use it was intended and has gone a long way to enhance an organisation's reputation for being fair.

A Public Relations Department traditionally was the main way in which the organisation passed on news and information to the media and other interested parties. In recent years, this role has been expanded to include close contact with the public. Requests for information about the organisation and its operations are dealt with by the Public Relations Department, which has developed a range of booklets and other materials for this purpose. Particularly in the field of education, many larger organisations have also developed teaching packs and other educational literature for supply on request.

It is the Public Relations Department which writes press releases and product news to be distributed to extensive mailing lists of newspapers, magazines, journals and specialist organisations. The Public Relations Department will also advise members of the management of the organisation as to how they should respond to questions from the media, and provide specialist support for conferences and seminars.

Individual activity

Carrying on from the previous tasks, again calculate the percentage of the employees engaged in this area of the organisation's activities.

In the role of Public Relations Officer of a road haulage company, you must prepare a statement to the public via the press, covering the following issues:

- New EC regulations state that the present limit of haulage vehicles has been increased from 38 to 44 tonnes.

- Your vehicles will still have to use their present routes through a number of small villages.

- In consultation with the Local Authority, you have discovered that there are no present plans to build a by-pass to avoid these small villages.

- You have already received a number of complaints from local residents regarding noise, damage to property and diesel fume pollution.

- Although you do not rely on local businesses or local residents as clients of your road haulage business, it is company policy to maintain and develop good community relations and avoid any bad publicity.

You should word process your statement to the press and then present this to the remainder of your group who will take the role of the local press and residents. You should be prepared to answer any questions which they may wish to pose.

The Community Projects Department

In many of the larger organisations throughout the UK a Community Projects Department has been set up with a responsibility to make sure that the local community is made aware of exactly what the organisation is doing. In some organisations this is carried out by a Public Relations Officer. Other areas in which it is involved are liaison with other local businesses, close contact with the local education service and maintaining an effective environmental policy. (*See* Fig. 2.15.)

Individual activity

Carrying on from the previous tasks, again calculate the percentage of the employees engaged in this area of the organisation's activities. Your organisations may not have a Community Projects Department, but working in pairs in the role of Community Projects Manager, you should consider the following request made by your Board of Directors:

- The Board wishes to donate £10,000 to a deserving local cause
- It would like you to identify at least five possible causes which would benefit from such a donation
- It would prefer the donation to be given to an organisation within an area of five miles from the site of the organisation
- It would like to receive as much publicity as possible in both the lead up to, and immediately after the donation has been made
- It would consider a split donation, but to no more than two different organisations

Prepare your findings in the form of a report which must include a brief section on each of the proposed organisations that you have chosen to nominate. You should also give reasons why you have chosen each of the organisations. In your recommendations you must offer your suggestions as

WOOLWORTHS IN THE COMMUNITY

Woolworths has always recognised the importance of putting something back into the communities in which it trades. This commitment is expressed through a wide range of activities. The enthusiasm with which Woolworths staff support worthy causes at both local and national levels has helped the company towards outstanding achievements in this field.

It was the company's proven track record which led Comic Relief to choose Woolworths as the high street focus for its Red Nose Days in 1989 and 1991, which raised over £40 million for famine relief in Africa and help for the homeless in Britain.

In recent years Woolworths company-wide appeals have generated over £500,000 for Help a Child to See (1989) and National Children's Homes (1990) through a combination of store-based and regionally co-ordinated events. In support of these campaigns Woolworths staff have climbed Britain's tallest mountains, covered thousands of miles on sponsored walks and organised countless Fun Days to encourage customers to contribute towards these causes.

Track and field athletics in the shape of the Young Athletes League became part of Woolworths community involvement in 1990. The company committed £700,000 over three years to help The YAL provide 20,000 youngsters from over 200 athletics clubs, with invaluable experience of competitive

athletics. And in 1991, as a result of Woolworths support, The YAL launched its first competition for girls.

Finally, the company's support for the YAL nationally saw individual Woolworths staff forging close links with local youth athletic clubs. The clubs received regular publicity through their local stores.

At the start of 1992 Woolworths

Fig 2.15 Woolworths value the local communities in which they trade and believe in putting something back into the community

adopted Barnardo's as the focus for its national fund-raising drive. This effort complements the company's successful sponsorship of Barnardo's Champion Children Awards – the longest established and most prestigious awards for British children – which recognise achievements in seven categories including bravery, music, sport and triumph over adversity.

But this is not the whole story of Woolworths support for good causes. At Christmas and Easter staff and customers in each of the company's stores are invited to nominate a local deserving cause to receive a giant box of chocolates or a giant Easter egg.

These are specially made by Woolworths suppliers to be raffled. The exercise raises an estimated £100,000 every year.

In addition to these activities schools are an important year-round focus for Woolworths.

For thousands of youngsters Woolworths provides their first work experience whether as Saturday assistants or on short work-experience placements while still at school.

Managers are often invited to give careers talks or conduct mock interviews and stores regularly provide prizes for school fetes.

Fig 2.15 continued

Element assignment

ORGANISATIONAL STRUCTURE AND DECISION-MAKING

Working in pairs, now collate all of the percentages that have calculated regarding the organisational structure of your two chosen organisations.

Your first task is to present this information in the most suitable format, with the emphasis on ease of reference.

Your second task is to consider the decision-making process within your two organisations, taking the following points into account:

■ How many people are involved in the initial decision-making process?

■ How many layers of management must a decision pass through before being acted upon?

■ Can the organisation plan effectively and ensure that any decisions are actually implemented?

■ How does the structure affect the quality of the decision making (you should think about this in terms of the negative effects a decision made at the top of the organisational structure has upon those at the bottom of it).

■ How does the structure of the organisation affect the speed of decision making?

■ How likely are decisions, which have been made by the hierarchy, to be changed beyond all recognition by the time they reach the bulk of the employees?

- If the organisation has a number of senior decision makers, how is responsibility for decision making organised?
- In order to make sure that a decision is implemented, the decision maker needs both power and authority. Are there any decision makers within your organisation that lack either power or authority? How do they operate?

Your findings should be presented using a formal report format.

UNIT TEST   Element 2.1

1 Give three features of a private sector organisation

2 Give three features of a public sector organisation

3 What is CCT?

4 Give three factors which might affect the structure of an organisation.

5 What is a hierarchical structure?

6 What are the features of a steep pyramid?

7 What are the features of a flat pyramid?

8 What is a cone structure?

9 What is line management?

10 What is the division of labour?

11 What is specialisation?

12 What is departmentalisation?

13 Give three functions of the Administration Department

14 Give three functions of the Accounts and Finance Department

15 Give three functions of the Sales Department

16 Give three functions of the Marketing Department

17 What is staff management?

18 Give three functions of the Production Department

19 Give three functions of the Personnel Department

20 What is the difference between the Public Relations Department and the Community Projects Department?

Element 2.2
Rights and responsibilities of employees and employers

PERFORMANCE CRITERIA

1 Employee rights and responsibilities and means of exercising them explained
2 Employer rights and responsibilities and means of exercising them explained
3 Legislation governing employee and employer rights described

RANGE

1 Employee rights and responsibilities: renumeration, safe working conditions, contract of employment, trades union membership, compliance with terms of contract and compliance with health and safety regulations
2 Employer rights and responsibilities: disciplinary action, working to terms of contract, health and safety at work, remuneration, employee consultation, and equal opportunities

LEGISLATION

Health and Safety at Work Act, equal opportunities, equal pay and employment law

EVIDENCE INDICATORS

An oral, written or dramatic account (supported by a script) which illustrates the rights and responsibilities of people in business organisations. The candidate must also identify the legislation which underpins employee and employer rights and responsibilities. Evidence should demonstrate understanding of the implications of the range dimensions in relation to the element. The unit test will confirm the candidate's coverage of the range.

EMPLOYEE RIGHTS AND RESPONSIBILITIES

The success or failure of an organisation will largely depend upon the balance struck between the employer and the employee.

Employers are very dependent on the people who work for them, in nearly all functions it will be these people who represent the interests of the organisation. Just how these people react to the requirements of the organisation, and how they respond to a variety of conflicting needs is a crucial concern.

The relationship between employers and employees is not left solely for the two parties to agree upon. There are a range of laws which govern the relationship. Equally, just as the employee may be protected from abuses, so too is the employer. We will look at this aspect of the relationship later. Nevertheless, the employee does have a range of responsibilities that is taken on when accepting employment.

We will firstly look at the employee's rights and responsibilities. Essentially, they fall into six major categories which cover most of the aspects of the relationship with the employer.

Group activity

Before reading any further in this section, in pairs try to think of at least three rights or responsibilities of both the employer and the employee. Compare your list with the rest of the group.

Remuneration

In the majority of cases, people work for pay. This may be in the form of:

- *Wages, paid weekly, sometimes in cash*
- *Salary, paid monthly, either by cheque or by bank transfer*
- *Commission, paid on performance, usually measured in sales volume generated by the individual*
- *Bonuses, paid according to whether specific targets have been met*
- *Performance related, an additional payment related to the individual's commitment beyond their usual job*
- *Profit related, linked to the overall profit made by the department or organisation as a whole*

Whatever the form of remuneration, the employer is essentially paying the employee for their time and effort. Some would say that employers are 'buying' a piece of the employee's life. This is true to some extent but we will see that this relationship is a two-way one.

There are, of course, some individuals who do not work for remuneration. These would include the following:

■ *Charity workers*

■ *Volunteers*

■ *Individuals who 'trade' their skills and time in return for someone else's expertise*

In the majority of cases, an employee would, quite rightly, expect a fair day's pay for a fair day's work. The key to this equation working is two-fold:

■ *The employer must be able to place a 'value' on the employee's time and effort*

■ *The employee must have a clear idea of what their time and effort are worth*

If the two parties can agreee, then this relationship should be a relatively easy one. In many cases, however, the two parties radically disagree. This can form the basis of conflict in the future. In later circumstances, the employer may find his only option is to pay the amount the employee demands. This may be because there is a shortage of skills and expertise. On the other hand, and far more commonly, it is the employee who finds it impossible to get the payment they believe is fair as there are too many people with the same skills and expertise chasing too few jobs on offer.

Group activity

In the past, many people operated on a barter system rather than receiving payment for goods or services. In pairs, research the barter system and try to work out when it really went out of fashion. Why do you think this was? Is there a place for it today?

Compare your findings with those of the rest of the group.

Safe working conditions

An employee can quite rightly expect to work in conditions that are neither hazardous to life or health. The central piece of legislation that protects the employee, and gives the employer strict guidelines to adhere to, is the Health and Safety at Work Act 1974 (this is covered in much greater detail later on).

It essentially sets out that the employee must work in an environment that is healthy, safe and considers the welfare of the individual. The employer is ultimately responsible for any hazards or accidents which may be caused by not taking note of the legislation. Very heavy fines may be incurred if the basics of the legislation are broken.

Safe working conditions include many of the more obvious dangers to the employee, such as:

- *Fitting protective guards on dangerous machinery*
- *Taking care that any hazardous or toxic chemicals are housed in safe and leak-proof containers*
- *Ensuring that the quality of the air is good enough*
- *Not requiring employees to carry out duties which could result in injury, such as falling from a gantry above the factory floor*

The laws, themselves, cover a multitude of situations: whether the employer is taking care to think about the health and safety aspects, as well as whether the training needs of employees are regularly monitored. The Health and Safety Executive sends out inspectors to make sure that nothing is amiss. Also an employee is given the task of being the organisation's Safety Officer. (Please look at the section on pages **56–59** for more detail).

Individual activity

In the role of Health and Safety Officer of an organisation, you have been presented with the following problem:

- The organisation for which you work is a small-scale manufacturing business
- Most of the employees are engaged on machine tool equipment
- All employees have been given health and safety training
- All employees have been issued with protective visors and heavy-duty gloves
- All machines are fitted with safety guards
- This morning, an employee has just lost two fingers from their right hand. They were not wearing gloves and the safety guard had been removed for maintenance purposes

You must write a memo to the Production Manager detailing the incident and with reference to the correct legislation (which you will find later in this Element) advise as to the following:

- Where the company stands in terms of responsibility
- What additional guidance notes must be given to supervisors
- What additional information must be passed on to machine operatives

You should also include in your memo a statement that the organisation should make to its insurance company.

Contracts of Employment

As we have seen so far, the employer has a number of duties towards the employee. This can be seen very clearly in the Contract of Employment. This really formalises the relationship and is seen as a legally binding document from both the employer and the employee.

- *A Contract of Employment should formulate all of the above points:*
- *Job role: what is the precise nature of the job?*
- *Job title*
- *Pay details: how it is paid, frequency of payment?*
- *Additional payment details, such as which salary/wage scale the individual will be placed on, when overtime can be undertaken, how bonuses and commission may be earned?*
- *Start times and finishing times of work*
- *Total number of hours worked per week before overtime*
- *Number of paid days off for holidays etc. Also are there any restrictions on when this may be taken?*
- *Sick leave details, duration and entitlement to sick pay and maternity leave*
- *Pension schemes, with details of contributions made by employer and employee*
- *Grievance procedures details, who is the Grievance Officer and the processes of the grievance procedure itself*

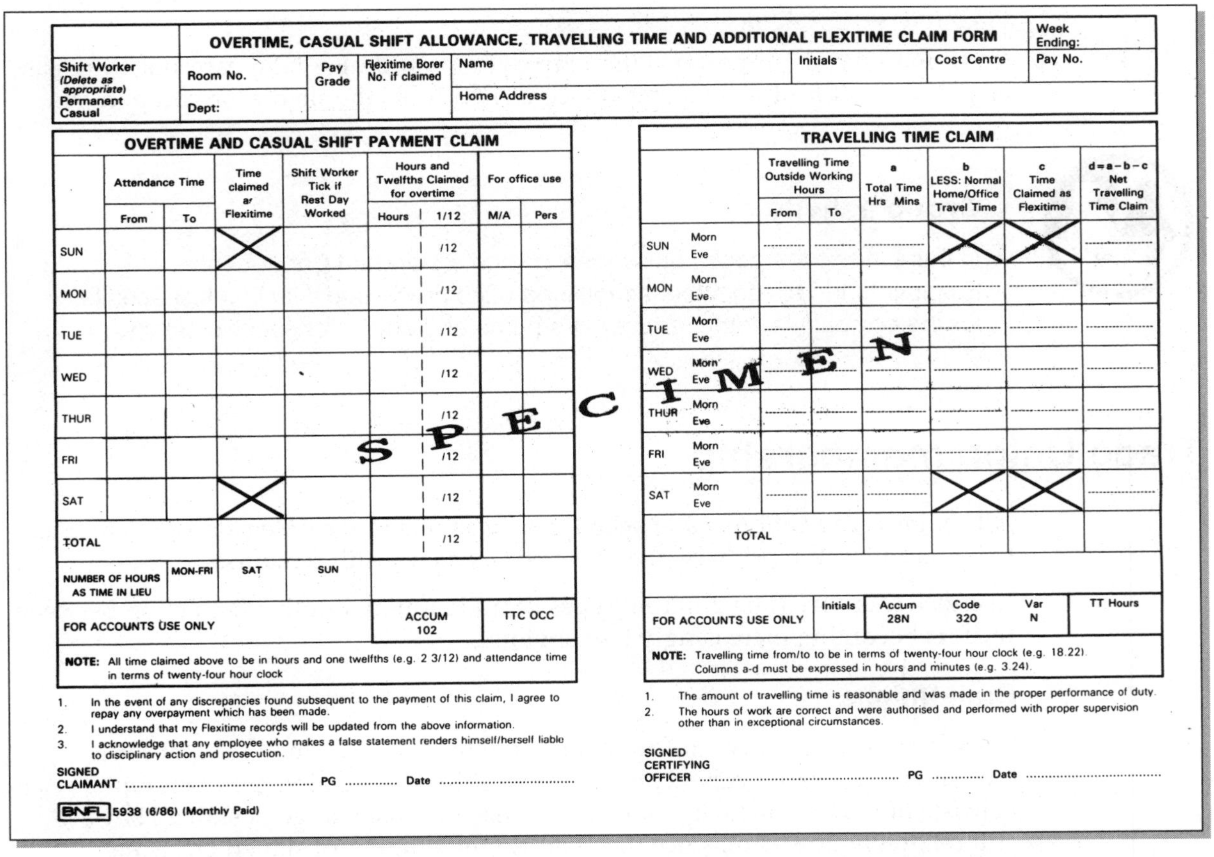

OVERTIME, CASUAL SHIFT ALLOWANCE, TRAVELLING TIME AND ADDITIONAL FLEXITIME CLAIM FORM

Shift Worker (Delete as appropriate) Permanent Casual	Room No. / Dept:	Pay Grade	Flexitime Borer No. if claimed	Name / Home Address	Initials	Cost Centre	Week Ending: / Pay No.

OVERTIME AND CASUAL SHIFT PAYMENT CLAIM

	Attendance Time From	Attendance Time To	Time claimed as Flexitime	Shift Worker Tick if Rest Day Worked	Hours and Twelfths Claimed for overtime: Hours	1/12	For office use: M/A	Pers
SUN			X			/12		
MON						/12		
TUE						/12		
WED						/12		
THUR						/12		
FRI						/12		
SAT			X			/12		
TOTAL						/12		

NUMBER OF HOURS AS TIME IN LIEU	MON-FRI	SAT	SUN

FOR ACCOUNTS USE ONLY	ACCUM 102	TTC OCC

NOTE: All time claimed above to be in hours and one twelfths (e.g. 2 3/12) and attendance time in terms of twenty-four hour clock

1. In the event of any discrepancies found subsequent to the payment of this claim, I agree to repay any overpayment which has been made.
2. I understand that my Flexitime records will be updated from the above information.
3. I acknowledge that any employee who makes a false statement renders himself/herself liable to disciplinary action and prosecution.

SIGNED CLAIMANT .... PG .... Date ....

BNFL 5938 (6/86) (Monthly Paid)

TRAVELLING TIME CLAIM

		Travelling Time Outside Working Hours From	To	a Total Time Hrs Mins	b LESS: Normal Home/Office Travel Time	c Time Claimed as Flexitime	d=a−b−c Net Travelling Time Claim
SUN	Morn / Eve				X	X	
MON	Morn / Eve						
TUE	Morn / Eve						
WED	Morn / Eve						
THUR	Morn / Eve						
FRI	Morn / Eve						
SAT	Morn / Eve				X	X	
TOTAL							

FOR ACCOUNTS USE ONLY	Initials	Accum 28N	Code 320	Var N	TT Hours

NOTE: Travelling time from/to to be in terms of twenty-four hour clock (e.g. 18.22). Columns a-d must be expressed in hours and minutes (e.g. 3.24).

1. The amount of travelling time is reasonable and was made in the proper performance of duty.
2. The hours of work are correct and were authorised and performed with proper supervision other than in exceptional circumstances.

SIGNED CERTIFYING OFFICER .... PG .... Date ....

Fig 2.16 BNFL's multi-purpose form for overtime, casual shift allowance, travelling time and additional flexitime claims

- *Period of notice to be worked/given*

- *Number of weeks or months notice required (by either side) in the event of resignation or termination of employment*

In addition to these legally required details, the employer may wish to inform the employee of the following:

- *Rules and regulations to be followed by employees*

- *Codes of behaviour expected of the employees*

- *The nature and availability of sports, social and welfare activities offered*

- *A full organisational chart so that the employee identifies where they fit into the overall scheme of things*

Compliance with contract – employee

Just as the employer will be expected to fulfil any obligations as set out in the Contract of Employment, so too will the employee.

The employee will be expected to comply with all of the aspects of the Contract of Employment, and furthermore will be required to accept responsibility for their action at work.

Confidentiality is important, the employee should also take care not to release any information of a sensitive or secret nature to the media or competitors.

Group activity

In pairs, using the above guidelines, design a standard Contract of Employment. This document should be word processed with blank spaces left for the company's name, employee's name and any other specific details.

Trade Union membership

Although Trade Unions have been the subject of a range of legislation to restrict their activities, the primary need for their existence still remains.

In effect, there are four different types of trade union, but the distinction between them is becoming increasingly less obvious.

Craft Unions

These are the earliest type of trade union, which were formed to cater for craftsmen who had received an apprenticeship. Craft Union membership consists of individuals who work with the same basic range of skills. They are still relatively powerful, since they control the number of skilled craftsmen entering the workforce. Craft unions restrict their membership by having very strict entrance qualifications and charging high membership rates.

Fig 2.17 Trades Union Congress meeting

It is still the case that you cannot work in a particular field unless you are a member of the specific union.

Industrial Unions

Traditionally, these unions were formed to cater for all employees (regardless of grade and job) within a particular industry. Good examples are the National Union of Mineworkers and the National Union of Railwaymen.

Occupational Unions

Contrary to the Industrial Unions, the Occupational Unions recruit from a wide range of different industries, but always from the same occupational group. A good example of this type of union would be the National Union of Public Employees, which recruits manual workers from hospitals, councils, schools and colleges.

General unions

Initially, these unions catered for those individuals not covered in the three categories above. The first general unions concentrated on unskilled workers, offering a wide range of benefits for a relatively low subscription rate. General unions have thrived in recent times as new industries have emerged and older, more traditional ones have declined. Often, these general unions are the result of several smaller, more specialist unions merging with one another.

Whatever type of union is involved at the work place, the basic functions remain the same. A union exists to protect and promote the interests of its members. It essentially does the following:

- *Acts as a pressure group, which promotes the interests of its members*
- *Acts as a pressure group, which protects the position of its members*
- *Acts as the main instrument of bargaining with the employer*

All unions are formed and financed by the members. They are run by full-time officials, voted or appointed into place by the members. Unions are independent of the employers, they do not rely on them for funding. The union must also organise its own facilities and not count on the employer offering space within their own premises.

Trade unions carry out a multitude of different tasks in the pursuit of looking after their members' interests. Some major functions include:

- *Protecting the wages of members, particularly in times of recession*
- *Negotiating the working hours required by the employer*
- *Negotiating the working conditions of the employees*
- *Monitoring health and safety*
- *Providing a range of benefits, including pensions, sick pay, unemployment pay and injury benefits*
- *Representing the interests of the members in times of dispute with the employers*

In addition to these tasks, unions undertake a number of political duties relating to employment. They will actively negotiate with the Government and opposition parties to further the cause of their members.

With a few notable exceptions, all employees are entitled to join a trade union and take advantage of the benefits, both in terms of protection and facilities offered.

Group activity

In groups of three, identify at least 10 unions which operate in your local area. You should also find out which type of union they are and what kind of employee they represent.

Compare your list with the rest of the group.

Compliance with health and safety – employees

Just as the employer must take heed of the requirements of these important series of Acts, so must the employee. Employees may suffer harm or injuries which are not necessarily the fault of the employer.

If an employee is negligent and causes injury to him- or herself or to another person, then the employer may be in a difficult position. The employee may claim that it was not really his or her fault. As long as the employer provides safe working conditions, then apart from accidents caused by negligence, there should be no real concerns here. We will look at the employer's role in preventing accidents later.

Fig 2.18 Health and safety hazards

Another possible area of concern is when an employee deliberately puts someone else's life in danger. Depending on the circumstances, they could find themselves not only dismissed, but the subject of criminal and civil proceedings.

Individual activity

With reference to the legislation detailed later in this Element, compile a Health and Safety Report based on the institution in which you are carrying out your studies.

You should highlight any potential dangers and compare these with any preventative procedures already in place. It would be useful to talk to the person who has responsibility for health and safety and to consult any documentation they may be able to supply.

EMPLOYER RIGHTS AND RESPONSIBILITIES

Rights and responsibilities work both ways in nearly all situations, no more so than in the case of employers and employees. An employee has a responsibility under the terms of the Contract of Employment, as does the employer.

The employer will, quite rightly, expect certain things of the employee, essentially they fall into seven different areas:

Disciplinary action

The Contract of Employment, between the employer and the employee, inevitabily must cease at some point. Many, but not all, relate to disciplinary matters. The key part is that one or other of the parties who signed the Contract of Employment has broken it. The employee may not be dismissed without good reason. Let us look at the dismissal reasons relating to the employee breaking the contract. (*See* Fig 2.19.)

DISCIPLINARY NOTICE

COMPANY NAME AND ADDRESS

Classification of Warning	Tick as appropriate
VERBAL WARNING	
WRITTEN WARNING	
FINAL WRITTEN WARNING	

Employee's Name: .... Date and Time of issue: ....

Issued by: .... in the presence of ....

Warning issued as a result of a disciplinary meeting held on ....

DETAILS OF OFFENCE:-

EMPLOYEE'S EXPLANATION:-

FUTURE ACTION REQUIRED FROM EMPLOYEE:-

THE EMPLOYEE has been informed of:-
(a) The right to be accompanied by a Friend or Colleague (who is also an employee of the Company) at all stages of the disciplinary procedure.
(b) The right to appeal, in accordance with the Company's Appeal Procedure against any warning.

Signed by person issuing: ....

Signed by Receiving Employee: ....

Fig 2.19 Proforma disciplinary notice. Note the multi-purpose nature of the form

Dismissal

This word basically means that the employer is terminating the contract of the employee for a particular reason, usually relating to their behaviour or conduct. The employer has to give the employee notice of his or her intention to dismiss them. In some cases, the dismissal may be instant, but this is usually restricted to very serious matters.

If the employer puts the employee in such a position as to make it impossible to stay with the organisation, this is known as Constructive Dismissal. Courts have found in favour of employees who have been put in this position by the unfair attitudes and actions of the employer. Such examples would relate to:

- *Changes in wages without informing the employee*

- *Changes in the location of the job without consultation*

- *Changes in duties required without negotiation*

- *Changes in job description without negotiation*

In all of these examples, the employer has decided, on their own, to change certain conditions of work. In some cases, this will break the original Contract of Employment. In some cases, an employee may resign as a result of a series of events. In these cases, an Industrial Tribunal would look carefully at the stages of events and decide whether this is Constructive Dismissal. Some of the breaches of the Contract of Employment may refer to sexual harassment or discrimination on the grounds of race or colour (for further details please see the relevant Acts later on in this element).

All contracts are a matter of interpretation, and we will look at this aspect shortly.

Unfair Dismissal

The right not to be unfairly dismissed from your job is a very important rule. The laws relating to this stop employers feeling that they have the right to hire and fire as they see fit. It is, however, a very complex issue. Whether an individual employee qualifies for claiming that they have been unfairly dismissed is a much argued subject.

Generally speaking, for an employee to qualify for a claim for Unfair Dismissal, the following requirements must be met:

- *The employee must have worked for the employer, as a full-time member of staff, for at least two years*

- *If a part-time worker, working eight hours a week or more, the employee must have been in employment for five years*

- *The individual must not be of pensionable age (currently 60 for women and 65 for men)*

- *Police Officers cannot claim Unfair Dismissal even though they may qualify in terms of service*

- *Individuals who are paid only a share of the profits are exempt*

- *Employees who work for the organisation outside the UK are exempt*

- *Employees on fixed period contracts are exempt (it will expressly state this in their Contract of Employment)*

- *Members of the Armed Forces are also exempt on service grounds*

In cases of dispute between the employer and the employee, an organisation called ACAS (the Arbitration and Conciliation Service) will assist and attempt to resolve the conflict. This individual, working for ACAS, will try to get the two parties to agree rather than having to resort to the courts for a settlement.

Causes of dismissal

There will nearly always be a reason for an employer dismissing an employee, whether the reasons are right or wrong. There are, essentially, five main reasons:

Capability and qualifications

These two reasons relate to the employee's fitness or competence to do the job. In this sense capability means skill, health, physical or mental ability. Qualifications, on the other hand, refer to the academic, technical or professional qualifications relevant to the job. Capability is an easier reason to define and explain. Basically, if the employee is shown to be incompetent or shows serious errors of judgement, then the employer has grounds for dismissal. Qualifications can be more complicated. If the employee is taken on by the employer on the basis that he or she must achieve a certain level of qualification, and then fails to, the employer may dismiss the employee.

Redundancy

If the employer closes down the business, or part of the business, they may no longer need the services of some or all of the employees. In such cases, the employer must consult the employees, have fairly selected those to be made redundant and offered them alternative employment if available. There are always ways around this problem of redundancy, for example the employer could freeze recruitment and redeploy the existing employees, or reduce the number of hours which all of the employees work.

Misconduct

Misconduct is a very wide area, it includes the following:

- *Absenteeism* – where an employee is away from work too often

- *Lateness* – where an employee constantly turns up late for work

- *Insubordination* – where an employee refuses to carry out instructions from a superior

- *Incompetence* – where the employee shows on several occasions the inability to do the job

- *Immorality* – where the employee behaves in such a way that is unacceptable, perhaps sexually or morally

- *Breaking safety rules* – where an employee endangers his or her life or the lives of others by not taking heed of the safety rules, perhaps deliberately

- *Theft* – where the employee has stolen the property of the employer

In reality, then, the employer can identify a number of reasons for dismissal due to misconduct. This may mean that the employee having an affair at work, an employee wearing offensive badges or T-shirts, or, indeed, an employee involved in questionable activities outside the work place could be dismissed under misconduct guidelines.

Statutory contraventions

This reason for dismissal relates directly to an employee doing something which breaks a legal requirement. Good examples of this would be a lorry driver who is banned from driving due to drink-driving, or even an employee who works for a butcher and grows a beard! (this would be against Hygiene and Food Legislation).

Other reasons

This broad area covers all other reaons not covered above, and in as much is a difficult category to cope with. Examples would include gradual deterioration in the output or performance of an employee, or in certain cases, the sexuality of the employee.

Fairness and dismissal

The employer really needs a valid reason for dismissing an employee. The employer's conduct must be fair towards the employee. The employer must not single out an individual because of their sex (for women, they have the right, of course, to be pregnant). If the employer chooses to dismiss an employee on the grounds of their sexuality, then there would have to be very strong reasons to link sexuality with the requirement and nature of the job. In one particular case, all of the employees were dismissed from a shop after stock had been disappearing over a number of months. A tribunal held that the employer could not do this as there were insufficient grounds to dismiss all of the employees when perhaps only one of them was the culprit. The employer had not 'proved' the guilt of all employees.

Within the category of fairness, it would be safe to assume that the following are 'fair' reasons for dismissal:

- *Sexual harassment of other employees or customers*
- *Racial harassment of other employees or customers*
- *Wilful destruction of the organisation's property*
- *Negligence*
- *Long-term bad timekeeping*
- *Sleeping at work*
- *Gross insubordination*
- *Inability to do the job that the employee was appointed to do*
- *Fraud including the falsification of records*
- *Inability to do the job as the employee is under the influence of alcohol*
- *Inability to do the job as the employee is under the influence of illegal drugs*

- *Fighting – when the employee has assaulted another person on the premises of the organisation*

- *Unauthorised entry to confidential computer records*

On the other hand, unfair dismissal may relate to the following:

- *Race* – an employer cannot dismiss an employee on the grounds of the employee's race

- *Religion* – an employee cannot be dismissed on the grounds of his or her religious beliefs

- *Sexual discrimination* – an employer cannot dismiss an employee because they are a homosexual or a lesbian, unless it affects the standard of the work, or the individual is sexually harassing other members of the workforce

- *Pregnancy* – as we have already said, a woman cannot be dismissed because she is pregnant. However, if the pregnancy affects her ability to do the job in total (e.g. the woman may be a labourer or have to carry heavy weights) then there are reasonable grounds

- *Criminal record* – if the employer finds out that an employee has a criminal record, but it does not relate to the job, then that employee cannot be dismissed. However, some criminal records may relate to the job, such as fraud and accountancy! In this case, the employer is within his or her rights to dismiss the employee

- *Trade union membership* – an employee cannot be dismissed for being a member of a union.

Disciplinary procedures

The approved disciplinary procedure, as recommended by ACAS, should be both fair and impartial. It includes the following features:

- *That all stages of the procedure should be written down as a record of events*

- *That copies of the procedures should be available to all employees*

- *That the employer should clearly state who operates the procedure within the organisation*

- *That the employer should clearly state who is involved*

- *That the employer clearly states what kind of disciplinary action will be taken against particular types of disciplinary matters*

- *That the employee has the right to have a friend, colleague or trade union representative present during all disciplinary interviews*

- *That in most cases, apart from really serious matters, an employee is not dismissed for a first 'offence'*

- *That the employee does have the right to appeal against a decision made by the employer*

- *That all proceedings should be administered in a fair way*

- *That the employee should not be unfairly discriminated against throughout the whole process*

Normally, the actual disciplinary procedure would work along the lines shown in the checklist.

Stages in a normal disciplinary procedure

- **Verbal warning** – if the employee's conduct, behaviour or performance does not reach suitable and acceptable standards, then they will be given a formal verbal warning. This is the first official stage of the proceedings, and will not last forever, providing the employee reaches acceptable standards. If the employee does so, then he or she will not move on to the next stage, and the matter will be dropped

- **Written warning** – If the employee persists with the same behaviour that resulted in their receiving a verbal warning, or if the 'offence' is serious enough, then a written warning will be issued. This is usually written by the employee's immediate supervisor

  The written warning details the complaint against the employee, and clearly states exactly what the employee must do to remedy the situation. The warning will also state how long the employee has to 'mend' his or her ways. If the employee persists then inevitably the next stage of the procedures will occur. Again, if the employee complies with the requirements of the written warning then the matter will be dropped. The employee may also appeal against this written warning through the usual channels

- **The final written warning or suspension** – if the employee continues to fail to improve his or her conduct, behaviour or performance, then normally a final written warning will be given. If the conduct has been sufficiently serious the employee may automatically be given a final written warning, rather than go through the first few procedures. Just as the written warning gives details of the complaint and a stern warning that dismissal is imminent should there be no satisfactory improvement, so too does the final written warning

  As an alternative, the employer may wish to suspend the individual for a maximum of five days without pay. This is known as Disciplinary Suspension

- **Dismissal** – the final stage in the disciplinary procedure is dismissal itself. To reach this point, the employee must have had to fail all the requirements as laid down in the written warnings. The employee's most senior but related line manager will make the decision to dismiss the employee. The employee will be given a written statement which includes the reasons for their dismissal and the date of termination of employment. Further, it will say how the employee may appeal

- **Appeals** – if an employee chooses to appeal at any stage in the disciplinary procedure, that employee must inform his or her superior within two working days. The manager will consider the appeal. However, the manager's decision is final. The manager may choose to uphold the decision to discipline the employee, but may not increase the severity of the action taken against the employee

It is recommended that all disciplinary matters should be considered at length and that employees have the right to state their side of the argument. As we have said, all disciplinary meetings or interviews should take place in the presence of a trade union official or colleague.

Normally, an employee is given two verbal warnings, followed by a final written warning before they are dismissed. It should be remembered that the disciplinary code of the employer must be reasonable and fair. If an employee thinks they have not had sufficient opportunity to state their case, then they may choose to refer the matter to an Industrial Tribunal.

Employers are not legally obliged to follow the above disciplinary process, but many have nevertheless. After all, employers are unlikely and unwilling to face the disruption and expense of an Industrial Tribunal.

Industrial Tribunals were set up by the Government as a kind of court. They are there to try to obtain an agreement between the employer and the employees and have the power to demand reinstatement of the employee or to award financial compensation if the former is not practicable. Over the years, Industrial Tribunals have heard matters arising from many of the laws and regulations detailed later in the book.

Group activity

In pairs, in the role of Personnel Manager, draw up a Disciplinary Procedure which details the following:

- Reasons why disciplinary action may be taken

- The grievance procedure

- The appeals procedure

You should try to present this information in the form of a flow chart and to indicate the Government legislation where necessary.

This information and flow chart should be in the form of a confidential memorandum, and will form the basis of a staff handbook to be issued at a later date.

Working to Terms of Contract

The employee has a responsibility to the employer to work in a loyal, conscientious and honest manner. The employee is also expected to accept any reasonable and legal directions from superiors. In essence, this means adhering to the terms of their Contract of Employment. As we have seen, the Contract of Employment can be a very detailed document and is considered to be a legally binding contract once both parties have signed. By law, all employees must have received a Contract of Employment within 13 weeks of beginning employment. The employer is required to exercise a duty of care over employees, provide sufficient work to do, pay the employee at due times and maintain a number of records on behalf of the employee. These will include:

- *PAYE deductions*
- *National Insurance contributions*
- *Pension scheme contributions*

The employer must take care when advertising a job, as it is considered to be the beginnings of the formation of the Contract of Employment. Once a candidate for a particular job accepts employment on the basis of the advertisement details, then much of the Contract of Employment has already been decided. Before the employer finally accepts a candidate as an employee, references will usually be taken up. In the former case, if the prospective employer receives unfavourable references about the candidate, then they are quite within their rights to withdraw the job offer. In reality, just how the employer interprets the contact of a reference is open to question.

A Contract of Employment is really like any other contract. It gives both parties rights as well as obligations. The contract, as we mentioned earlier, identifies formally what was really agreed during the interview or selection process. Normally, a Contract of Employment will contain the following, either directly, or by inference:

- *The employer will pay wages*
- *The employer will provide work*
- *The employer will pay any reasonable losses or expenses incurred by the employee in the course of their work*
- *The employer will provide a reference if required by the employee*
- *The employer will provide safe working conditions and working practices*
- *The employer will not act in such a way as to breach the trust and confidence given of the employee*
- *The employer will provide necessary information relating to the employee's work, pay, conditions and opportunities*
- *The employer will always act in good faith towards the employee*

In addition to the obvious obligations the employee may have, he or she will also be expected to:

- *Act in good faith towards the employer*
- *Account for any cash received from other sources (this is to make sure that the employee does not accept bribes or fees in the pursuit of their normal activities from external organisations)*
- *Keep trade secrets confidential*
- *Obey any reasonable orders and give faithful service to the employer*

Compliance to health and safety at work

We will be looking at health and safety in much greater detail later, but essentially, employers and employees have an obligation to ensure a safe working environment. If the legal requirements are broken by either party, in effect one side or other have been negligent, then the aggrieved party may begin legal proceedings. In effect, the health and safety requirements are:

- *To provide a safe working environment*
- *To provide adequate welfare facilities*
- *To ensure entrances and exits are safe*
- *To ensure equipment and systems used are safe and regularly serviced*
- *To make sure that items needed for use in handling or storage are safe*
- *To make sure that dangerous or toxic materials are housed in safe containers*
- *To provide instruction, training or supervision regarding working practices and materials used*
- *To ensure that all accidents are rigorously investigated and the causes promptly dealt with*

Remuneration

Remuneration is the level of payment for a particular job. Normally, the level of payment is arrived at to ensure the following:

- *That it attracts suitable staff*
- *That it retains staff for a considerable period of time*
- *That it motivates staff by offering a reasonable payment package, or the ability to earn extra related to individual or organisational performance*
- *That it helps towards the general objectives of the organisation, in terms of competitive rates of pay and linking pay increases and bonuses to overall organisational performance*

As we have already said in the previous section, an employee can reasonably expect to be paid for their labour at times stated in the Contract of Employment.

Employee consultation and participation

Many organisations have formed a Joint Consultative Committee in which the employees are given the opportunity to involve themselves in the organisation's decision making.

These committees will meet regularly where decisions made by the management are relayed to the workforce and a forum for discussion is provided. In other cases, the committees meet to discuss and negotiate on matters relating to industrial relations, such as working conditions, disciplinary procedures and pay.

These committees will either take the form of:

- *An advisory body*
- *A consultative body*
- *A negotiating body*

If the committee is of the last type, then usually decisions made by that committee are binding on the organisation.

An alternative form of employee consultation is known as employee participation. This has come about because employers have recognised that the workforce has considerable skills and good ideas which could be used for the mutual benefit of employer and employees. (*See* Fig 2.20.)

There are various versions of employee participation, and include the following:

Fig 2.20 A detail from St. Michael News, the Staff newspaper of Marks & Spencer. Long-service employees are held in high regard as this clipping shows

- *Quality Circles* – where employees meet on a voluntary basis to discuss their work and how systems and procedures may be improved

- *Employee briefing sessions* – where the employees are given useful and relevant information regarding the objectives of the organisation

- *Transferring of responsibility* – when employees take on some of the management-related decision making

- *Worker councils* – which are largely consultative and generally concentrate on welfare issues and can often be an alternative to unions

- *Worker Directors* – where employees attend meetings of the Board of Directors. In Europe, this idea has proved to be very successful in improving the quality of decision making at Board level. It also gives the Board the opportunity to hear the workforce's views at first hand rather than relying on the various layers of management to relay the employees wishes and ideas. Further, this system tends to mean that the employees are more committed to decisions made by the Board. Finally, it helps reduce employer/employee conflict, as the employees have a greater idea of the overall problems faced by the organisation

Group activity

In pairs, in the role of Managing Director and his assistant, you have been asked to prepare a report for the Board detailing the following:

■ The Board wishes to involve the employees in the decision-making processes of the organisation

■ It has heard about Joint Consultative Committees and Worker Directors, for example, but has no real idea of what they are and how they work

It is your task to research the various forms of worker participation within an organisation, and to try to recommend one which you think would be the best.

Whichever form of worker participation you choose, the Board will adopt for a trial period of six months. In the light of this, you may discover that some of the forms of worker participation need longer to operate in order to see if they are actually valuable. If this is the case, then you should detail in your report this fact.

Your report should be word processed.

Welfare

A good employer will offer a range of social facilities to their employees. In some cases, this does not go beyond a Christmas party. The ideal employer would provide many of the following:

■ *Sports and Social Club*

■ *Company outings*

■ *Season ticket loans*

■ *Subsidised crèche or nursery facilities*

■ *Regular health checks for employees*

■ *Interest in the welfare of the employees' family*

■ *Understanding regarding compassionate leave (perhaps in the event of a death in the family)*

■ *Understanding regarding paternal leave (for the father of a newborn child)*

■ *Subsidised canteen facilities and meals*

■ *Staff discounts*

A further, more recent addition to the list of welfare facilities is staff appraisals. While these are considered by some with suspicion, a good employer will use staff appraisals in a positive manner. On the one hand, they do look at staff skills and assess how good the employee is at doing a job, on the other hand, they try to look at the ambitions of the employee.

Regular staff appraisals will consider the following:

- *The employee's ambitions within the organisation*
- *The employee's concerns about the job he or she is doing*
- *The interests the employee may have, and the direction he or she may wish to go in*
- *The promotion prospects of the employee*
- *How the job may be improved to give further satisfaction to the employee*

Equal opportunities

Even in these modern times, there are many individuals who are discriminated against on various grounds. Within employment, employees are protected to some extent by a series of laws and regulations, which we look at in some detail later. The main groups who suffer from discrimination are:

- *Women*
- *Ethnic minorities*
- *Disabled*
- *Those with an alternative sexual orientation*
- *The young*
- *The old*
- *Certain religious groups*

Many organisations have adopted equal opportunities policies, although they are not yet required to do this by law. The Equal Opportunities Commission has designed a standard policy which employers can use. This covers a variety of different situations, and includes the following:

- *That to have an equal opportunities policy is a desirable thing*
- *That it should be strictly adhered to*
- *That all forms of direct and indirect discrimination are clearly defined*
- *That the organisation states its commitment to equal opportunities and, further, states that it is in the best interests of the organisation and its employees*
- *That all employees are made aware of the policy*
- *That staff are trained to maintain the policy*
- *That any preconceived ideas which employees may have regarding those who are subject to discrimination are addressed*

- *That both recruitment and promotion is equal for all*
- *That training is offered on an equal basis to all*
- *That the employment contract does not inadvertently discriminate against anyone*
- *That the organisation's facilities are open to all*
- *That an individual is nominated to monitor the policy*
- *That the policy is regularly reviewed and updated according to need*
- *That any grievances relating to discrimination are dealt with in a prompt and fair manner*
- *That no individual suffers victimisation in the course of their duties within the organisation*

Group activity

Discuss the following statement as a group:

'An individual should not be protected by a series of laws and regulations. They should be able to stand on their own two feet.'

EMPLOYMENT LEGISLATION

Employment legislation is considered by many people to be a minefield of legal requirements and restrictions. Many of the laws have been designed to protect the individual employee in situations where they may be unfairly treated by a powerful employer. Some may say that the laws have only served to reduce the number of full-time employees, as employers move towards part-time and short-contract labour, which is not so comprehensively protected by law. All of the following laws are currently in force in the UK, although another whole batch of laws and regulations are contained within the EC's proposed Social Chapter (which at the time of writing the UK Government has opted not to accept).

Disabled Persons (Employment) Act 1958

An employer with 20 or more employees must employ a minimum of three registered disabled persons. Certain organisations can obtain an exemption certificate due to the hazardous nature of their work. On the other hand, certain organisations are required to give disabled persons priority in selection and recruitment, e.g. electronic switchboard operators, etc.

The Factories Act 1961

This Act covers a wide range of different organisations, focusing on the use of machinery. The key features of this piece of legislation are:

- *The employer must provide toilet and washing facilities*
- *Premises should be adequately heated and ventilated*
- *The employer must make sure that floors, stairs and passageways are not obstructed in any way*
- *All floors should have a non-slippery surface*
- *Potentially dangerous machinery should be fenced off to protect employees*
- *The employer must ensure there are adequate fire escapes, well signposted and regularly maintained*
- *Fire doors themselves should never be locked or obstructed*

The Offices, Shops and Railways Premises Act 1963

This Act concentrates on conditions within shops and offices and provides a number of clear guidelines to the employer, including:

- *In work areas, the temperature must never drop below 16°C*
- *The employer must ensure that there is an adequate supply of fresh air*
- *Following on from the Factories Act 1961, this legislation states that the employer must provide enough toilet and washing facilities in relation to the number of staff. He must also make sure that there is hot and cold running water as well as soap and clean towels*
- *Again, following on from the Factories Act 1961, this legislation states that an employer has to provide suitable lighting wherever employees are expected to work or move around*
- *The employer must ensure that there is at least 12 square metres of working space per employee*

Equal Pay Act 1970

This important Act states that women, performing a similar job to men, should be treated in every way equally. This includes not only pay and conditions, but opportunity for promotion and recognition.

Race Relations Act 1970

This very complicated piece of legislation aims to protect individuals against discrimination on the grounds of race, colour, nationality, national origin or ethnicity.

The Rehabilitation of Offenders Act 1974

Individuals who have criminal convictions need not necessarily mention these on their job application forms or during interviews. Some convictions, after a certain period of time, are considered to be 'spent' (no longer applicable). If an employer subsequently discovers that an employee has 'spent' convictions and decides on dismissal, this is illegal.

Health and Safety at Work Act 1974 and EC Directives on Health and Safety

Before this Act, employees had been protected against hazardous working conditions under a number of different pieces of legislation. HASAW aimed to bring together and extend the protection of employees under a single Act. The main points were:

- *State general duties of an employer across all types of industry and commerce*

- *Create a system by which HASAW could be enforced (by the Health and Safety Executive and Local Authorities)*

- *The formation of the Health and Safety Commission which aimed to help employers understand the regulations and develop codes of practice*

- *The Act was backed up by imposing a series of legal duties on the employer who ran the risk of criminal proceedings being taken against him if he failed to follow them*

- *The imposition of minimum safety regulations and improvement to the working environment were introduced*

The work of HASAW has been followed up by a number of EC Directives covering such areas as safety signs at work, employees handling hazardous materials and guidance regarding avoidance of major hazards.

New regulations and codes of practice are being designed continuously and now cover nearly all work activities, both in the private and public sector. Steps are now being taken to cover any gaps in the legislation, or to make it easier to understand and implement.

Sex Discrimination Act 1975 and 1986

This Act covers discrimination on the grounds of gender. It is equally applicable to both males and females. The Act also covers discrimination relating to marital status.

The amended Act of 1986 extended protection against discrimination to employers employing five or less people. It also included for the first time employees working in a domestic capacity for private employers and employees working for professional associations.

Employment Protection (Consolidation) Act 1975 and 1978

The original Act, substantially amended in 1978, covers the main features of a Contract of Employment. In addition, it requires employers to provide a Contract of Employment within 13 weeks of commencement of employment. We have looked at Contracts of Employment in much more detail earlier in the book.

Employment Acts 1980–1990

Since 1979 successive governments have taken steps to limit trade union power. The main points of each of the laws are as follows:

1980   Picketing (attempting to prevent other employees, customers, deliveries, etc., from entering or leaving the premises during industrial action) was restricted to the premises involved in the dispute and none of the other organisation's premises. The Act also restricted 'blacking' (employees refusing to handle goods from an organisation whose employees are in dispute). It also became illegal to sack an employee who refused to join a trade union, before this certain occupations required compulsory membership of a Trade Union (known as a 'closed shop'). These 'closed shops' were further restricted by the law requiring 80 per cent of employees to agree that there should be one in existence.

1982   This law restricted the reasons behind an industrial dispute being called in the first place. The reasons had to be related directly to employment matters and could in no way be political. A more damaging part of the Act, as far as trade unions were concerned, was that they could now be sued by employers for any loss of business to other organisations as a result of industrial action.

A trade union's funds were now open to seizure by the Courts to pay for damages.

Following on from the restrictions made on 'closed shops' in 1980, the law stated that trade union members must vote as to whether 'closed shops' should continue.

1988   For the first time, individual trade union members were given the right to take their union to court to prevent industrial action. This only applied when the union itself declared there should be industrial action, and a ballot had not been taken. Union members were also protected under this law against disciplinary procedures for not having taken part in industrial action. Employees could now work for organisations which had 'closed shops', and not join the union, in the knowledge that they would keep their jobs.

1989   This amended Act required employers to provide some form of document which stated the terms and conditions under which an individual is employed. This is not a Contract of Employment, and does not have all the detail of one.

1990   This Act outlawed the dismissal of an individual who refused to join a union. Secondary action (union members taking industrial action in support of other union members) was made illegal. Unions became responsible, legally and financially, for any unofficial industrial action taken by members. All industrial action had to be approved by a majority of members in a secret ballot. Any union members involved in unofficial industrial action could be singled out by the employer and dismissed.

Trade Union Act 1988

This Act clearly stated that all industrial action must be agreed in advance by a majority of union members in a secret ballot.

EC Directive 'An Employer's Obligation to Inform Employees of the Conditions of Employment Relationships' 1991

The most important feature of this EC Directive is a change to the nature of the Contract of Employment. Employers are now required to provide a range of information, as detailed below, within two months and not the original 13 weeks.

- *The location of the work*
- *The job title*
- *The type of job (by categories)*
- *A job description*
- *Paid leave entitlements*
- *Hours of work*
- *Collective agreements made organisationally/nationally*

This is the first stage of a comprehensive range of legislation designed to ensure that employees throughout the EC have an employment contract, and know exactly what is required of them. The intention is also to treat employees working on a part time basis as equals to full-time employees in most respects.

Trade Union Reform and Employment Rights Act 1992

This law was designed to assist the rapid creation of jobs by clearly stating exactly what an employer has to provide for the benefit of the employee. This includes a written statement which covers their main conditions of employment (pay, holiday entitlement and hours worked).

Female employees are entitled to take 14 weeks maternity leave in the knowledge that their job is secure for them to return to it should they desire to do so after the pregnancy.

Employees who have responsibility for ensuring that health and safety regulations are adhered to and find themselves in a position where their employers have broken those regulations, are protected under this law from having the employer take action against them.

Management of Health and Safety at Work Regulations 1992

This major piece of legislation aims to provide a systematic and well-organised set of guidelines in relation to health and safety. They include the following:

■ *Employers are required to assess any potential risks employees may have to face and take preventative measures to cope with them*

■ *This risk assessment must be continually monitored by a group of employers working closely with at least five employees*

■ *Employers are required to employ specialists whose sole responsibility it is to implement the preventative measures, as well as providing information for all other employees within the organisation*

■ *Employers are further required to carry out regular screenings of their employees to make sure that they have not suffered from any ill-effects as a result of carrying out their duties. If appropriate, any health hazards which have been identified should be addressed immediately*

■ *Employees who have been given the duties of Safety Representatives should be regularly consulted, provided with time and space to carry out their investigations and given the authority to act on them*

Health and Safety (Display Screen Equipment) Regulations 1992

This Act is designed to protect employees who spend considerable amounts of their working hours in front of a computer screen. The main points of the legislation are:

■ *Employees receive sufficient breaks from the screen*

■ *Work should not be repetitive and the employee should be given a variety of tasks*

■ *Basic safety requirements must be satisfied as regards the screen itself, the design of the keyboard, as well as the shape and height of the desk and chair being used*

■ *Regular eye tests must be provided by the employer and if the employee needs special spectacles in order to carry out their tasks, they should be provided by the employer*

■ *Efficient lighting should be provided in the room where the employee is using the computer, as should proper ventilation*

Provision and Use of Work Equipment Regulations 1992

This Act covers all equipment from major production line machinery to hand-held tools. The legislation requires employers to:

■ *Take into consideration how and where equipment will be used, and choose the least hazardous methods of production*

■ *When purchasing equipment it must conform with any applicable EC Safety Directive*

■ *Ensure that employees are given sufficient information to safely use any equipment. Where appropriate, training and retraining should be offered*

■ *All equipment must be regularly serviced*

■ *Potentially dangerous machinery should have appropriate guards to prevent injury*

■ *When using hazardous materials protection must be available*

■ *The employer is responsible for ensuring that work is carried out in an environment which has sufficient light*

■ *The employer must display any relevant warnings regarding potential dangers*

Manual Handling Operations Regulations 1992

These regulations were implemented to assist in the avoidance of unnecessary injury at work. This directive covers lifting, pushing, pulling, carrying and moving objects at work, and offers advice as to the correct manner by which these should be carried out.

Personal Protective Equipment at Work Regulations 1992

The term 'personal protective equipment' includes life-jackets, harnesses, head, hand and foot protection, glasses and goggles, and clothing designed to be visible at all times and in all conditions. The Directive states that the protective equipment must be fit for the purpose for which it is intended, as well as actually fitting the employee. The equipment must conform with EC regulations and it must be suitably stored, cleaned regularly and replaced if defective. In addition, employees must be trained in the correct use of the equipment.

Individual activity

In the role of Personnel Manager, or Health and Safety Officer, which of the following situations relate to the Acts as detailed above:

■ A word processing operator has complained of constant migraines since being issued with a new computer

■ There has been a complaint regarding noxious fumes in the factory

■ The temperature in the office has dropped to 10°C

■ It has been rumoured that an employee has a criminal record of which you are officially unaware

■ A female member of staff has been receiving sexually abusive telephone calls at work. Investigations have shown that the calls have been made from another extension within the organisation

Element assignment

'THE IDEAL JOB'

One of last year's level 2 students recently started a new job. It seemed to be just what Rachel was looking for. She loved to work with people and was always happiest when she was busy. MacMillans Estate Agency in the high street had selected her from no less than 20 other applicants. It was true that her job was not exactly glamorous, at the moment, but the potential was there to learn and to gain valuable experience.

Her official job description was that of a Trainee Sales Negotiator. In effect though, she was the office dogsbody! 'Photocopy this Rachel', 'Get me a sandwich Rachel', 'No, I don't want to talk to him, take a message Rachel'. Frankly, after just a month, it was getting her down.

Rachel had been brooding about the whole problem for the entire weekend. Somehow she managed to pluck up the courage to at least walk to Mrs MacMillan's office door. Mrs MacMillan seemed to be an understanding type of person, but always too busy to give Rachel anything other than a smile. The promise of training had never materialised. Rachel was just left to pick things up as best she could. She hesitated in the corridor outside the door, then suddenly found herself gently knocking the varnished wood.

'Come in', she heard. 'Oh, it's you, Rachel, what can I do for you? I hope this won't take long, I need to see a client across the other side of town in half an hour.' Rachel obviously looked embarrassed, confused and disillusioned. Mrs MacMillan picked up the telephone and rang through to the front office to rearrange her meeting.

'Sit down, what's wrong?'

Firmly, Rachel replied, 'I have decided to pack this job in.'

'What? You have only been here a month! I thought that you were happy. You seem to fit in OK. I have got lots of plans for you in the future. I think you would make a great Sales Negotiator,' protested Mrs MacMillan.

'I just haven't got a clue what I am supposed to do. No one tells me anything. No one really talks to me. If I do something wrong they just shout at me. I just can't handle it any more,' Rachel poured out.

Having read the above situation, try to answer the following questions and solve the problems posed:

- *Should Rachel have waited this long before seeing Mrs MacMillan?*

- *Should the company have offered Rachel some training before throwing her in at the deep end?*

- *Whose fault is the situation? Mrs MacMillan's or Rachel's?*

After some discussion with Rachel and the other members of the organisation, Mrs MacMillan decided to take Rachel under her wing and train her personally. In the role of Mrs MacMillan, how would you organise this Training Programme? What do you think Rachel needs to know before being left to her own devices?

Working individually, prepare a draft Training Programme on behalf of Mrs MacMillan to ensure that Rachel is fully informed about office procedures, communication with staff and clients and is aware of what to do in circumstances when she cannot personally handle an enquiry.

UNIT TEST - Element 2.2

1 What is remuneration?

2 State two potential hazards at work

3 Give four items you would expect to find on a Contract of Employment

4 What is a craft union?

5 Name three well-known general unions

6 State three functions of a trade union

7 What is negligence?

8 What is dismissal?

9 Give three reasons why an employee could be dismissed due to misconduct

10 What is statutory contravention?

11 Give two examples of unfair dismissal

12 What is the normal disciplinary procedure and its stages?

13 How soon must an employee appeal after dismissal?

14 What is meant by 'acting in good faith'?

15 What do you understand by a 'safe working environment'?

16 What is a Joint Consultative Committee?

17 What is a Quality Circle?

18 What is compassionate leave?

19 What are equal opportunities?

20 What is picketing?

Element 2.3
Job roles

PERFORMANCE CRITERIA

1 Job roles in business organisations are described
2 Functions of different job roles are identified
3 Tasks undertaken by different role holders are identified

RANGE

1 Job roles: directors, managers and team members
2 Functions: design and production, personnel, finance, administration, sales and marketing and distribution
3 Tasks: decision making, problem solving, setting targets and achieving targets

EVIDENCE INDICATORS

A description of two different job roles, identifying tasks undertaken in their roles. Evidence should demonstrate understanding of the implications of the range dimensions in relation to the element. The unit test will confirm the candidate's coverage of range.

JOB ROLES

Having identified the different types of structure of organisations, employer and employee responsibilities and any legislation relating to employment, we will now look at the specific job roles of individuals within an organisation. We will begin by looking at the senior members of an organisation. The following should be borne in mind throughout all of these explanations of job roles:

- *The employer has clearly identified exactly what the employee should do*

- *At the same time, the employee is well aware of what the employer is expecting of them*

- *The employer, and for that matter the employee too, are contented that the employee is capable of doing the job. If not, then whatever steps need to be taken must be taken to ensure that the employee can perform to the best of their ability*

There are a number of key phrases that we will use continuously in describing exactly what the individual job roles are. These are:

- *Authority* – can the individual command others to carry out tasks? In other words, does the individual have any real power?

- *Accountability* – who is the individual responsible to? How many superiors have responsibility for the individual?

- *Responsibility* – what exactly are the tasks or duties related to the job?

- *Rights* – what should the individual reasonably expect from the employer? What should the employer reasonably expect from the employee? This has already been looked at in much greater detail earlier in the book.

THE MANAGING DIRECTOR

This Director is the most senior member of the Board of Directors. In some cases, the Managing Director is also the Chairman of the organisation. In this role, it is the responsibility of the Chairman to preside over every meeting of the Board.

The main roles of the Managing Director are:

- *To exercise all the powers and duties of a Director*

- *To exercise power and responsibility in the name of the rest of the Board on a day-to-day basis.*

The Board itself will have agreed certain guidelines of conduct and policy which it will expect the Managing Director to adhere to.

The Managing Director is chosen by the other members of the Board, who will be looking for an individual with a number of important qualities. Among these may be the following:

- *Wide business experience*
- *A proven track record of success*
- *The ability to make the right decisions under pressure*
- *To answer for any decisions made and stand by those decisions*
- *To be accountable to the Board and ultimately the shareholders (the Board itself is answerable to the shareholders)*
- *A clear idea of the policies and objectives of the organisation and the ability to work towards the fulfilment of these objectives*
- *Excellent communication skills and the ability to be a good ambassador for the organisation in a variety of situations*

The Managing Director is responsible for the implementation of policy formulated by the Board, and represents the Board at all times. To some extent, the Managing Director has to interpret the wishes of the Board, and develop a clear programme of organisational objectives. Further, the Managing Director must be aware which key members of staff can be relied upon to follow through his or her policy decisions to a successful completion. At all times, the Managing Director must keep the Board informed of any problems, decisions, or crises which it should be aware of.

Group activity

Working in groups of three, in the role of the Board of Directors, draw up a list of qualities you would be looking for in a Managing Director. Compare your list to those of the rest of the group.

THE DIRECTORS

Depending on the type of organisation, there must be at least one Director. In the case of private companies, there need only be one, but a public company requires a minimum of two. A Directorship has a dual function, that of direction itself and, of course, management. The main difference between these two functions is that direction tends to relate to longer-term aims, while management concerns the day-to-day decision making. (*See* Fig 2.21.)

Direction is essentially the implementation of the Board's policies. If a Director is an Executive Director, this means that they are full time and have responsibility

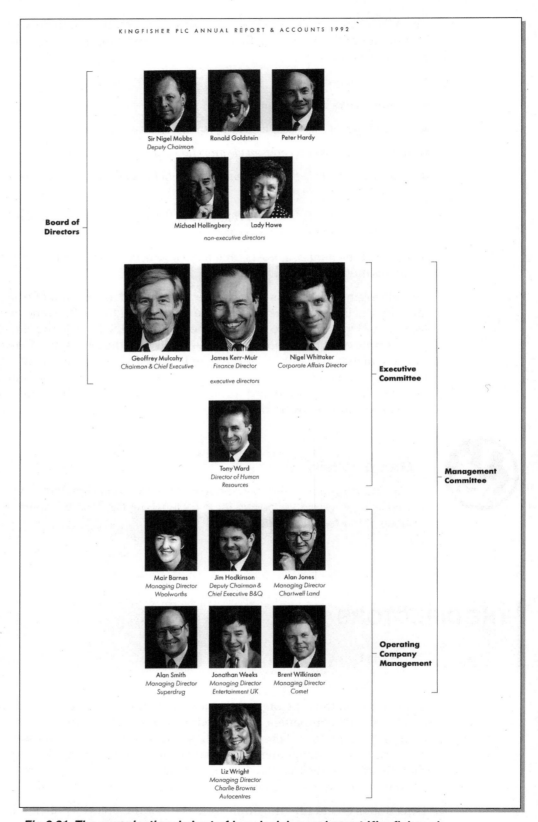

Fig 2.21 The organisational chart of key decision makers at Kingfisher plc

for a particular part of the organisation. On the other hand, a Non-Executive Director may be part time and may concentrate on a particular aspect of policy with which they are experienced.

Management by Executive Directors is, as we have seen, related to day-to-day decision making. Many Executive Directors find it very difficult to separate the direction and management roles that they are faced with. They may have a good idea of the nature of the organisation's policies, and have a clear impression as to how this policy may be achieved. Unfortunately, day-to-day decision making may mean that the Executive Director has to make decisions at odds with organisational policy. One way around this problem is to organise the Board of Directors into two separate units. Board members will serve on one or other of the units (with the exception of the Managing Director, who will serve on both). One unit of Directors will deal with overall policy and the other unit will concentrate on day-to-day implementation of policy. In this way, any conflict between policy and management of decision making is avoided.

The main duties of a Director are:

■ *To exercise their power and authority in good faith and for the benefit of the organisation*

■ *To put aside their personal interests and always consider the organisation first*

■ *To endeavour not to be casual or off-hand when managing the affairs of the organisation*

These duties essentially mean that a Director should display care and skill at all times. Obviously, Non-Executive Directors who have been included on the Board for their experience and expertise in a certain area are expected to be even more professional in their conduct on behalf of the organisation. At the same time, these Non-Executive Directors may not have the skill or expertise of being a Board member. In such cases, they are often assisted by an employee who can guide them as to the processes and procedures required of them.

Group activity

Consider this statement and discuss with the other members of your group:

'The only useful Director is one who spends all of his or her time involved in the company's business. Part-time Directors are worthless and can walk away from problems, leaving the full-time Directors to sort out their mess.'

THE COMPANY SECRETARY

Both public and private limited companies are required by law to have a Company Secretary. Essentially, this is an administrative post. Depending on the size of the organisation, a Company Secretary may have a variety of different duties. The most common duties are:

- *To keep all records, as required by law, which include a register of members of the organisation, plus minutes of Board and other Directors' meetings*

- *To keep all of the organisation's legal documents and the 'seal' secure. The 'seal' bears the organisation's name and registration number.*

- *To arrange organisation's and Directors' meetings*

- *To ensure that information, as required by law, is sent to the Registrar of Companies*

- *To enter into legally binding contracts on behalf of the organisation*

Group activity

In pairs, make a list of legal documents which you think a Company Secretary should be responsible for. Compare your list with those of the rest of your group.

THE AUDITORS

Annually, there is a legal requirement to look into the financial affairs of the organisation. This is undertaken to ensure that any facts or figures relating to finance made by the organisation are true and accurate. This auditing is done mainly for the benefit of the shareholders.

It is usual for the auditors to be a professional organisation, not related in any way to the organisation being audited. Only registered auditors can carry out auditing work and there are a number of limitations regarding who may act as an auditor for an organisation. These are:

- *The Auditor must not be an officer or servant of the organisation being audited*

- *Equally, an Auditor may not be the partner of, or employed by an officer or servant of the organisation*

- *This exclusion of officers and servants extends to any subsidiaries of the organisation and their employees and partners*

- *Finally, any individual who has any relationship with the organisation being audited is also excluded*

The Auditor, having been appointed, looks at two main areas. First, the organisation's accounts, and second what the organisation has said in relation to these accounts to the members of the company.

Individual activity

In the role of an Auditor, which documents would you expect to be given open access to when completing the audit? Make a list and compare this to those in the rest of the group.

MANAGERS

Below the level of Director, are a number of layers of Managers. It is the duty of a Manager to undertake tasks and duties as delegated to them by a Director. In effect, it is the Manager who takes responsibility for the day-to-day decision making and implementation of organisational policy. A Manager will be accountable to a Director, and ultimately the Board and shareholders via any other Managers senior to them.

A Manager would usually have a far better working knowledge of the organisation than a Director. It is therefore the case that Directors tend not to interfere with basic decision making and are happy to delegate their authority to the various levels of Management.

The exact duties of a Manager are totally dependent upon the level of responsibility, the department for which they are responsible, and the exact nature of the organisation they belong to. We shall look at specific managerial job roles at a later stage.

Group activity

As a group, discuss the following statement:

'Managers are the ones who do all the hard work. Directors just grab the glory, but blame their Managers if things go wrong.'

TEAM MEMBERS

It is rare to find employees working in any organisation alone. It is much more often the case that teams are created, either formally or informally to carry out specific tasks. A team is basically a group of individuals working together towards a single, common objective. When working as a member of a team there is a need to know which members of that team have power and authority. In other words, who is actually directing the joint efforts of the team. A successful team member needs to be able to communicate with others easily as the whole point of a work team is the interaction between its members. Many organisations spend considerable time and effort in training and retraining their staff in inter-personal skills.

Employers have also recognised the advantages of team building and may well be prepared to pay for residential training programmes aimed at enhancing team building.

JOB FUNCTIONS

The jobs people actually do within an organisation are clearly dependent upon three major criteria:

- *The size of the organisation*
- *The type of the organisation*
- *The function of the organisation*

Perhaps a good starting point in trying to assess exactly what a job entails is to try to discover what an organisation needs. Once this has been done, jobs can then be designed to fulfil the various functions required by the organisation. However, things are not always this simple. The majority of organisations have evolved over a number of years and the jobs undertaken by individuals working for them have changed as well. In fact many jobs have expanded to incorporate other different duties to those they were originally intended to do.

The result of this change is that some employees find themselves extremely over-worked, whilst others cope well with the tasks required of them, yet others still are under worked (perhaps because technology has replaced the bulk of their original duties). An organisation which allows such an imbalance of work to persist will find that it may well adversely affect the smooth running of the organisation.

The solution appears to be simple, but not often taken advantage of. Each time an individual leaves their job, there is an opportunity to evaluate exactly what the job entailed and assess whether certain duties can be merged or re-allocated elsewhere. A normal course of action in the more progressive-thinking organisa-tion is job review and evaluation. This process aims to look in detail at each job role and see if any features of the job need to be changed to take account of developments in working practices, new or different demands and technological breakthroughs.

The smaller the organisation, the more complex each individual employee's job may be. Employees may have to be capable of carrying out a wide variety and number of unrelated duties. The owner of a small business will not only be a Managing Director, but may have to cope with recruiting, training and promo-tion of employees, supervise all aspects of the organisation's operations and work out wages and other financial requirements. This individual will rely on his/her small number of employees to carry out their duties largely unaided, but will be able to turn to a number of professionals to cope with certain complex situations. Good examples would be an Accountant, Bank Manager or Solicitor.

In the case of larger organisations, different functions of that organisation tend to be split into distinct areas. These will include many of the departmental divisions looked at earlier in the book. It would be useful to look at the various layers of management and authority before considering these divisions in detail;

- Directly below the level of Director are the Senior Managers. In consultation with the Directors they will set any necessary policies or procedures to achieve the organisation's objectives. These Senior Managers, as we have mentioned previously, may well be Executive Directors.

- The task of implementing organisational policies and procedures is left to the Middle Managers. On a day-to-day basis they will liaise with both the Senior Managers, in order to clarify organisational objectives, and Supervisory Managers, who are directly responsible to them.

- The Managers who deal directly with the workforce are known as Supervisory Managers. These are responsible for ensuring that tasks, as directed by the Middle Managers, are carried out promptly and efficiently.

- The individuals who make up the bulk of the organisation are the workers. Alternatively, these may be referred to as subordinates. It is their role to actually deal with the job at hand. They are often called simply 'staff' to make a distinction between all types of Managers and these employees.

It is commonly held that there are effectively only five different types of job related to skills required to carry them out. These are:

Professional

This category includes Solicitors, Accountants, Dentists, Doctors and Architects, all of whom display a certain degree of specialist knowledge of a given area. In recent years, although many professionals would strenuously disagree, new professionals have joined this group. They are in the main related to new areas of work, as opposed to the more traditional professional. Examples of these would be Computer Analysts, Personnel Managers, Marketing Executives and a wide variety of Business Consultants.

Managerial

This category is a very wide one but essentially features managerial and supervisory posts. Some occupations which we have already mentioned as being professional can also be referred to as managerial, such as Personnel Directors and Marketing Managers.

Technical

This relatively recent category of occupational type (although ever since there have been machines this group has existed) essentially refers to those individuals who are responsible for the setting-up and maintenance of machinery and technological equipment. Within this category we will find Computer Programmers, Television Cameramen and Sound Recordists, and Production Line Technicians.

Administrative

This category is also a fairly wide one, which includes any job that could be considered clerical or administrative. Typical examples are Typists, Secretaries, Receptionists, Word Processor Operators and Switchboard Operators.

Manual

Essentially, this category covers all manual workers who operate various types of equipment and machinery. It is further broken down into three sub-sections, which are:

- *Skilled* – in this sub-section, we would find tradesmen such as carpenters, plumbers, bricklayers and roofers or tilers. It is usually the case that members of this sub-section belong to a Guild or Association for their specific trade.

- *Semi-Skilled* – in this sub-section we would find workers who have not been fully trained in a particular trade, but who have been trained to use the equipment or machinery they use regularly for their job. Typically skilled manual workers' assistants or 'mates' would be found in this category.

- *Unskilled* – in this sub-section we would find workers who are not trained for a specific job and fulfil the role of labourer, factory operative, warehouse packer or cleaner.

Group activity

In pairs, write down all of the occupations undertaken by your family and friends. Now try to place them in one of the categories given above. Which of the categories covers most of the occupations? Compare your findings with those of the rest of the group.

We will now look in detail at the job roles within each major department, and try to identify any key operations covered by them.

The Administration Department

Chief Administration Officer/Office Services Manager

This person will oversee all major functions of the department, allocate work received from other departments (and routine administrative duties) and carry the responsibility for the smooth running of the department.

Secretariat Supervisor

The Secretariat Supervisor will allocate and monitor all work carried out by the secretaries, audio typists, shorthand typists, word processor operators and typists.

Word Processor Operator

Under the guidance of the Secretariat Supervisor, the Word Processor Operator will undertake work from a variety of different sources and will be responsible for the presentation, safe storage (on disk or hard copy) and ensuring that any deadlines related to the work are met.

Secretary

This job usually refers to an individual who works directly for one or more managers. It is the Secretary's responsibility to ensure that any information in the form of messages, memos, letters, reports, etc., are brought to the attention of the Manager. In addition, a Secretary will also be responsible for routine letter and note taking on behalf of the Manager, as well as keeping track of all the manager's diary commitments (sometimes the personal diary too!). The Secretary may also arrange meetings for which his or her manager may be responsible. At all times the Secretary will ensure that only relevant information and individuals which really need the time of the Manager are brought to his or her attention.

A Secretary's skills may include the capacity to work with audio tape, word processors and shorthand.

Audio Typist

The Audio Typist will be responsible for working for several people in the organisation, possibly based in a 'pool'. The Audio Typist's duties will include typing from audio tapes which have been prepared by various individuals and he or she will need to ensure that this work is completed to the given deadline, in a neat and accurate way.

Shorthand Typist

A Shorthand Typist will also work for several individuals within the organisation. The Shorthand Typist will take dictated notes from the Manager and will have the responsibility of transcribing them and typing up the document in a neat and accurate way. It is usually the case that a Shorthand Typist will be present to note the decisions taken at any company meetings.

Typist

This job will involve the typing of routine documents within the organisation. To a great extent this role is gradually being replaced by Word Processor Operators as, increasingly, organisations are tending to buy word processors rather than typewriters.

Messenger

This job involves the distribution of both internal and external documents. The role is particularly useful in organisations which have a number of closely situated sites, or in situations when the organisation's customers are located in the immediate vicinity. Messengers are still used traditionally in the City of London, however, many functions of the Messenger have been replaced with the availability of facsimile machines, modems and electronic mail.

Records Supervisor

The primary responsibility of this individual is to ensure that all necessary documents are safely, securely and accessibly stored. Despite the fact that technology has substantially reduced the need to store vast amounts of paper documents, there are many reasons why organisations still prefer to have hard copies of documents available for inspection. Upon receiving a request for information, the Records Supervisor will instruct a Records Clerk to retrieve and deliver the required documentation.

Records Clerk

The Records Clerk will be allocated work by the Records Supervisor. It will be the Records Clerk's responsibility to retrieve the required information and ensure its safe delivery by internal mail, personal delivery, or by a Messenger. The Records Clerk will also take note of who has requested the information, the date of the request and the date of return. This 'out card' is completed in order to keep track of the documents and ensure their safe return.

Librarian

This individual is responsible for acquiring and maintaining resources relevant to the organisation's activities. These may take the form of books, reports, periodicals and newspaper cuttings. This resource is then available to all members of the organisation who may need to research into a specific area related to their work. It is the Librarian's task to ensure that the information is as up to date as possible and that all staff are aware of its availability.

Mail Room Supervisor

This job entails the handling of all internal and external mail and may commonly be known as The Post Room. This location acts as a central collection point of letters, packages and parcels. Some may be bound for literally any part of the world and others may be internal mail or bulletins. The various pieces of mail will either be collected by the Mail Room Assistant, or delivered by various individuals within the organisation. It is the Mail Room Supervisor's responsibility to make sure that all outgoing mail is weighed, franked and made ready for collection by the Post Office. The Mail Room Supervisor will also note (for internal cost allocation) the postage totals for each department within the organisation.

Mail Room Assistants

Working under the instruction of the Mail Room Supervisor, the Mail Room Assistant may complete a variety of different tasks:

- *There may be mail to be collected from the various departments*

- *Mail received each morning must be delivered to the relevant person(s). Before this can be done, the mail needs to be sorted and perhaps re-routed to another site*

- *All outgoing mail needs to be weighed, franked and put into the correct Post Office bag ready for collection or delivery to the Post Office*

- *Taking note of postage spent by each department and ensuring that the Mail Room Supervisor has up-to-date figures for this cost*

- *Ensuring that the Post Office leaflets kept in the Mail Room show the current postal rates*

Telephone/Switchboard Supervisor

Since many organisations rely heavily on the external and internal telephone systems, this key post is vital to the smooth running of most operations. This Supervisor ensures that all telecommunication needs are met and that the switchboard system is capable of fulfilling all the demands of the organisation. In addition, the Supervisor will make sure that the switchboard is constantly 'manned' and at times when the organisation is closed for business, that answerphone messages can record incoming calls, or give useful information to the caller. (*See* Fig 2.22.)

FOR:	**FROM:**	
OF:		DATE:
TEL:	FAX:	TIME:
		TAKEN BY:

TELEPHONED ○   PLEASE RING BACK ○   RETURNED YOUR CALL ○   WILL RING BACK ○   WOULD LIKE TO SEE YOU ○   URGENT ○

Fig 2.22 A telephone message form as used by Mercury Communications

Switchboard Operator

In many cases, a customer's first contact with an organisation is via the telephone. It is therefore most important that the Switchboard Operator answers the calls swiftly and is helpful and responsive to the caller. A good Switchboard Operator will instantly know exactly who the caller needs to speak to (despite the fact that the caller may not ask for a named individual) and will know from memory the extension number of most members of staff.

Cleaning Supervisor

All organisations, whether or not they have a constant flow of visitors, need to ensure that the premises are kept as clean and tidy as possible. Organisations which have sensitive technological equipment may even need to ensure that the work areas are as dust-free as possible. The Cleaning Supervisor will allocate his or her cleaning staff according to the demands which each particular work area will make. Periodically, floors and windows may need to be given special attention and may require specialist equipment/sub-contractors to carry out the necessary work.

Cleaners

A cleaner is usually given a particular area of the premises for which they are responsible. The main cleaning duties will include emptying of bins, clearing away of empty boxes and packing materials, hoovering and dusting and routine general cleaning duties. Specialist cleaners may be employed to sanitise telephones, clean word processors with anti-static sprays and clean carpets or polish floors.

Individual activity

Draw up an organisational chart which shows the operations of an Administration Department which includes all of the above posts.

Indicate on this chart who has responsibility for decision making.

The Accounts/Finance Department

Company Accountant

It is the Company Accountant's responsibility to maintain an up-to-date record and analysis of income and expenditure. The Company Accountant will have a number of accounts specialists who will be monitoring, on his behalf, various financial aspects of the organisation. At any time, the Company Accountant may be asked for detailed information regarding the financial status of the organisation, and must be able to respond immediately. There are a number of legal and statutory requirements which organisations must fulfil and it is the responsibility of the Company Accountant to ensure that any of these obligations are met. The Company Accountant is directly accountable to the Board of Directors for his or her actions and decisions.

Accountants

There are a variety of accounts specialists who are employed to carry out specific monitoring and analysis of financial data. These Accountants will oversee the flow of data received regarding sales, purchases, running costs and other expenses. In addition, they will provide essential accounting information such as gross profit, net profit, turnover and relative profitability of different areas of the organisation. In larger organisations they may keep track of the performance of investments in other organisations and regularly monitor the financial strengths and weaknesses of subsidiary companies.

Credit Controller

This individual will monitor the orders placed and payment history of customers in order to establish their reliability as payers. Each customer will have a set credit limit (rather like an agreed overdraft) and the Credit Controller will endeavour to make sure that customers do not exceed this limit. In cases of late or non-payment of invoices, it is the Credit Controller who will contact the customer in question in an attempt to secure payment. The Credit Controller will take into account how long the customer has been purchasing from the organisation and may well look back into the past to see if there has been any problems with regard to payment before.

Accounts Clerk

An Accounts Clerk carries out the routine day-to-day accounting duties, as directed by either the Chief Accountant or Senior Accountants. This may involve either manual figure work, or the use of the increasingly popular range of accounting software. It is usually the Accounts Clerk's role to prepare figures for analysis by the more senior Accountants.

In some organisations, one duty of an Accounts Clerk will be to maintain and issue petty cash to those who request it by the presentation of a validly signed voucher (e.g. for the purchase of sundry office items).

Payroll Clerks

Working closely with the Personnel Department, the Payroll Clerk is responsible for ensuring that the correct wages or salaries are paid to every member of staff. The Payroll Clerk must be familiar with Income Tax and National Insurance and pension scheme contributions. Depending on the size of the organisation, the Payroll Clerk may have to undertake these tasks manually, or in the case of a larger organisation, he/she may be assisted by a software package. In some organisations where the wages structure is complex, or is related to performance and output, this job may not be as straightforward as one may imagine. (*See* Fig 2.23.)

Inland Revenue PAYE — Employer's permanent record of employees

Name of employee	Works or payroll no. etc.	National Insurance number	Date of birth	Date started	How Tax Office notified (P45(3) or P46)	Date P45 (3) or P46 sent to Tax Office	Date left	Date P45 (1) sent to Tax Office	Notes

P13   Dd 8261763-800M-10/82—900193-Ghead

This form is for optional use by the employer.

Fig 2.23 A P13 form which details the employer's record of employees. Issued by the Inland Revenue for **PAYE records**   (Crown copyright)

Individual activity

In the role of an Accounts Clerk, what action would you take in the following situations:

- You are processing a cheque which is unsigned

- You receive a telephone call from a customer who has exceeded their credit limit, but require further goods for a special exhibition they are attending next weekend

- You have received some petty cash vouchers which do not correspond with the attached receipts

In each of the above cases you may simply choose to refer the problem to your immediate superior, but even in this event, you should offer suggestions of how the situation should be dealt with.

Compare your solutions to the three problems with those of the rest of the group.

The Sales Department

Sales Manager

This job entails the co-ordination of the organisation's sales efforts. The Sales Manager is usually located at the Head Office with an administration staff who monitor the performance of the various national, regional and area Sales Managers and teams. In occupations such as this, a considerable amount of the salary is related to sales performance. Periodically, the Sales Manager will visit his sales team in the field to assess their effectiveness and to keep in touch with current customer demands.

Assistant Sales Manager

Deputising for the Sales Manager, this individual will take on a range of sales related responsibilities and may often be the first point of contact for the various members of the sales force. It will be the Assistant Sales Manager's role to help the Sales Manager formulate the sales policy of the organisation.

National Sales Manager

In larger organisations, there is a need to co-ordinate the sales effort on a country by-country basis. National Sales Managers are usually given considerable freedom to formulate sales policy which is the most effective for the country in which they operate. Normally, a National Sales Manager will have a wide knowledge of the country in which they work and may even be a national of that country. Other organisations may not have National Sales Managers, as they may have entered into an agreement with a foreign company who will represent the interests of the organisation in the field. (*See* Fig 2.24.)

Regional Sales Manager

Just as different countries have their own peculiarities, regions within a country also have theirs. Different sorts of industry and commerce tend to cluster around

Fig 2.24 Mercury Communications application form for residential telephone installation

particular towns or cities. The Regional Sales Manager will have an intimate knowledge of the needs of these businesses, which may be different from the national needs. The Regional Sales Manager will be located within the region for which he or she has responsibility and will be required to regularly analyse any changes in the local economy which may affect sales.

Area Sales Manager

Working under the direction of the Regional Sales Manager, an Area Sales Manager will be responsible for a part of the region. In some cases, this may mean a single city or county. Again, a good working knowledge of the needs of the area is essential in co-ordinating the sales effort. The Area Sales Manager will regularly accompany Sales Representatives when they visit customers and be able to offer on the spot advice and guidance.

Sales Representatives

These individuals form the backbone of the sales team. Constantly on the road, visiting both customers and potential customers, they will be in direct contact with their Area Sales Manager via mobile or car phones. Since the bulk of their salary is directly related to the sales which they generate, they are always under pressure to meet their targets in order to achieve their bonuses. The image of the Sales Representative in his company car, is one that is easy to visualise. In reality, they may be very well trained salespeople, with an expert knowledge of their field and extremely useful to their customers. They are, after all, the first point of contact and may well become a useful 'partner' in building up a business.

Tele-Sales Assistants

Working from central, national, regional or area offices, these individuals will not only take direct orders for goods and services from the customer, but will also receive regular orders from the Sales Representatives. Operating with up-to-date lists of customer contacts from the Sales Representatives, they will attempt to gain new sales or arrange for one of the Sales Representatives to visit the business. They will be particularly well trained in telephone skills and have any useful information to hand via a desktop computer.

Invoice Clerk

The role of this individual is to process all orders generated by either the Sales Representatives or the Tele-Sales team. Essentially, the documents produced will form both a list of required products for the warehouse to despatch and a record of products sold for the Accounts Department. The Invoice Clerk will be in regular contact with the warehouse to ensure that the sales team is aware of the stock levels of each product.

Group activity

In the role of Sales Director, working in pairs, prepare a memorandum which answers a note received from the Personnel Department. This note states that you will lose the services of your Invoice Clerk at the end of the month.

Prepare your memorandum which clearly states why you should keep your Invoice Clerk.

The Marketing Department

Marketing Manager

Marketing Managers are responsible for planning, organising, directing and controlling the marketing efforts of the organisation. Increasingly, they are professional individuals who are well-versed in formulating a marketing plan which is workable within the limitations of the organisation. In effect, they are responsible for establishing the organisation's marketing objectives (known as the Strategy) and deciding how the overall objectives may be achieved (known as the Tactics). All organisations have a 'Corporate Image', which means that everything the organisation produces from letterheads to finished products, has the same overall look. The Marketing Manager will decide exactly how the Corporate Image relates to each and every aspect of the company.

Assistant Marketing Manager

Deputising for the Marketing Manager, and co-ordinating the efforts of each of the Product/Brand Managers are the main responsibilities of the Assistant Marketing Manager. It will be this individual's role to implement the marketing strategy across all aspects of the organisation and to ensure that the Corporate Image is consistent.

Product/Brand Manager

A Product Manager is responsible for co-ordinating the marketing plan relating to a single product.

A Brand Manager, on the other hand, may be responsible for a range of products which have the same brand name.

In both cases, the individuals will have to organise all activities relating to their product(s) including advertising, sales promotions, launches, relaunches and packaging.

Marketing Research Analyst

Millions of pounds are spent each year on Marketing Research. Nearly 10 per cent of the retail price is spent on Marketing Research alone. Marketing Research is the systematic collection and analysis of data which looks specifically at the customer's attitudes, needs, opinions and motivation and anything which influence these. In order to minimise the risks of launching a new product, the organisation needs to know as much about the potential customer, competition and any other factor which may affect sales. This specialist will use existing statistical data, as well as commissioning new market research as may be required.

Advertising Manager

An Advertising Manager will be responsible for co-ordinating the advertising budget of the organisation. Working in close co-operation with various other members of the organisation, the Advertising Manager should be able to identify the best media for the advertising of the product. Additionally, the Advertising Manager will negotiate with magazines, newspapers, radio and television companies to achieve the best possible price. In many organisations, the Advertising Manager's function is taken by an Advertising Agency who place and co-ordinate all advertisements. (*See* Fig 2.25 *overleaf*)

Promotions Manager

There is a narrow line between what a Promotions Manager does and an Advertising Manager's responsibilities. Essentially, the Promotions Manager will

Fig 2.25 An example of BNFL's commitment to enhance their organisation's public image

co-ordinate all other marketing strategies apart from advertisements. These will include special offers, competitions, trial offers, money-off vouchers, point of sale material and exhibitions.

Individual activity

In the role of Promotions Manager, devise a leaflet to be handed out at the local train station, which gives customers your recent change of telephone number. To assist you in the design of this leaflet, refer to the brief details below.

- Name and address of company – Brewster's DIY, 22–27 Golden Lane, London EC4

- Opening hours – 0830–1900 Mon–Sat

- New telephone number – 071 254 1212

Include any further information you feel necessary.

The Information Technology/Computer Services Department

Departmental Manager

It is the responsibility of this Departmental Manager to provide a round-the-clock and comprehensive service back-up for the organisation's computing and data processing requirements. Within his or her area of influence, the Manager will co-ordinate the design of computer programs to manipulate data for the various departments.

Assistant Departmental Manager

Under the direction of the Departmental Manager, this Assistant Manager will be responsible for acquiring and maintaining all computer software and hardware. In order to carry out this task, the Assistant Manager will delegate various aspects to specialist managers. In co-ordination with the Departmental Manager, they will ensure that sufficient support is given to all computer-based communication systems within the organisation.

Data Processing Manager

This individual will maintain a detailed record of the organisation's stored information, which will be constantly updated and always accessible. The Manager will also ensure that sensitive information is protected from access by any unauthorised person. On a regular basis, the Data Processing Manager will also make sure that back-up copies of all data stored have been made and kept in secure and fire-proof locations.

Computer Services Manager

The Computer Services Manager will keep a constant overview of new developments in order to inform the Departmental Manager of more efficient ways of storing and manipulating data. It will also be this individual's responsibility to install and maintain new or updated versions of software as they become available. Further, their team of servicing engineers will regularly check all of the organisation's computer equipment. In some organisations, this service function has been bought-in from computing service specialists.

Computer Programmers

These specialist individuals will create computer software needed by the various departments, so that information may be processed and analysed according to changing needs.

Computer Operators

These individuals will be responsible for the inputting of data and manipulation of existing information at the request of various departments within the organisation. Routinely, they will update information from a variety of sources, deleting or modifying as required. Increasingly, organisations have become more reliant on computer-based information and will need constant access to reliable and contemporary data.

Group activity

Discuss with your group the following statement:

'Computers have taken the human factor out of too many business decisions. We have lost the personal touch.'

The Research and Development Department

Research and Development Co-Ordination Manager

It is the responsibility of this Manager to co-ordinate the development of products and services to prototype level. All products and services must be rigorously tested before they are put into production and offered to the customer. The type of individual who will fill this post is likely to be a technical expert within a specific field. They will be aware of the technological requirements and any production problems related to these. Normally, this Manager will be given clear instructions as to the organisation's requirements for a new product or service, but will have to work very closely with the Production Manager in order to develop a product which the organisation is capable of producing.

Researchers

Once the Departmental Manager has been given a brief to develop and test a new product or service, Researchers will then investigate all aspects relating to this product or service. They will refer to any scientific reports allied to the area of interest, as well as investigating competitors' products. In effect, they will produce a report which offers a series of alternatives from which the Developers can work. This report will also be circulated to any other interested party in the organisation.

Product/Service Developers

These individuals will again be specialists in their own field. They will have been chosen for their knowledge and application of skills. It is their responsibility to work from the information given to them by the Researchers and to develop a working version or versions of the product. This product will then be subjected to exhaustive testing to ensure that it meets the requirements of the organisation, safety tests and the needs of the customer. At all stages of the development, the Production Department will advise the Developer regarding any production considerations.

The Production Department

Production Manager

The Production Manager's responsibility is to manufacture products to the correct specification, quality, price and safety levels. Production Managers tend to be quite technical individuals, who understand the production process intimately. They will work closely with the Research and Development Manager, as well as the Sales Manager. It is the Production Manager's role to turn new product ideas into finished products and supply the regular needs of the Sales Department.

Assistant Production Managers

These individuals will be given the responsibility by the Production Manager to oversee the smooth running of the various production lines. They will work in close co-operation with the Production Line Managers to ensure that production levels and product quality are maintained in relation to demand. The Assistant Production Managers will be technically competent and may have a good working knowledge of the machinery.

The Buyer

The Buyer is required to ensure that he or she has purchased sufficient stocks of raw materials and components to enable the production lines to run efficiently. The Buyer must be able to predict demands for all raw materials, components and machinery by close examination of sales figures, past, present and projected. An essential duty of the Buyer is to obtain all items at the best possible price. The Buyer may be able to negotiate favourable extended credit terms from regular suppliers. He or she will also be responsible for making sure that all items ordered are received in good time.

Production Line Manager

A Production Line Manager is responsible for the smooth running of a part of the Production Department which produces a single product or product range. The

Production Line Manager will be given quotas to achieve from the Production Manager or Assistant Production Manager and will have to organise their staff to meet the deadlines.

Production Line Supervisor

It is the Production Line Supervisor's responsibility to deploy the members of his or her work team to the maximum possible effect. The Supervisor will monitor the performance of both the work team and the machinery and regularly report to the Production Line Manager with regard to any potential problems. This Supervisor is the main point of contact between the employees and the management structure of the organisation. In the event of potential problems with the machinery, they will liaise with the Service Engineers.

Service Engineers

It is the Service Engineer's role to ensure that any defects or breakdowns in machinery within the Production Department are swiftly and efficiently dealt with. They will inform the Production Manager and the relevant Production Line Manager regarding any need to close down a production line for the purposes of maintenance, servicing and cleaning. The Service Engineers will need to keep a stock of basic components in order to repair machinery on the spot.

Production Line Operatives

Depending on the type of production employed by the organisation, the Production Line Operatives will either be responsible for a repetitive task, or a series of related tasks. Many production lines have been developed so that only routine duties need to be carried out by humans. In these cases, Production Line Operatives tend to merely feed the machines with raw materials and components and do not actually take part in the production process itself. In situations when the production is less automated, Production Line Operatives will be involved in the production of goods to completion. Many organisations run their production lines continuously and therefore require their Production Line Operatives to work shifts.

Group activity

In the role of Production Manager, and working in pairs, design a timesheet for use on the factory floor by production operatives. The production operatives are paid on piece-work only, and up to this point you suspect there have been a number of false claims for work carried out. The total number of products finished is much smaller than the claim total. Try to design a system which would eliminate this problem. Compare your form to those designed by the rest of the group.

The Distribution/Transport Department

The Distribution Manager

The Distribution Manager's duty is to design, run and maintain a cost-effective way of ensuring that products reach their correct destination, in a suitable state, at the right time. The Distribution Manager will work in close co-operation with the Sales Department which will report orders placed by customers, as well as expected delivery dates. The Distribution Manager tends to control the operations of the warehouse and all storage facilities. He or she will inform the Production Department when stock levels reach the reorder level. This information will be received from the Warehouse Manager. (*See* Fig 2.26 *overleaf.*)

The Transport Manager

The Transport Manager's responsibility is to maintain and run the delivery fleet of vehicles which service the distribution requirements of the organisation. He or she will liaise closely with the Distribution Manager, the Warehouse Manager and the Sales Department. The Transport Manager will also be responsible for keeping service records and vehicle registrations, as well as any related insurance for the fleet. He or she will also negotiate any leasing or purchasing agreements relating to vehicles and will directly co-ordinate the efforts of the drivers, vehicle service engineers and the administration staff within his or her department.

The Warehouse Manager

The Warehouse Manager is responsible for the smooth running of the warehousing facilities of the organisation. He or she will co-ordinate all warehouse staff in an effort to ensure that goods both inwards and outwards are dealt with in a quick and efficient manner. The Warehouse Manager will design the storage facilities in such a way as to enable easy access to the most used items. He or she must also keep a close eye on the stock levels of all stored equipment, products, components and raw materials.

Operatives/Drivers

The Warehouse Operatives will take their instructions from the Warehouse Manager. It will be their responsibility to report any problems to their immediate Manager, and to ensure that they carry out their tasks in a quick and efficient manner. Upon receiving an order via the Sales Department, Warehouse Operatives will then 'pick' the order and pack it ready for distribution. Others may be concerned with the goods inwards part of the warehouse operation, and will check Goods Received against orders made by the organisation. Should there be any discrepancy, the Warehouse Manager should be informed and will contact the relevant person. Some Warehouse Operatives will operate machinery such as fork-lift trucks.

The Drivers will be directly answerable to the Transport Manager, who will issue them with delivery rounds. In certain cases, particularly in larger organisations, there may well be a need to have regional distribution points which will have small warehousing facilities and attached drivers/delivery men.

Group activity

There are many rules and regulations which control the operations of a driver. Working in groups of three, try to find out as many laws and restrictions which relate to drivers. Compare your findings with those of the rest of the group.

WOOLWORTHS DISTRIBUTION NETWORK

Satellite communications and computerised ordering are key to today's distribution network.

The company's two distribution centres supply the chain with 64 million products each year.

The efficiency of the distribution network was recently recognised by the British Standards Institute.

In 1992 Woolworths became the first retailer to be awarded British Standard 5750 for its Distribution Quality Management system.

Continuous monitoring and spot checks by distribution personnel ensure these standards are maintained and that techniques and systems are continually updated.

Running an all year-round operation from its two centres at Swindon and Castleton, distribution aims to make delivery to a store within 48 hours of receiving an order through an electronic messaging system. Speed and accuracy are crucial to the success of the operation which works to achieve an error rate of less than half of one per cent.

During 1992 a new transport fleet was introduced and it is estimated that drivers will cover eight million kilometres a year. The new fleet not only helps to further improve the speed and efficiency of distribution, but by using more fuel-efficient vehicles, reduces the environmental impact of the operation.

Fig 2.26 Woolworth's two main distribution centres supply some 64 million products to their stores per year

The Personnel (or Human Resources) Department

The Personnel Manager

The Personnel Manager is ultimately responsible for the recruitment, retention and welfare of all staff. In this role the Personnel Manager will be involved in the designing of job descriptions and job specifications, the interview process, any training required by employees, staff problems and handling any necessary documentation relating to termination of employment for whatever reason. The Personnel Manager will also be involved in the co-ordination of staff facilities such as catering, sport, leisure and social activities. He or she will monitor and fulfil any staff development requirements. It is the Personnel Manager who is the main point of contact with the management structure with regard to trade union negotiations.

The Assistant Personnel Manager

The Assistant Personnel Manager will deputise for the Personnel Manager in a variety of situations, and will have regular duties delegated to him or her. The Assistant Personnel Manager will usually be the first point of contact for employee problems and individuals enquiring about possible vacancies within the organisation. Between the Assistant Personnel Manager and the Personnel Manager, a confidential counselling service will be offered to all employees. The Assistant Personnel Manager will also be responsible for the maintenance of comprehensive staff records.

Clerical Assistants

Routine personnel duties, such as the maintenance of staff records and work logs are carried out by Clerical Assistants in the Personnel Department. Various duties will be delegated to them by either the Personnel Manager or the Assistant Personnel Manager and it is essential that these are carried out with confidentiality.

Group activity

Working in pairs, assume the role of Assistant Personnel Manager. You have been asked by the Personnel Manager to draft the details of a job advertisement for your organisation. The post to be filled has the following features:

- Job title – cleaner
- Hours – 0700–0930 daily (except Sundays)
- Payment – £2.73 per hour
- Previous experience preferred

Use a word processor to make the advertisement look as attractive as possible.

The Customer/Public Relations Department

The Public Relations Officer

Increasingly, organisations have recognised the need to project a strong, positive image to the public. The Public Relations Officer will be responsible for fostering a good relationship with the media, in the hope that it will consider giving the organisation both editorial space and favourable news reporting. He or she will maintain a comprehensive database of media contacts, from which extensive mail shots will be made. The Public Relations Officer is also responsible for the writing of press releases and will also produce a range of booklets and leaflets concerning the operations of the organisation.

BNFL **Press Release**

QUALITY AWARD FOR BNFL COMPUTER OPERATIONS SECTION

The Computer Operations section at British Nuclear Fuels plc has become the Company's first computer department to attain BS5750 Part 2 certification, with TickIT for "quality in the Data Centre."

TickIT is the IT sector interpretation of BS5750, supported by the Department of Trade and Industry and the British Computer Society, and the achievement of the Risley-based section follows a year of concerted effort by CMS Computer Operations and QA teams.

The Risley Data Centre provides computing services to BNFL and Facilities Management to a variety of external custmers. The award demonstrates that customers can have confidence in the Data Centre's quality management systems.

Information Systems Director Lesley Ottery said: "This is an achievement for which everyone can feel proud. It represents a lot of hard work and gives tangibile recognition to the professionalism of the Data Centre's staff."

CMS are now planning to extend the scope of the BS5750 certification to other areas of activity within the department.

- ENDS -

BNFL/892/93   29 January 1993

For further information contact the BNFL Press Office on (0925) 832450.

Evenings and Weekends: Bill Anderton (0942 493320)
                          Judith Charlton (0925 764008)
                          Harold Ashurst (0942 492591)
                          Alison Broadbent (0925 418064)

British Nuclear Fuels plc
For further information, contact: The Press Office,
Information Services Directorate, British Nuclear Fuels plc, Risley, Warrington, Cheshire WA3 6AS
Telephone: Padgate (0925) 832450, Telex: 627581

Fig 2.27 BNFL's company policy is to constantly inform the Press as to any interesting development regarding the organisation

The Customer Relations Officer

Whilst the Public Relations Officer is concerned with media and news coverage, the Customer Relations Officer concentrates on existing and potential customers. He or she will respond to customer enquiries, providing a range of information packs which may be sent on request. In addition, the Customer Relations Officer will co-ordinate activities with the Community Projects Department. In cases where a customer has a serious complaint regarding the products or services provided by the organisation, then the Customer Relations Officer will be available to assist in the solving of any problems.

Individual activity

In the role of Customer Relations Officer, write a letter in response to one received from a customer complaining that their car was broken into and their radio cassette stolen while parked on the premises of your organisation.

It is company policy to point out that there are notices clearly visible which state that you take no responsibility for damage or theft from vehicles while parked.

Your letter should be word processed and in the correct business format (this is explained in Unit 4 of this book).

The Community Projects Department

The Community Projects Officer

Many organisations, having recognised the need to form a closer relationship with the local community, have appointed a Community Projects Officer. In several respects, the duties of this individual are somewhat similar to the Customer Relations Officer, however, the Community Projects Officer tends to concentrate on the immediate locality. He or she will organise, with the assistance of other local organisations, a range of activities in order to heighten the public's awareness and appreciation of the organisation. This may take the form of sponsoring local events, financing community projects, or offering the organisation's facilities to local groups.

JOB TASKS

In order to be a successful employee, or, for that matter, a successful Manager, you need to display a wide range of different skills. In this sense, if you were a Computer Programmer, we are not necessarily talking about your skills in computer programming. We are looking at more basic skills, such as decision making, managing your own time, whether you need to delegate tasks to anyone, your problem solving skills, how you would manage problems like conflict with other individuals, how do you manage stress, can you set targets, and how do you achieve them?

Forward Job Plan

For guidance on how to use this form consult:
- Report Form A Notes for Guidance B6-B11
- Report Form B Notes for Guidance B9-B11.

Name of Job Holder

Period covered

Grade   Division   Date

1 Purpose

Describe in a few words how your job fits into the work of the unit.

2 Main Duties

Set out under a number of headings in order of importance. Remember staff management and training responsibilities.

3 Specific Objectives

List specific work-related objectives agreed with your Reporting Officer. Be realistic - they should be a challenge but possible.

4 Resources managed and changes planned

Only a broad indication is required, such as the total number of staff you are responsible for and how much expenditure you advise upon and control directly. Are you planning changes eg. to get better value for money?

Keep a copy of this form and note alterations agreed throughout the year on the back.

DTI 2083 (999-9115) Mar 1991

15

Fig 2.28 The DTI's forward job plan aimed at focusing employee's efforts to attain special objectives

Decision making

To be a good manager or supervisor, or for that matter an employee, you need to be able to make decisions easily. The more senior position you hold within an organisation, the more decisions are likely to fall on your own shoulders, and more decisions will have to be made by you on behalf of other people. The lower down the organisation, the less decisions you will have to make of a very important nature, but they may very well be important all the same, after all successful decision making will make your life easier or much, much harder.

It is generally accepted that decision making goes through five particular phases. These are:

■ *Deciding on your aims and exactly what you want to achieve by making the decision*

■ *To look at the various strategies or options you may have in overcoming the problem and making the decision*

■ *To choose the best option that is available to you.* This may mean trading off perhaps the cheapest way of doing something for the most efficient way of doing something. In other cases it may be a case of choosing the least difficult way of doing it, or the one that may take you the least amount of time

■ *Actually implementing the decision.* Having decided on the course of action you then need to follow it through, bearing in mind of course that you could always change your mind if this particular way of solving the problem turns out to be ineffective

■ *Looking back at what you decided to do and assessing whether you made the right decision* and whether, given a similar set of circumstances in the future you would choose the same way again. Perhaps you would not

Managing time

Most of us, if we are honest, would admit that we do not really stop to make a decision about how we are using our time. We may get into a pattern of life or a pattern of working and just continue to take it from day to day, basically being content to let things go on as they are. So what does managing time, or time management actually mean. Here are some variations on definitions:

■ *Making better use of the time that you have*

■ *Getting more done in the time that you have got*

■ *Only to concentrate on important things and to ignore things that are irrelevant*

■ *Take control over the time itself and allocate things particular amounts of time*

■ *Spend more of your time on what is important*

■ *Try to avoid getting into the situation where you have to rush things at the very last minute*

Managing time itself means taking more control over how we spend our time and trying to make a sensible decision about how we are using time. There are three major causes of bad time management:

■ **Crisis management** – This is where people avoid making any decision about anything until they absolutely have to. In turn, this causes stress and we will look at this a little later on

■ **Priorities** – you make yourself too available to other people, they will constantly interrupt you. They have their own priorities, you should have your own. By allowing other people to control how you spend your time, you will find yourself in a situation where you are constantly behind with your work, causing unnecessary stress and mistakes

■ **The treadmill** – This is when you have got behind with your work. You are making no real attempt to catch up on your work, but always working a few days or a few hours behind, constantly. Again, this causes stress, but more importantly it causes frustration, not just for yourself, but for those who work with you. It also does not give you an opportunity to take advantage of situations as they arise, because you miss them. There are some ways of getting out of this:
    – To clearly set your own goals
    – To choose your own priorities and to stick with them
    – To make decisions at the right time instead of putting them off

So how do you make time work for you? There are two basic tools which a good employee or a good manager will use:

■ *A diary for long-range planning, and to make a note of any appointments you may have*

■ *To make a list. This will help you plan day by day, week by week, month by month. First get into the habit of making a daily list, and then checking your progress against that list midday and at the end of the day*

The next step is to identify any tasks that you have which have a deadline. Essentially there are two sorts of deadline. A fixed deadline is when something has to be completed by a certain time. Secondly, a natural deadline. This refers to things that have to be done before something else can be done after it. So a progression of different things have to be tackled in a particular order.

To summarise

The *first* stage is planning, whether you use a diary or list. These should help to jog your memory as to what you have to do to be able to keep track of several jobs at once, deciding how long you need to spend on something, deciding on what order to do things and how to plan your next step in a series of tasks.

The *second* stage is to order these plans. Some things that you may need to do are urgent, others are important. Put them into some sort of logical order.

The *third* thing is to know that plans cannot always be achieved and not to get frustrated about them if you have not managed to achieve them.

Fourth is the ability to deal with regular disruptions of your plans. Establish which individuals are going to waste your time, and try to avoid them. Also try and work around things which take up a large amount of your time. Allocate them only the time they need.

Fifth consider using a time log. This consists of a daily or weekly planner where you meticulously note exactly how much time you are using on a particular task. The information that it contains can help you get an idea of time management and whether you need additional training or assistance or resources to carry out the tasks that you are expected to cope with.

Individual activity

Individually, keep a diary of your activities for a week. At the end of the week review the entries and answer the following questions:

■ How many hours, on average, do you devote to your studies?

■ How many hours, on average, do you devote to your leisure activities?

■ How many hours, on average, do you spend sitting in front of the television?

■ Can you identify any times during the week when you managed your time badly?

■ Can you identify any times during the week when you managed your time well?

Compare your weekly diary of activities with those of the rest of the group.

Now, draw up an action plan for yourself to help you use time more efficiently.

Delegation

Delegation is a very practical skill. Some people just think of delegation as passing the buck and getting someone else to do your work for you. A more positive way of looking at delegation is to define it along these lines – giving someone else the responsibility and authority to act on your behalf. The two key words in that sentence are responsibility and authority, but you also must make sure that you have given them the resources to carry out the task. There are a number of advantages in delegating responsibility to other people, these are:

■ *It does allow other people to demonstrate their own ability*

■ *It will give other people a wider and more varied experience of work*

■ *It helps people feel involved and trusted at work and to feel that they are valued*

■ *It does enable other people to get a wider picture of what is going on*

Many managers seem reluctant to delegate responsibility to people. In effect, you do lose some control over the situation. Some things to bear in mind are:

■ *What should be delegated?*

■ *To whom should you delegate it?*

■ *What should never be delegated?*

You should always remember that although you have delegated the responsibility to someone, the ultimate responsibility still lies with you.

Delegation itself is essentially a very difficult balancing act. You can either under delegate, or over delegate. Let's look at the problems from both points of view.

Under delegation

If you do not give sufficient authority and responsibility to those who work for you, this can result in a number of things:

- *You may end up doing too much work for yourself*

- *You will always be over worked, and you will not be taking advantage of other individuals skills at completing tasks*

The main reasons why people under delegate are:

- *It is often less bother to do the job yourself*

- *You pride yourself in your own decision making, and you do not feel confident enough to allow your own reputation to be damaged by a bad decision made by someone else*

- *You may lack confidence in your employees' abilities*

- *If you delegate too much you may feel insecure and afraid that you can be replaced*

Over delegation

This is when you pass on too much of your responsibility to others which means you are losing control over the situation. People tend to over delegate because:

- *They lack experience in their job*

- *They are poorly motivated*

- *They are too frightened of making mistakes themselves and would prefer to 'pass the buck' to other people*

So how can you delegate effectively? The most effective way is to approach someone in a tactful and helpful manner. First of all, you should know exactly what it is you want to be done, how and when you want it done and any other restraints that may apply. You need to explain this fully to the person you are delegating to, and make sure that they understand it. Give them sufficient authority to carry out the task.

Individual activity

In the role of a busy Manager, which of the following would you decide to delegate and why. You should tackle this task in groups of three and agree your course of action:

- Attendance at regular weekly management meetings

- Attending the wedding of your ex-secretary

- Attending the staff appraisal interviews of your staff

- Attending the monthly health and safety committee meeting

Compare your answers with those of the rest of the group. You should be prepared to back up your decisions with reasons for your choices.

Problem solving

This skill is at the heart of any good employee, whether they be a manager or clerk. It is an essential feature of problem solving to be able to clearly identify the problem facing you, then to consider all possible options to cope with the problem. Perhaps to order them in your own mind or in consultation with others. To consider which of the solutions you are offering to solve the problem is the most appropriate for the situation and then to move into the decision-making process that we have looked at earlier.

Problem solving is a difficult skill. In many cases individuals will not even realise that there is a problem which needs to be solved. It is only when the problem emerges and is in danger of seriously affecting the work that people recognise the problem is there.

Problems need not necessarily be big ones. They can be simple problems of not having enough staff on a particular shift. They can be running out of stationery. They can be the telephone system breaking down. Whichever kind of problem we are considering, solutions have to be arrived at in a swift and efficient manner. In order to do this, as we have said, a manager or employee needs to be good at decision making. They may also need to be good at managing their own time in order to be able to devote necessary time to problems as they emerge. Equally, they may have to be willing to delegate responsibility of solving a problem to another person who is adept at coping with that particular kind of situation.

Managing conflict

Organisations, just like families, have problems. Few managers enjoy a career which is not full of conflict. Resolving conflict itself can be very exhausting. The process usually works something like this:

- The manager has to be skilful enough in the beginning to notice a potential conflict brewing. Perhaps there are changes in someone's behaviour, or absenteeism

- Once the manager has noticed a potential conflict growing, or has perhaps actually been confronted by it, he or she has to take steps to sort it out. The common way is to talk on an individual basis to each of the members of the group who are involved in the conflict. After all, the manager needs to hear each different side to the story

- The next stage is to try and find a solution which is fair to everybody, then to bring together all of the people involved in the conflict and suggest a possible solution. Most important in this particular part of managing conflict is to get the agreement of all involved. After all, having defused one situation, it may not be to the advantage of everyone, and therefore certain members of the group may continue to feel aggrieved and further conflicts may occur

- In extreme circumstances it may be necessary to 'transfer out' the person who is deeply involved in the conflict

Here is the progression of managing conflict.

■ *Always be fair and impartial*

■ *In order to gain the confidence of all of those involved, you have to be trustworthy and sensitive to their grievances*

■ *Be equally fair to all members of the group involved in the conflict*

■ *Try to find out the root cause behind the problem and try to figure out a way to avoid these causes from reoccuring*

■ *Any decision you come to about managing the conflict needs to workable and fair*

■ *It is important that all members of the group accept the conflict resolution willingly*

■ *If it can be avoided, all individuals involved in the conflict must win or loose equally. Any loss of faith of any members of the group would be disastrous*

■ *Once the conflict has been resolved, it needs to be monitored and seen to be working*

■ *If absolutely necessary, transfers or changes in job role should be considered*

Coping with conflict at work can be one of the most stressful parts of a manager's job. It needs a good manager with excellent communication skills to cope with some of the more complicated conflicts. Also, in extreme cases, it may be worthwhile bringing in an independent person who can look at the two sides, or indeed several sides, of the argument and help the manager resolve them fairly.

Group activity

In the role of a Supervisor, and working in pairs, prepare an action plan to cope with the following problem:

■ Two members of your workforce seem to have a serious personality clash. They continually argue and find it almost impossible to work together. On several occasions, this has caused difficulties to other members of the team, and has held up the production for a short time

■ Each of the individuals involved have been warned that their behaviour is unacceptable and that it is causing problems. For a while things improved, but now it seems to have 'flared up' again

■ The arguments are beginning to get out of hand and it seems that one particular individual is being quite vindictive

After drafting your action plan, discuss it in groups of four.

Managing stress

Every year literally thousands of people suffer from stress-related illnesses. These can be as extreme as a heart attack or mental breakdown or even depression. Many people do eventually recover from the stress-related illnesses, but in many cases, the cause of the stress could have been prevented and avoided. Some of the more common causes of stress are the following:

- Not having enough responsibility – where an individual is doing a job which is not stretching them sufficiently they may become frustrated, which inevitably leads to stress.

- Giving someone too much responsibility can give almost exactly the same results. They may have to work far too many hours in order to carry out a task because they have been promoted too quickly.

- A person who has literally too much to do and is overloaded with work will inevitably suffer from stress.

- Having poor or little guidance from managers can also be a cause of stress. If an individual does not know exactly what is expected of them and is not helped in any way by their manager, then stress again is a common result.

- Individuals may be excluded from certain decision making or meetings. They may only receive basic memos and be excluded from circulation lists of information within the organisation. Again this is a cause of stress as the individual feels threatened by feeling they are not being included in the full decision-making process of the organisation.

- Not having a very clear job description – where an individual does not have a clear set of responsibilities they may suffer stress on the basis that other people do not know exactly what they are doing and therefore when they do achieve and carry out a task well they are not rewarded and recognised for having done a good job.

- If an individual is in a situation where they meet too many people or are responsible for too many people and are perhaps told by their manager to involve themselves in every decision, this will also cause stress as the individual is trying to juggle too many things at one time.

So, how can stress be handled? First, you need to be aware of what kind of types of stress there are, and what kind of behaviour stress brings out in an individual. This could be:

- *Being very irritable*

- *Making lots of mistakes*

- *Absenteeism*

- *Drinking or smoking too much*

- *Crying easily*

- *Appearing to be nervous in many situations*

- *Fall in work output*

Once any of these signs have been noticed, then the individual involved needs to be counselled very carefully. In this interview the causes of the stress need to be discovered. The manager interviewing the individual under stress may need to reappraise that person's job role or responsibilities and look at what kind of things immediately cause stress to that individual. Hopefully, once the situation has been resolved, this person needs to be carefully and sensitively protected for a while at least, to ensure that the symptoms do not reoccur.

There are some ways that everyone can avoid stress. These are:

- *Eating regularly and sleeping enough*
- *Pacing yourself throughout the working day*
- *Taking up a sport or a hobby*
- *Establishing a good balance between your work and your leisure*
- *Trying to keep a sense of humour at all times*
- *Perhaps doing relaxation exercises*

A manager who knows how to handle stress should be able to handle the stress that his or her employees or colleagues may suffer.

Group activity

Working in pairs, and assuming the role of Personnel Manager and Assistant Personnel Manager, prepare a single page of hints and tips for employees to avoid and cope with everyday stress.

Compare your list with those of your fellow students.

Motivation and motivating people

Depending on what position you hold in an organisation, your definition of motivation may be a very different one.

- *It may be to actually get a job done, which refers to self-motivation*
- *It may be to organise and control the people that work for you, which refers to being a good organiser and controlling the situation*
- *It may be to get your employees to perform tasks which meet the objectives of the organisation*
- *It may be to make it possible for employees to get the most satisfaction out of their work*
- *It may be to manage your employees so that any objectives are reached and that the task is carried out to the best ability of your employees*

We have looked at five definitions of motivation, rising from self-motivation through to motivating other people and, as we said, your idea of motivation is going to be dependent upon the position you hold within an organisation. You may take a narrow view if you are a relatively lowly member of an organisation, or you may have to take a wider view if you are a key manager.

There are lots of ways that you could attempt to get people to do things. You could force them to do it. You could shout at them. You could coax them. You could plead with them. You could praise what they have done so far. You could appeal to their better nature. You could say how important this particular task is. You could try and make the job they are doing more enjoyable. You could tell them it is their duty. You could reward them. You could threaten them. You could tell them what would happen if they did not do it and leave it up to them to decide. In reality, motivation is somewhat more complicated than any of those options that we have just mentioned.

It may mean getting someone to do what you want them to do. It may mean making us want to do something. It may be an inward driving force. It may be a desire to achieve an objective, or it may be an incentive that makes us do something. We have mentioned a couple of very key words here – incentive and desire. When we consider those two words we consider that motivation is nothing to do with threatening people. It is nothing to do with making people do something. It is making sure that people want to do something.

There have been a number of theories written by management theorists over the years such as McGregor, Maslow or Hertzburg, all of which consider that motivation is a key factor in improving people's work output, job satisfaction and ultimately their loyalty to the organisation.

Maslow put forward the idea that there are five levels of motivation, running from physiological, safety, love, esteem to what he called self-actualisation. What these actually mean are a little more easy to understand.

- *Physiological means that all of us need such things as air and water and sleep and if they are provided we will be motivated to a certain extent*

- *We are even more motivated by the safety factors being provided by the job. These include security or stability at work*

- *The third is love. By this he means being accepted, belonging to the organisation and achieving some level of friendship with colleagues within the organisation*

- *Then there is esteem. This means being recognised for your qualities and also to have self-respect and confidence and actually to be achieving something at work*

- *Finally, is self-actualisation, which is doing a job in which you are developing and fulfilling yourself*

Maslow's hierarchy of needs

1	**Physiological needs**	satisfaction of physical needs such as hunger, sleep, etc.
2	**Security needs**	protection against threats and danger
3	**Affiliation needs**	need for love and affection and status within a group
4	**Esteem needs**	needs for self-respect and recognition from others
5	**Self-actualisation needs**	the need for self-fulfilment

What Maslow is saying is that everyone is at a place somewhere on the five levels of motivation.

In other words, we can look at this theory in the following way:

The main reason that people work is to earn enough money to live on. Once individuals have reached a point where their income is sufficient to support them, they tend to start looking for additional benefits from work. Here are some of the more common:

- *The need to survive is the most common reason for people going to work, as work brings in the money for clothes and food and housing*

- *Interacting with other people is often only satisfied by going out to work. In many cases, an individual's work relationships are the most important ones they have*

- *Work tends to fulfil the needs of security and safety that many people have. When someone is out of work then they feel insecure*

- *To be accepted by other people is also very important to an individual. Working within a group helps fulfil this*

- *A person who reaches a sense of fulfilment and achievement in their work can consider this to be one of the primary reasons that they go out to work. This, too, is closely allied with self-respect where an individual feels proud of what they have done*

- *Most of us seek some kind of recognition for performing certain skills and showing certain abilities. We spend a lot of time at work and should not be surprised that people tend to look at the work situation as being the main place that they fulfil this aspect*

Many other people would say that we all try to develop ourselves over the years. Work means that we are often given the opportunity to develop our skills, abilities and experience. This again is a common motivator.

Another theorist called MacGregor looked at the various ways in which people are motivated to work. To make his theories as concise as possible, there are five main points:

1 *He realised that people do not really dislike work. It is just the conditions of work that may make them unhappy*

2 *If an individual is committed to the objectives of an organisation, then they will direct themselves, rather than having to be controlled by their superiors*

3 *People will be committed to these objectives of the organisation if they are getting enough personal satisfaction from the job itself*

4 *An individual can learn to take on responsibility providing the conditions of the working situation are correct*

5 *Generally speaking, an individual's creativity and ability to solve problems are very much under used*

Another theorist, Hertzburg, identified five main determinants of job satisfaction. These are:

- *Achievement* – which is the personal satisfaction gained from completing a task or solving a problem

- *Recognition* – having successfully completed a task or solved a problem that someone shows appreciation for the fact that it has been completed well

- *Satisfaction* from the work itself. This means that the job needs to be varied and to give some opportunity to be creative

- *Given responsibility* – the more responsibility an individual has, up to a point, the more motivated they may feel as they have authority and responsibility

- *The chance to be promoted within the organisation* – obviously the more an individual gains promotion, the more freedom they has to show their skills in decision making and problem solving.

Hertzberg's hygiene factors and motivators

Hygiene Factors *(leading to dissatisfaction)*	**Motivators** *(leading to satisfaction)*
■ Policies and Administration	■ Achievement
■ Supervision	■ Recognition
■ Working Conditions	■ Responsibility
■ Money	■ Growth
■ Job Security	■ Development
■ Status	
■ Relationships with Peers and Subordinates	

Another way of looking at how people are motivated in their work is to look at what they expect from the job itself. It is usually held to be the case that if an individual's motivation is high, their performance is very good. But improved performance can only come from the efforts of motivated workers, not from workers who are being forced to do a job they do not enjoy. We can look at it in terms of a circle, which has motivation leading to effort leading to performance leading to greater rewards which again leads to higher motivation and continues round the circle which is rising at all times. If we have a break in this circle, we have problems with all of the elements which make up the circle, and something has to be done in order to mend the breaks. Otherwise, just as the circle was gradually ascending when all elements were working together, so the circle can now gradually decline with each of the elements dragging the circle down.

In situations when people do boring, monotonous jobs there are a number of effects that this has on an individual.

- *When they do boring jobs they tend to make more mistakes*

- *When they loose concentration they are liable to have accidents and hurt themselves*

- *When there is no scope for development in the job and it cannot be done any better because it is so repetitive, then they are prone to react violently when there are changes in the working practices*

- *There is very likely to be a high labour turnover*

One way around this is to improve the nature of the job itself. This can be done in a number of different ways:

- *Job rotation* – switching people regularly between a number of different jobs. Although the jobs will be very similar it does give the opportunity to change from one part of an assembly line to another

- *Job enlargement* – adding more tasks of a similar nature to a particular job to give a little bit more responsibility

- *Job enrichment* – adding a series of more complex tasks over a period of time. This gives the individual an opportunity to use skills and abilities which they have not had the chance to use before

Ensuring that employees are sufficiently motivated often falls to the person who is supervising them. A good supervisor should always attempt to do the following:

- *Plan the work in advance*

- *Organise the work area so that any equipment or materials are available as and when they are needed*

- *Make sure all the employees are properly trained*

- *Give clear information and instruction about what is required of the employee*

Rewarding employees is also a very good motivator, as we have mentioned before. This can be done in a number of different ways:

- *They can be praised*

- *They can be thanked*

- *The supervisor should recognise the needs of an individual, and not treat all employees in the same way*

- *The social aspects of work could be improved by organising the work area so that it is easy for members of the same group to communicate*

- *Recognising that an individual has put in extra effort to a particular job or task*

- *Giving responsibility to an individual when they deserve it and want it.*

Delegation also falls within this category and can be used as a useful method of helping to motivate employees. So how can the motivation of employees be measured? Here are some useful ways:

- *Reduction in lateness*

- *Reduction in absenteeism*

- *Reduction in time lost due to accidents within the work place*

- *Bonuses earned*

- *The amount of wastage*

- *The value of sales achieved*

- *The quality of work*

- *The number of customer complaints*

- *The number of sales made or the volume of production*

Individual activity

Again, in the role of Personnel Manager and Assistant Personnel Manager, devise a programme of activities to help cope with a growing motivation problem which your organisation is encountering on the shop-floor. The following points may assist you in this task:

- More people have been arriving late for work and do not seem concerned about it
- More people have taken the odd day off
- Productivity is down
- Breakages and wastage of raw materials is increasing
- Social events organised by the company are very badly attended, although they used to be very popular

You should present your recommendations in the form of a memorandum to the Board of Directors, which has voiced concern about the problem and has ear-marked funds if necessary.

Setting and achieving targets

Several years ago, a particular management technique was designed which aimed to try to assess and monitor how targets and objectives were set. This became known as management by objectives and results. It is not so popular now, but still some of the ideas behind it are very useful to think about. How is a target set? (*See* Fig 2.29.)

- *Design a plan of action which can be easily followed*

- *Ensure that you have enough information to work with*

- *Make sure that you do not substantially change your original plan while you are trying to achieve it*

- *Ensure that communications are good between anyone involved in trying to achieve the plan*

- *Ensure that employees involved in trying to achieve the objective are sufficiently motivated and have a clear idea of what the organisation's overall objective is*

- *Try to make sure that problems outside your control do not adversely affect your move towards achieving the objective*

Having said all of this, some of the problems which will get in the way of achieving an objective are, by their very nature, beyond your control. It may mean that no matter how carefully you have planned and organised all the factors to help you achieve the objective, there may still be problems that will arise which are insurmountable.

In reality, then, setting and achieving objectives boils down to just four main considerations. These are:

- *That you should be determined to see the plan through*

- *That you should be prepared to negotiate with all individuals involved in trying to achieve the objective*

- *That you should constantly monitor progress towards the objective, making adjustments as and when required and put in extra resources as necessary*

- *That you should consider adjusting your overall plan should there be significant problems in achieving the objective in the first place*

Section 3 — Assessment of Aspects of Performance

Reporting Officer's Assessment

See Guidance Notes C14–29 and Note 1 on page 8

3.1 Give a rating for aspects of performance.
Comments would be helpful.
Write "not applicable" against any aspect of performance not tested by the job.

Performance rating

1	Outstanding
2	Performance significantly above requirements
3	Performance fully meets normal requirements of the grade
4	Performance not fully up to requirements; some improvement necessary
5	Unacceptable

	1	2	3	4	5	Comments
Accuracy						
Output						
Quickness on the uptake						
Reliability						
Willingness to take responsibility						
Supervision of staff						
Relations with others						
Oral expression						
Written work						
Figure work						
Application of skills						

Overall Performance

3.2 Give a rating of 1 to 5 (using the performance rating scale as described in Section 3.1).

See Guidance Notes C30–52

Important

3.3 If you have given a 4 or 5 marking for Overall Performance explain what action has been and will be taken to improve the Job Holder's performance and attach a copy of the written warning(s) you have given.

See Guidance Notes C44–52

3.4 Comment if you wish on any features of the Job Holder's performance not already covered and make any general comments you feel add to your overall assessment.

See Guidance Note C53

➤ **Reporting Officer to pass report to Countersigning Officer**

The Job Holder has worked for me for _____ years _____ months

Signature _____ Telephone number _____

Name in CAPITAL LETTERS _____

Grade _____ Date _____

3.5 Refer to how much and what is seen of the Job Holder's work. Indicate whether you endorse the mark for overall performance in section 3.2 and how far you agree with the rest of the Reporting Officer's assessment.

See Guidance Notes D8–10

Countersigning Officer's comments on Performance Assessment

4

Fig 2.29 Pages from the DTI's staff appraisal report form. Note performance rating

Individual activity

Consider the diary you kept in a previous activity. Choose one aspect of time management that you know you are not very good at. Set yourself a realistic target relating to that aspect of your life. Promise yourself that you will do your best to reach this target and to show a great improvement within the next month. As a further incentive, promise yourself a small reward for having achieved this target. You may wish to also deny yourself something should you fail!

Element assignment

JOB ROLES

Your task is to carry out an in-depth interview with two members of different departments. You may chose to use members of organisations that you investigated in Unit 2.1. Your interview should focus on the following:

■ Their exact job description and job role

■ How they see themselves within the organisation

■ What tasks they carry out on a day-to-day basis

■ Which departments they regularly liaise with

■ What organisational documents they complete in carrying out their duties

■ Can they identify another job role within the organisation which they would like to be involved with?

■ How do they see their future in relation to promotion prospects, either within or outside the department in which they work?

You should now compile a profile of the job role of the two individuals and compare their activities, achievements, prospects and goals. You should present this information as attractively as possible on a single sheet of flipchart paper.

UNIT TEST   Element 2.3

1 What is accountability?

2 What is the difference between an Executive and a Non-Executive Director?

3 Give two important duties of a Director

4 Who, or what, is the Registrar of Companies?

5 What is the role of an Auditor?

6 List three attributes of a good team member

7 Give three occupations that could be considered as professional ones

8 Give three occupations that could be considered as technical ones

9 Give two examples of semi-skilled workers

10 What is the difference between an audio and a shorthand typist?

11 What is the role of a Company Accountant?

12 What is the difference between a Regional and an Area Sales Manager?

13 What does an Invoice Clerk do and in which department would you expect to find them?

14 What are the differences between strategies and tactics?

15 List at least five different forms of media that would be handled by a Promotions Manager

16 What is the role of a Data Processing Manager?

17 In which department would you normally find a Buyer?

18 Who would be responsible for fulfilling staff development requirements?

19 What are the five phases of decision making?

20 What is meant by the term 'under delegation'?

UNIT 2   End Test

1 What is CCT?
- (a)   Computer Calculation Technology
- (b)   Credit Control Transactions
- (c)   Compulsory Competitive Tender
- (d)   Credible Conscious Teamwork

2 What are the main determinants of an individual's position in a hierarchical structure?
- (a)   Power and authority
- (b)   Pay
- (c)   Holiday entitlement
- (d)   Years of service

3 Which of the following is not a function of the Personnel Department?
- (a)   Staff salaries and wages
- (b)   Discipline and grievance procedures
- (c)   Budget controls
- (d)   Staff welfare

4 Which of the following is not a trade union?
- (a)   TGWU
- (b)   GMB
- (c)   ACAS
- (d)   NUM

5 Which of the following are grounds for fair dismissal?
- (a)   Religion
- (b)   Gender
- (c)   Drunkenness
- (d)   Pregnancy

6 How soon must an employee appeal after dismissal?
  (a)   3 months
  (b)   7 days
  (c)   1 month
  (d)   6 months

7 What is an auditor?
  (a)   A secretary with audio/typing skills
  (b)   An external individual who checks financial transactions
  (c)   An individual responsible for checking personnel records
  (d)   A non-executive director

8 In which department would you normally find a buyer?
  (a)   Purchasing
  (b)   Personnel
  (c)   Sales
  (d)   Accounts

9 What is underdelegation?
  (a)   An individual who delegates only to one person
  (b)   An individual who delegates only to his/her secretary
  (c)   A system of monitoring progress
  (d)   An individual who does not allow others to carry out tasks for him/her

10 In which department would you find an Invoice Clerk?
  (a)   Sales and Accounts
  (b)   Personnel and Production
  (c)   Distribution and Warehousing
  (d)   Research and Development and Production

Unit 3
FINANCIAL TRANSACTIONS
Intermediate Level

Element 3.1

Identify and explain financial transactions and documents

Element 3.2

Complete documents for financial transactions

Element 3.1
Financial transactions and documents

PERFORMANCE CRITERIA

1 Reasons for financial recording in business organisations are explained
2 Purchases transactions and documents are explained
3 Sales transactions and documents are explained
4 Payment transactions and documents are explained
5 Receipts transactions and documents are explained
6 Security checks for payment documents are explained

RANGE

1 Reasons: keeping records, producing annual account, ensuring security and monitoring business performance
2 Purchases: materials, services, wages; orders placed, goods received note and purchase invoice
3 Sales: goods, services; orders received, delivery note, sales invoice and statement of account
4 Payment methods: cheque, cash, credit card, debit card, credit (includes hire purchase); pay slip and petty cash voucher
5 Receipts: receipt, cheque, paying-in slip and bank statement
6 Security: authorisation of orders, invoices against orders and goods received notes and authorised cheque signatories

EVIDENCE INDICATORS

An explanation of the purposes of financial recording, of the financial documents regularly used in business, and of security checks for payment documents. Evidence should demonstrate understanding of the implications of the range dimensions in relation to the element. The unit test will confirm the candidate's coverage of range.

Element 3.2
Documents for financial transactions

PERFORMANCE CRITERIA

1 Purchases documents are clearly and correctly completed
2 Sales documents are clearly and correctly completed
3 Payments documents are clearly and correctly completed
4 Receipts documents are clearly and correctly completed
5 Reasons for the correct completion of documents are explained

RANGE

1 **Purchases documents: orders placed, goods received note and purchase invoice**
2 **Sales documents: orders received, delivery note, sales invoice and statement of account**
3 **Payments documents: pay slip, cheque and petty cash voucher**
4 **Receipts documents: receipt, cheque and paying-in slip**
5 **Reasons for correct completion: accuracy and importance of reliability of data**

EVIDENCE INDICATORS

A set of completed financial documents for a simulated or real business over a period of time, together with an explanation of the importance of the correct completion of documents. Evidence should demonstrate understanding of the implications of the range dimensions in relation to the element. The unit test will confirm the candidate's coverage of the range.

REASONS FOR FINANCIAL RECORDING

When any financial transaction takes place, it is essential that a record is kept by the organisation. These records have to be stored safely and securely, and must be easily accessible and up to date. Financial transactions are recorded for the following reasons:

- *So that there is evidence that the transaction has taken place – it is not sensible to rely on the memory of those people involved in the transaction. The records can then be checked at a later date*

- *So that the Accounts Department can pay the bills and collect any money owed to the organisation*

- *So that the Accounts Department has a record of the transactions in order that it can produce the Annual Accounts for the organisation*

- *So that the business performance of the organisation can be monitored – the Accounts Department will want to work out the profit or loss figures so that an idea of how well the organisation is doing can be gained*

- *A public limited company has to legally keep records so that it can inform its shareholders as to how the organisation is performing*

- *The VAT can only be assessed by the Customs and Excise office if it has access to the organisation's records of financial transactions*

- *The income tax (for small businesses) and the corporation tax (for limited companies) can only be assessed by the Inland Revenue office if it has access to the organisation's records of financial transactions*

The reasons listed above are general to most organisations. Let us look at a few of them in more detail:

The Annual Accounts

As we have said, all organisations have to keep a record of their financial transactions so that they can be assessed for various reasons. Depending on the size of the organisation, this may be carried out in different ways. Larger organisations will have their own Accounts Department which will deal with the financial transactions, whereas a sole trader may do his own accounts, or employ an Accountant on a part time basis. This Accountant must be registered and qualified in order to cover legal requirements. On the other hand, a limited company legally has to have its accounts audited (either by an Internal Auditor, or a company specialising in auditing the accounts of different organisations).

The Annual Accounts can be broken down into two areas – the Balance Sheet and the Profit and Loss Accounts.

Before we look at these in more detail, there are some terms which it may be useful to explain.

Assets

Assets can either be cash, money in the bank, stock or buildings and equipment. In addition, any money the organisation may be owed by another organisation is also known as an asset (customers who owe an organisation money are known as debtors).

Liabilities

This is the money owed by the organisation to suppliers (known as the organisation's creditors).

Gross Profit

This is the difference between the price of buying the raw materials and the selling price of the finished product.

Net Profit

This is the Gross Profit, less the expenses incurred in the production of the product (e.g. electricity, wages and salaries for the employees and the cost of heating the premises).

Profit and Loss Account for the year ended 31 December 199-			
	£	£	£
Sales			70,000
Cost of sales			
Purchases		31,000	
Less: Closing stock		3,000	
			28,000
Gross trading profit			42,000
Other income			
Rent			60
Total profit			42,060
Selling and distribution expenses			
Salesmen's salaries	12,000		
Motor expenses	2,000		
Depreciation - motor vehicles	1,800	15,800	
Administrative expenses			
Rent	6,000		
Office salaries	10,800		
Insurance	350		
Light and heat	1,000		
General expenses	300		
Depreciation - furniture and fittings	225		
		18,675	
Financial expenses			
Bad debts	180		
Provision for doubtful debts	178	358	
Total overhead expenses			34,833
Net Profit			7,227

Fig 3.1 A profit and loss account

The Profit and Loss Account

All the financial transactions of the organisation for the year will have been recorded. At the end of the financial year (this will vary from organisation to organisation, but will be the same date each year), the Accountant will prepare a Profit and Loss Account. This will include a summary of all the transactions, both for expenditure (money paid out) and income (money coming in). The difference between the income and expenditure is known as either the Profit or the Loss (*see* Fig 3.1).

The Balance Sheet

The Profit or Loss the organisation has made during the year is transferred from the Profit and Loss Account to the Balance Sheet. The Balance Sheet will also list all the organisation's Assets and Liabilities at the end of the financial year (*see* Fig 3.2).

GROUP BALANCE SHEET – STERLING

Consolidated balance sheet					£ million
Fixed assets	1987	1988	1989	1990	**1991**
Tangible assets					
Exploration and Production	8,980	11,732	12,584	11,099	**11,615**
Refining and Marketing	3,007	3,343	3,871	3,664	**4,134**
Chemicals	879	1,000	1,189	1,279	**1,526**
Nutrition	419	454	553	544	**562**
Other Businesses and Corporate	2,187	2,397	1,088	895	**844**
	15,472	18,926	19,285	17,481	**18,681**
Intangible assets	1,031	1,874	1,672	1,447	**1,309**
Investments	1,973	1,437	1,497	1,413	**1,854**
Total fixed assets	18,476	22,237	22,454	20,341	**21,844**
Current assets					
Stocks	2,716	2,503	3,381	3,476	**2,993**
Debtors	4,399	4,243	5,361	6,259	**6,238**
Investments	601	157	151	152	**502**
Cash at bank and in hand	682	183	268	469	**215**
	8,398	7,086	9,161	10,356	**9,948**
Creditors – amounts falling due within one year					
Finance debt	(1,829)	(2,319)	(2,531)	(1,713)	**(1,647)**
Other creditors	(6,404)	(5,659)	(7,037)	(7,897)	**(7,857)**
Net current assets	165	(892)	(407)	746	**444**
Total assets less current liabilities	18,641	21,345	22,047	21,087	**22,288**
Creditors – amounts falling due after one year					
Finance debt	(3,740)	(4,864)	(5,758)	(5,207)	**(6,507)**
Other creditors	(1,426)	(1,719)	(1,936)	(2,144)	**(2,142)**
Provisions for liabilities and charges	(2,206)	(2,630)	(2,912)	(2,495)	**(2,685)**
Net assets	11,269	12,132	11,441	11,241	**10,954**
Minority shareholders' interest	(576)	(614)	(656)	(240)	**(300)**
BP shareholders' interest	10,693	11,518	10,785	11,001	**10,654**
Represented by					
Called up share capital	1,503	1,536	1,346	1,353	**1,360**
Share premium account	1,388	1,685	1,752	1,826	**1,902**
Capital redemption reserve	—	—	197	197	**197**
Reserves	7,802	8,297	7,490	7,625	**7,195**
Capital and reserves	10,693	11,518	10,785	11,001	**10,654**

Fig 3.2 A consolidated balance sheet
(Courtesy of British Petroleum)

Security

We mentioned earlier that the transactions must be recorded and kept safely and securely. It is very important that an organisation has security high on its list of priorities. Not everyone is honest, and money kept in an insecure way may tempt such people. On the other hand, there are different reasons for an organisation to take steps to ensure security measures are complied with.

The organisation will have to have information readily available for the Income Tax/Corporation Tax/VAT officials to inspect on a regular basis, sometimes with little notice.

If any errors are made, either by the organisation itself, or a debtor or creditor, these can easily be traced.

To avoid fraud or theft. It is much easier to commit fraud now than it used to be. When people only dealt with cash, this was more difficult to trace if lost. Nowadays, with credit cards being a popular method of payment, the opportunity for fraud has been increased.

Monitoring business performance

We have already said that financial transactions must be recorded so that the organisation can monitor the business performance for the financial year. This is different to the reason for keeping the records so that profit or loss can be identified. An organisation needs to know what the position is on a day-to-day basis. In order to do this, an organisation must have easy access to financial records on a regular basis.

One of the roles of the Accountant will be to organise a budget for the organisation. This is very similar to the type of budget you or your family may have to keep to on a weekly or monthly basis. The Accountant will set a budget for the organisation, and it will be the responsibility of each of the Departmental Managers to ensure that their staff do not exceed the stated amount of money. For example, the Purchasing Department will not be allowed to purchase any items which would be too expensive, and would mean they would go over their budget limit.

Each month, the Accountant checks the income and expenditure of the organisation against the budget set. A budget is a form of financial plan for the organisation.

Individual activity

Thinking back to the activity when you prepared an income and expenditure analysis for your own money. Now we would like you to try and prepare a budget for next week. Think about where you are spending money unnecessarily. What items do you have to pay for and which could be excluded? Answer making two lists – essential items and luxuries.

So, it is vital that an organisation has an efficient way of recording information from financial transactions. There is, however, no point in keeping such a strict system if the documents stored are either incomplete, inaccurate, illegible, unchecked or unreliable. It is obviously essential that those involved in the completion of such documents are aware and motivated enough to see the value of them. Let us look at the five reasons above in more detail.

Completing documents

It is very important that a document is completed. This may seem like an obvious statement, but it is more detailed. For example a cheque without the date added is useless and will not be accepted by a bank. The same applies to documents such as invoice or order forms. In order to try and avoid documents being sent out incomplete, most organisations use a Proforma. This means that their documents have headings and spaces where all the relevant information has to be inserted. These documents will be used throughout the organisation, and are part of its 'Corporate Image'.

Accuracy

Again, this may sound obvious, but it is vital that documents are completed accurately. One incorrect figure, or a decimal point in the wrong place could cause enormous problems, not only for the organisation itself, but also for the customer. The same would apply to the address – it can cause unnecessary delay and inconvenience if a document goes astray in the post because of an inaccurate address. Some organisations design their documents in duplicate or triplicate so that such inaccuracies can be spotted easier.

Neatness

Everyone thinks that their handwriting is legible, but this may not always be the case. An organisation needs to ensure that all documents leaving their premises are clearly legible. This is not so important with handwriting itself, but it is vital with figures! The outcome could be disastrous if a figure is mistaken for another – perhaps this is why the French in particular distinguish their 1 from their 7?

Checking

All documents should be checked thoroughly before being issued. This should be done by the person completing the document, although this is not easy to do. Sometimes one simply cannot see one's own mistakes and it is more efficient to either get someone else to check it, or to read it to them and they check the figures and data.

Reliability

We said earlier that some organisations prepare their documents in duplicate or triplicate. In some cases, the document will have several copies, e.g. an order form. This is done so that several departments in the organisation will have a copy. An order form will be distributed as follows:

- *The top copy will go to the supplier of the goods*

- *One copy will be kept by the Purchasing Department for its records*

- *One will be needed to check the goods when received to ensure the order is complete and accurate*

- *One will be sent to the Accounts Department so that it can pay for the goods when received*

Because so many copies are being used by so many different people, it is vital that the information contained in them is correct, accurate and reliable.

Individual activity

Look at the seven cheques included in this section (*See* Fig 3.3). There is a discrepancy on each of them. In other words, each one has a mistake which will mean that the bank will not accept it. Thinking about all the reasons why a cheque needs to be accurate, write a list of the mistakes you can find.

SPECIMEN ONLY Issued by Bank Education Service

25|6|1993   25 June 1993   **70-19-85**

J Sutherland   **TECHNICAL BANK LIMITED**
                                HOMETOWN

Pay _____ or Order

Seventeen pounds 50p – | £ 17-50 |

£ 17-50   DE Canwen

000331   ⑈000331⑈ 70⑈1985⑈ 41707365⑈

Fig 3.3(a)

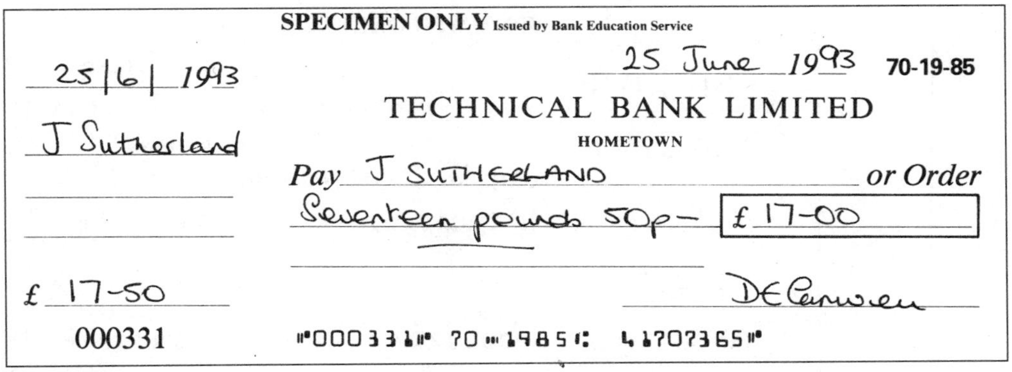

25|6| 1993

J Sutherland

£ 17-50

000331

SPECIMEN ONLY Issued by Bank Education Service

25 June 1993   70-19-85

TECHNICAL BANK LIMITED

HOMETOWN

Pay J SUTHERLAND _____ or Order

Seventeen pounds 50p— £ 17-00

D E Canwen

⑆000331⑆ 70⑈1985⑉ 41707365⑈

Fig 3.3(b)

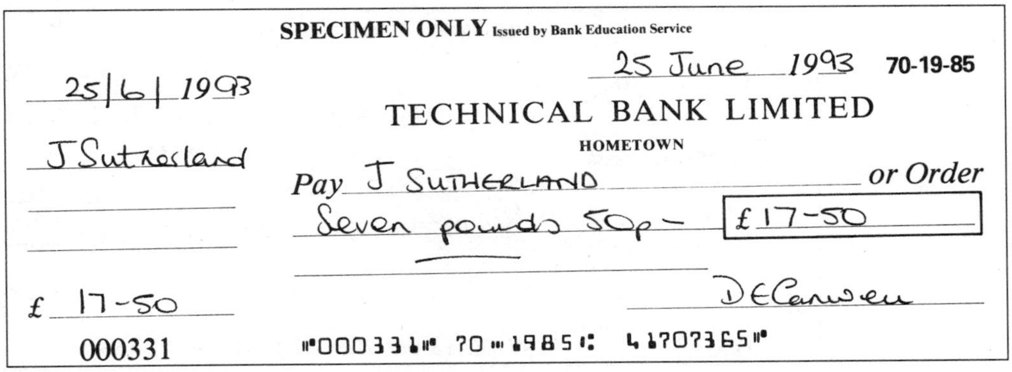

25|6| 1993

J Sutherland

£ 17-50

000331

SPECIMEN ONLY Issued by Bank Education Service

25 June 1993   70-19-85

TECHNICAL BANK LIMITED

HOMETOWN

Pay J SUTHERLAND _____ or Order

Seven pounds 50p— £ 17-50

D E Canwen

⑆000331⑆ 70⑈1985⑉ 41707365⑈

Fig 3.3(c)

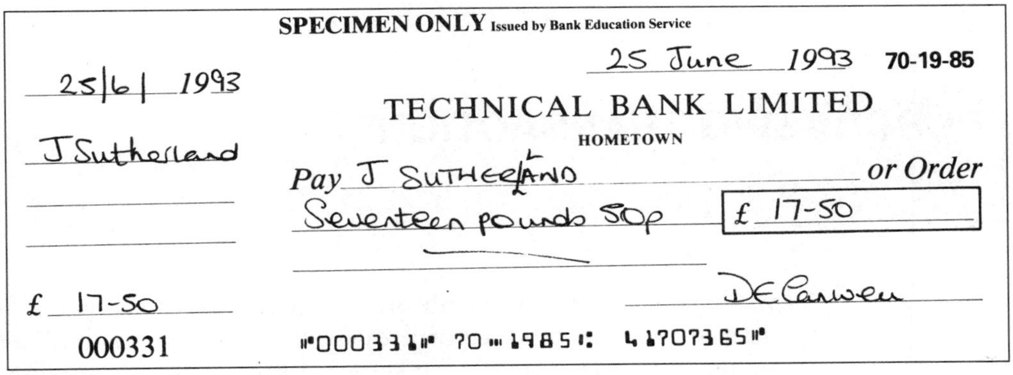

25|6| 1993

J Sutherland

£ 17-50

000331

SPECIMEN ONLY Issued by Bank Education Service

25 June 1993   70-19-85

TECHNICAL BANK LIMITED

HOMETOWN

Pay J SUTHERLAND _____ or Order

Seventeen pounds 50p £ 17-50

D E Canwen

⑆000331⑆ 70⑈1985⑉ 41707365⑈

Fig 3.3(d)

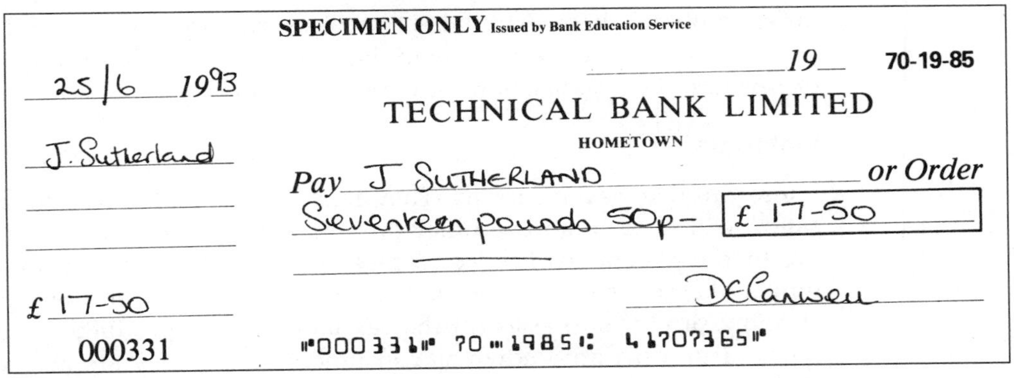

25|6 1993

J. Sutherland

£ 17-50

000331

SPECIMEN ONLY Issued by Bank Education Service

19__   70-19-85

TECHNICAL BANK LIMITED

HOMETOWN

Pay J SUTHERLAND _____ or Order

Seventeen pounds 50p— £ 17-50

D E Canwen

⑆000331⑆ 70⑈1985⑉ 41707365⑈

Fig 3.3(e)

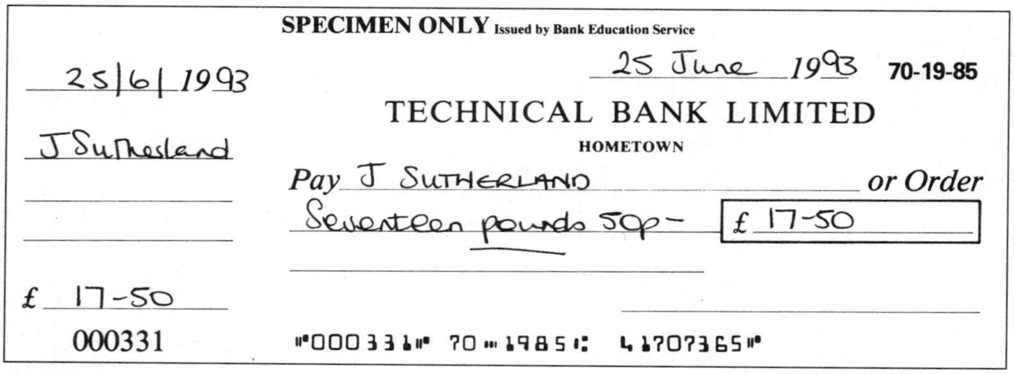

SPECIMEN ONLY Issued by Bank Education Service

25/6/1993

J Sutherland

£ 17-50

000331

25 June 1993   70-19-85

TECHNICAL BANK LIMITED

HOMETOWN

Pay J SUTHERLAND _____ or Order

Seventeen pounds 50p —   £ 17-50

⑆000331⑆ 70⑈1985⑇ 41707365⑈

Fig 3.3(f)

SPECIMEN ONLY Issued by Bank Education Service

25/6 1993

J Sutherland

£ 17-50

000331

25 June 19__   70-19-85

TECHNICAL BANK LIMITED

HOMETOWN

Pay J SUTHERLAND _____ or Order

Seventeen pounds 50p —   £ 17-50

DEConwen

⑆000331⑆ 70⑈1985⑇ 41707365⑈

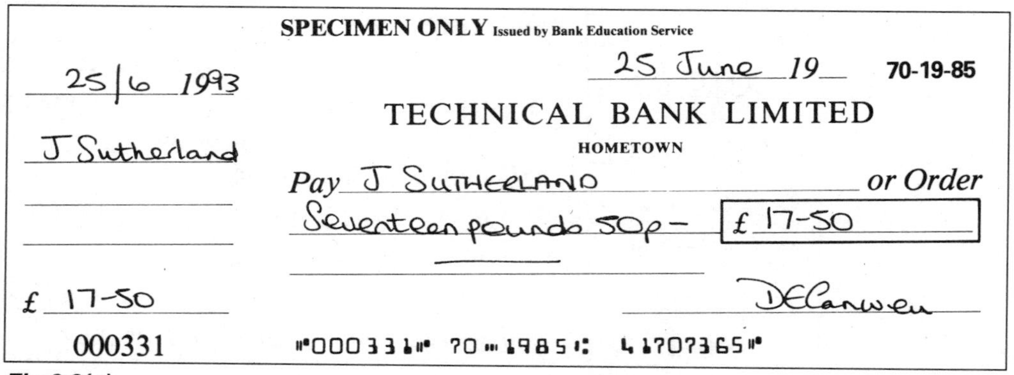

Fig 3.3(g)

PURCHASING TRANSACTIONS

As we have said previously, all organisations need to buy raw materials and services in order to produce or provide their own goods and services. These materials and services may take several forms – raw materials needed on their production line, the services of specialists, e.g. cleaners or consultants. In order to obtain these materials or services, the organisation will have to complete documents requesting them. First, let us break down the types of goods or services the organisation may need to request:

Materials

These can take several forms. They may be raw materials, which the organisation will need to add to other raw materials in order to produce its product, e.g. potatoes needed to make oven chips. Materials may, however, be things like headed paper needed to produce letters from the organisation, or cleaning products to assist in the sanitation of the production lines. These types of product are known as consumables, and they are all ordered on an Order Form.

Capital items

An organisation will also need to purchase such items as office furniture, new computer equipment, new buildings, etc. These are dealt with in a different way to materials, and a special purchasing system will be in effect within an organisation to deal with these purchases.

Services

In order to purchase a service from an individual or another organisation, it would be necessary to complete a contract. The organisation raising the contract would state clearly the terms of the contract, and this would be signed by a representative of the organisation, plus the person providing the service. This contract would be legally binding on both sides.

So, the Purchasing Department would be responsible for buying materials or services for the organisation. This involves a series of processes and the completion of a series of documents. Before we look at these documents in detail, there are a number of terms which you may find helpful.

Trade discount

This discount is given to an organisation because it is placing a large order. It may also be given if the organisation buys goods on a regular basis from the same company, or if that company is in the same field as the organisation itself.

Prompt payment discount

This discount is given to an organisation if it pays its bill on time. The term – five per cent per one month – means that the organisation can deduct five per cent from its bill if it pays within one month of receiving the goods ordered.

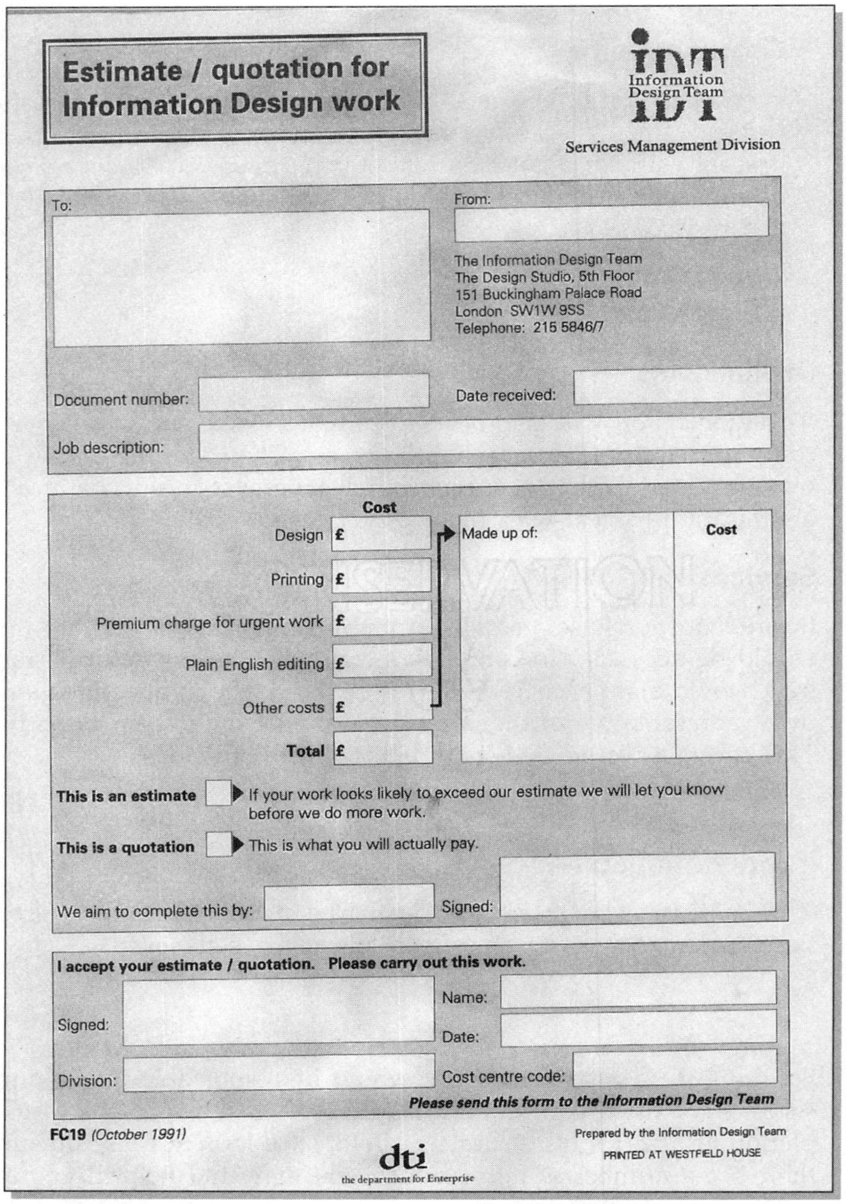

Estimate / quotation for Information Design work

IDT Information Design Team

Services Management Division

To:

From:

The Information Design Team
The Design Studio, 5th Floor
151 Buckingham Palace Road
London SW1W 9SS
Telephone: 215 5846/7

Document number:

Date received:

Job description:

	Cost
Design	£
Printing	£
Premium charge for urgent work	£
Plain English editing	£
Other costs	£
Total	£

Made up of:	Cost

This is an estimate ▶ If your work looks likely to exceed our estimate we will let you know before we do more work.

This is a quotation ▶ This is what you will actually pay.

We aim to complete this by:

Signed:

I accept your estimate / quotation. Please carry out this work.

Signed:

Name:

Date:

Division:

Cost centre code:

Please send this form to the Information Design Team

FC19 *(October 1991)*

dti the department for Enterprise

Prepared by the Information Design Team
PRINTED AT WESTFIELD HOUSE

Fig 3.4 Proforma estimate/quotation form used by the DTI

Cash discount

This discount is given if the organisation pays its bill immediately. The term – two and a half per cent cash discount – means that the organisation can deduct two and a half per cent from its bill if it pays by cash or by cheque immediately the goods are received.

Let us look at the buying process.

Quotation

If the organisation wants to purchase an expensive piece of machinery, then it may ask several companies to give a quotation. This will state the price of the goods required, the expected date of delivery and any discounts the company may offer. The organisation will then choose the company with the best price, terms and delivery times.

Estimate

As with a quotation, the organisation may ask several companies to offer estimates for a piece of work that it requires. This is not as accurate as a quotation, but again the organisation would choose the company offering the best deal. (*See* Fig 3.4.)

Tender

It may be that an organisation puts a piece of work, or a service, out to tender. This means that any company interested in doing the work will 'offer' to do the job for its price. There will be a closing date for tenders to arrive with the organisation, and on that date all tenders will be opened. Again, the organisation will choose the company offering the best deal.

Many companies issue catalogues of the goods, products or services they provide. Purchasing Departments would keep stocks of these catalogues, and would need to update them when new price lists are issued.

Individual activity

Look at the three quotations received from suppliers (see Figs 3.5(a), (b) and (c)). If you worked in the Purchasing Department and were responsible for ordering these goods, which one would you choose and why?

Once the Purchasing Department has decided which company it intends to order its goods from, it will issue an order form to that company.

Order forms

All the details of the order form will be completed accurately and neatly, stating exactly what is required. The clerk completing the document will check with the catalogue and price list, or the quotation, to ensure the price and details are correct. Then the order form will be sent to the supplier. Once this has been done, it is a firm commitment that the organisation requires the goods. Sometimes, if goods are required urgently, and the organisation has dealt with the company before, an order can be placed over the telephone. In this case, a completed order form still has to be sent to the supplier, so that the buyer and the seller both have written confirmation.

Individual activity

Look at the example of a completed order form (*see* Fig 3.7). For each of the headings, state why you think the information is required.

QUOTATION

REFERENCE NUMBER   411   DATE   19 Nov 19..

TO
      Sutherland Sportswear
      124 South Street
      LONDON
      SE2 4DC

In reply to your letter dated 15 November 1993
we have pleasure in quoting you for the following:

4 MAHOGANY OFFICE DESKS @ £375.00 EACH –
TOTAL £1500.00

Prices include delivery by: COMPANY VAN
Delivery: WITHIN 3 WEEKS
Trade Discount: 2.5%
Cash Discount: 2.5%
VAT: Value Added Tax at 17.5% must be added to the price
     quoted.

Fig 3.5(a) Quotation 1

QUOTATION

REFERENCE NUMBER   411   DATE   17 Nov 19..

TO
      Sutherland Sportswear
      124 South Street
      LONDON
      SE2 4DC

In reply to your letter dated 15 November 1993
we have pleasure in quoting you for the following:

4 MAHOGANY OFFICE DESKS @ £399.99 EACH –
TOTAL £1599.96

Prices include delivery by: COMPANY VAN
Delivery: WITHIN 4 WEEKS
Trade Discount: 2.5%
Cash Discount: 1.5%
VAT: Value Added Tax at 17.5% must be added to the price
     quoted.

Fig 3.5(b) Quotation 2

QUOTATION

REFERENCE NUMBER   411   DATE   29 Nov 19..

TO
      Sutherland Sportswear
      124 South Street
      LONDON
      SE2 4DC

In reply to your letter dated 15 November 1993
we have pleasure in quoting you for the following:

4 MAHOGANY OFFICE DESKS @ £350.00 EACH –
TOTAL £1400.00

Prices include delivery by: COMPANY VAN
Delivery: WITHIN 8 WEEKS
Trade Discount: 1.5%
Cash Discount: 1.5%
VAT: Value Added Tax at 17.5% must be added to the price
     quoted.

Fig 3.5(c) Quotation 3

ORDER FORM

TO	ORDER NUMBER
	DATE

DELIVERY ADDRESS	SPECIAL INSTRUCTIONS

REF NO	QUANTITY	DESCRIPTION	UNIT PRICE	AMOUNT

ORDER AUTHORISED BY: ....

Fig 3.6 Order form

ORDER FORM

TO Sutherland Sportswear 124 South Street LONDON SE2 4DC	ORDER NUMBER ST448 DATE 25 JANUARY 19 . .

DELIVERY ADDRESS AS ABOVE	SPECIAL INSTRUCTIONS NONE

REF NO	QUANTITY	DESCRIPTION	UNIT PRICE	AMOUNT
A4 154	14	REAMS OF WHITE A4 PAPER	£3.01	£42.03
D11	10	PACKS OF D11 SIZE ENVELOPES	£2.00	£20.00

ORDER AUTHORISED BY: ....*A. Smith*...

Fig 3.7 Completed order form

Goods received note

This document will be completed by the person receiving the goods when they are delivered. That person may not have a copy of the original order form, so all they will do is check that the Goods Received Note states correctly what has actually been delivered. They will check the number of boxes or packages to the quantity stated on the goods received note. It may be that the two do not tally, in which case the items will need to be unpacked and counted. It could be that any of the following may occur.

GOODS RECEIVED NOTE			
NO	DATE RECEIVED	ORDER NO	DELIVERED BY
QUANTITY	DESCRIPTION	NUMBER OF PACKAGES	STORES REF
RECEIVED FROM	ENTERED INTO STOCK		RECEIVED BY
	DATE	INITIAL	
SUPPLIER			STOREKEEPER

Fig 3.8 Goods received note

Missing goods

It could be that the goods were not sent because the supplier was out of stock at the time, or that it forgot to send them. If it was out of stock, then the goods received note should state 'to follow' or 'discontinued'. If this is not the case, then the Accounts Department would need to be informed of the shortage of goods, so that they do not pay for what they have not received. The supplier would then need to be contacted to find out why some goods have not been received.

Additional goods

Any goods received which were not stated on the original order form, but were listed on the goods received note should be returned to the supplier. It may be that this could be done immediately, by returning them with the company's delivery van, or they may have to be sent separately.

Incorrect goods

Again, if the goods received are incorrect, they will have to be returned to the supplier. This will be easy to identify because the goods received note will differ from the order form.

Damaged or faulty goods

It is usually possible to exchange faulty or damaged goods immediately the supplier is notified. Sometimes the goods received note will include a section for the person receiving the goods to complete, should there be any problem with the goods on arrival.

Goods ordered in error

This is quite difficult. If goods have been ordered by mistake, and are supplied in good faith by the supplier, then it is under no obligation to take them back. However, if the organisation and the supplier have had a long-term working relationship, and the organisation has spent a lot of money and paid regularly, then the supplier would rather take the goods back than lose the custom.

Individual activity

Look at the completed goods received note (*see* Fig 3.9). Why do you think the headings are necessary?

Compare the goods received note with the order form in the previous activity. Do the two agree? Are there any discrepancies? If you find some mistakes, make a list of them.

Find out the different names an organisation might call the special point allocated for receiving goods.

Purchase invoice

Once the goods have been delivered to the buyer, the supplier will send a copy of the Purchase Invoice. This invoice will list the quantity and description of the goods sent, as well as the total price owing. The invoice will also state a time by which the payment should be made, and will list any discounts made available to the buyer. The organisation buying the goods will check the invoice against the order form and the goods received note to ensure that they all tally. They will check for the following:

- *The order number is correct*
- *The goods listed match those delivered*
- *The quantity listed matches that delivered*
- *The price listed matches that quoted*
- *The calculations are correct*
- *The discounts are as agreed*

GOODS RECEIVED NOTE

NO	DATE RECEIVED		ORDER NO	DELIVERED BY
367	30 JANUARY . .		ST448	COMPANY VAN
QUANTITY	DESCRIPTION		NUMBER OF PACKAGES	STORES REF
A4 154	REAMS OF WHITE A4		10	BAY 56
D11	PACKS OF D11 ENVELOPES		10	BAY 55

RECEIVED FROM	ENTERED INTO STOCK		RECEIVED BY
	DATE	INITIAL	
SUPPLIER			STOREKEEPER

Fig 3.9 Completed goods received note

INVOICE

TO			NUMBER		
			DATE		
			TERMS		
YOUR ORDER NO			DESPATCH DATE		
QUANTITY	DESCRIPTION		UNIT PRICE	TOTAL PRICE	VAT
	Gross Value				
	LESS Trade Discount				
	Net Value of Goods				
	PLUS VAT @ %				
	INVOICE TOTAL				

E & O E

Fig 3.10 Invoice

All invoices contain the letters E&OE at the bottom of them. This stands for 'errors and omissions excepted' and helps to ensure that the supplier can send a further invoice if a mistake is found.

Individual activity

Look at the example of the completed invoice (*see* Fig 3.11). Why do you think the headings given are necessary?

Compare the invoice to the order form and goods received note. Do they all agree? If you find any discrepancies make a list.

INVOICE

TO Sutherland Sportswear
      124 South Street
      LONDON SE2 4DC
YOUR ORDER NO   ST448

NUMBER   5/149/dec
DATE   28 February 19 . .
TERMS   2.5 %
DESPATCH DATE   30.1.19 . .

QUANTITY	DESCRIPTION	UNIT PRICE	TOTAL PRICE	VAT
14 Reams	A4 A54 WHITE A4 PAPER	£3.01	£42.03	£7.35
10 Boxes	D11 ENVELOPES	£2.00	£20.00	£3.50

Gross Value	£62.03
LESS Trade Discount	£1.55
Net Value of Goods	£60.48
PLUS VAT @ 17.5%	£10.85
INVOICE TOTAL	£71.33

E & O E

Fig 3.11 Completed invoice

Supplementary Invoice

In the case of items having been delivered, but been missed from the invoice, the supplier will send a Supplementary Invoice to cover the difference. A supplementary invoice will also be sent if the customer has been undercharged for some reason.

Credit Note

Should the supplier list items on the invoice by mistake, meaning that the invoice total is too high, then it will send the customer a Credit Note. This will also be issued when any faulty goods have been returned. (*See* Fig 3.12.)

CREDIT NOTE

TO			NUMBER		
			DATE		
ORDER NUMBER			INVOICE NUMBER		
QUANTITY	DESCRIPTION		UNIT PRICE	TOTAL PRICE	VAT
		Gross Value			
		LESS Trade Discount			
		Net Value of Goods			
		PLUS VAT @ %			
		CREDIT NOTE TOTAL			

Fig 3.12 Credit note

Group activity

How could you check whether an organisation is registered for VAT?

In pairs, prepare a flow chart showing the purchasing process of an organisation.

What do you think would happen if a company had been given discount provided it pays within 28 days, and then it did not pay?

SALES DOCUMENTS

As you know, the Sales Department works very closely with the Marketing Department. Once the Marketing Department has done its job, and advertised and promoted the organisation's products, then the Sales Department sells the product to the customer.

The documents dealt with in the Sales Department link very closely with those dealt with in the Purchasing Department. The difference is that the organisation is now the supplier of the goods or services, rather than the customer. However, all the rules about the completion and checking of documents still apply, and all transactions need to be recorded accurately and neatly.

The Sales Department would deal with the following documents:

Orders received

As in the case of placing an order, this can be done over the telephone, and a written order form must be sent by post to confirm. If the Sales Department receives an order over the telephone, it would ask the customer to state an Order Number from their Order Book. This would then be recorded in the Sales Department, and 'married' to the written order form when it arrived.

When the Sales Department receives an order form, it would be checked for the following:

- *Is the catalogue number correct?*
- *Is the price correct and the most up to date?*
- *Is the customer new to the organisation, or an existing one? If the customer has dealt with the organisation before, it may be entitled to credit.*
- *Is the customer allowed any discount, either trade or cash?*
- *Is the order straightforward, or are there any special instructions attached, e.g. the delivery address or times?*

Once the order form has been checked and processed, then the goods will be sent to the customer.

Delivery Note

This will often accompany the goods when they are sent to the customer. A Delivery Note will not state the price of the goods or the total of the order. The customer will check the goods (although if they do not have time to do this they can sign it as 'goods received and not examined') and sign the delivery note to say the goods have been received. The goods are then the property of the customer. (*See* Fig 3.13.)

Group activity

Look at the example of a delivery note (*see* Fig 3.13). Why do you think all the headings are necessary? Write down your answers.

What do you think an organisation should do if it receives goods which are damaged or incorrect? Discuss this in a group and then write down your findings.

Using the findings from your group discussion, write a letter to the supplier. Your letter should include an explanation of the problem and your opinion as to how the problem may be resolved.

DELIVERY NOTE

TO   NUMBER
                                            YOUR ORDER NUMBER
                                            DATE

THE FOLLOWING ITEMS HAVE BEEN DESPATCHED TODAY TO _____
_____ BY RAIL/COMPANY VAN/POST*

QUANTITY	DESCRIPTION	NUMBER OF PACKAGES

I certify that the goods received have been checked and are in good condition

Signed: .... On behalf of: ....
Date: ....

I certify that the number of packages delivered is correct according to the number
stated above, but that the goods have not been checked

Signed: .... On behalf of: ....
Date: ....

* Please delete as appropriate

Fig 3.13 Delivery note

Sales Invoice

The Sales Invoice is often sent out at the same time as the goods. Once again, it is
vital that the information contained on the sales invoice is correct, legible and
contains all the necessary information. It is to the advantage of the supplier to
send out sales invoices promptly, so that payment is made as quickly as possible
after the goods are despatched. Obviously, if the sales invoice contains errors, it
will not be paid but will have to be reissued or amended.

How quickly the customer pays a sales invoice will depend on the terms with which it ordered the goods. It may want to take advantage of the prompt payment discount, or be entitled to the cash or trade discount. The VAT will also have to be calculated on the sales invoice:

■ *VAT is charged on the goods plus the delivery charge*

■ *VAT is added to the total price of the goods, less any discounts available*

Individual activity

Can you remember what we have already said about discounts? Write down the difference between trade, cash and prompt payment discounts.

Should there have been any discrepancy between the goods received by the customer, and the invoice sent by the supplier, then a credit note will be sent by the Sales Department.

Statement of Account

Once a month, usually at the end of each month, the supplier will send out a Statement of Account to each of its customers. This statement will list the transactions that have taken place between the two companies. It will show the totals of each of the sales invoices sent to the customer, plus any payments made by the customer during the month. The balance shown at the end of the statement is the amount of money still to be paid by the customer to the supplier.

Statements of account are important to an organisation for two reasons:

■ *They keep a check of what a customer still owes it*

■ *They keep a check of what it still owes a supplier*

Individual activity

Look at the completed Statement of Account (*see* Fig 3.14). Why do you think the headings are necessary?

How much does the organisation actually owe? How much has it already paid?

You are responsible for checking the Statements of Account when they are received by your organisation. You are going to be away on a course for a month, and need to leave instructions for your stand-in. Write your list of instructions to ensure that the job is carried out correctly.

Draw up a flow chart of the selling process. You may work in pairs if you prefer.

STATEMENT

TO
    Sutherland Sportswear
    124 South Street
    LONDON
    SE2 4DC

DATE   28.2.19. .
NUMBER 32
TERMS   2.5 %

DATE	DETAILS	DEBIT	VAT	CREDIT	VAT	BALANCE
10/2	Balance					£120.60
15/2	Goods	£519.40	£77.91			£717.91
18/2	Returns			£171.50	£25.73	£520.68
20/2	Cheque			£220.68		£300.00

Payments received after the end of the month will not be shown on this statement.

Fig 3.14 Statement of account

PAYMENT METHODS

Obviously, we all need money of some description on a day-to-day basis, and depending on our circumstances, we pay for the goods we buy in a variety of ways. It is the same, to some extent, in business organisations. Usually, there are six ways that a customer may choose to pay for goods or products they have bought:

- *Cheque*
- *Cash*
- *Credit card*
- *Debit card*
- *Credit sales*
- *Hire-purchase*

Although cash, cheque and debit card are different methods to us, they are still regarded as being 'cash' payments because the supplier receives the money for the goods immediately.

A credit card payment gives the supplier the money instantly, but the credit card company may not receive the money from the customer for some time.

Let us look at these methods of payment in more detail:

Cheque payments

We already know how much safer it is to carry a cheque book than to carry cash – cash is irreplaceable, while a cheque book can be 'stopped' by a bank or building society should it get stolen or lost.

Individual activity

What would you do if you had your cheque book stolen? Discuss this in groups.

It is better in some ways for a supplier, because a receipt is not needed by the customer, as they have their cheque stubs or counterfoils as evidence of payment. The customer will also receive a Bank Statement to show that the cheque has been cashed, therefore having proof of payment.

A cheque can be sent through the post quite safely, whilst cash should never be sent. Should a cheque get lost while in the post it is of no use to anyone except the Payee, unlike cash (which is of great use to everyone!).

When someone opens a current account at a bank or building society, they are issued with a cheque book and a cheque guarantee card (we will look at the cheque guarantee card in more detail a little later). The cheque book will contain a number of cheques, each of which are identical in every way, except for the serial number printed on them.

SPECIMEN ONLY Issued by Bank Education Service

_____19___   70-19-85

_____19__

TECHNICAL BANK LIMITED
HOMETOWN

Pay_____ or Order

£_____

£_____

000331   ⑈000331⑈ 70⑈1985⑆ 4170736 5⑈

Fig 3.15 Blank cheque

Individual activity

Look at the blank cheque example (*see* Fig 3.15). Write down all the areas on the cheque and state why they are necessary. Which number is the cheque number, which the bank sort code and which the account number?

Now look at the completed cheque (*see* Fig 3.16). Who is the drawee? Who is the drawer? What do the vertical lines on the cheque mean?

Why do you think the amount has to be written in words and figures?

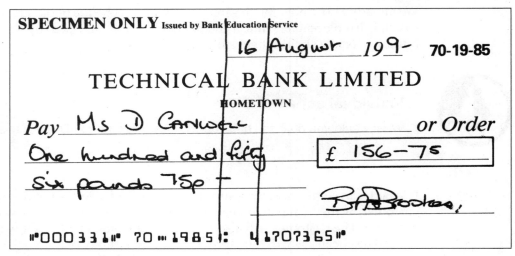

Fig 3.16 Completed cheque

Writing a cheque

- Complete the date section. If a cheque is not dated it will not be accepted by the bank or building society

- Write in the name of the person or company to whom you wish the money to be paid (this is known as the payee)

- Write the amount to be paid in figures in the box. Keep your figures close together so that they cannot be amended by anyone else

- Write the amount to be paid in words along the two lines. Ensure that the amount in figures and in words are the same. If they are not they will not be accepted at the bank or building society. Some people write the word 'only' after the amount in words to show that it is completed. You could also draw a horizontal line to the end of the space for writing the amount in words

- Sign the cheque. The person signing the cheque is known as the drawer, and the bank with whom they have their account is known as the drawee. It will not be accepted by the bank or building society if it is not signed

- Complete the counterfoil. This is the section of the cheque book that the owner keeps as their record of any transactions made. They will check this against the Bank Statement when it is received

Individual activity

Using a blank cheque, make out a cheque for you to sign for the following:

- The Payee is John Brown
- The date is 25 January 19–
- The amount is £35.68
- The cheque is for the purchase of a pair of trainers

Group activity

Now hand your cheque to a fellow student and ask them to check the details. Your colleague can take the role of the supplier and write the cheque guarantee card number on the back. They will also need to know the date of expiry of the card.

You should then hand your cheque guarantee card to the supplier of the goods you are purchasing.

Cheque Guarantee Cards

It is almost impossible nowadays to pay by cheque unless you have a Cheque Guarantee Card to accompany it. The card guarantees that the bank or building society (the drawee) will honour the cheque on behalf of the drawer, even if the cheque book and card are stolen, or if there are insufficient funds in the current account. Once a cheque guarantee card has been used, it is impossible to 'stop' the cheque, so don't buy anything you might change your mind about!

A crossed cheque is one which has two lines drawn or printed down the centre, and the words 'Account Payee' written between these lines. This means that the person receiving the cheque will have to pay it into their bank account and cannot 'cash' it anywhere else. By doing this, the banks and building societies are making it more difficult for people to steal cheques and cash them.

Most organisations tend to pay their bills using a cheque book. In larger organisations, several designated people will be the only ones allowed to sign cheques. We will deal with this area of cheque payment later.

Cash payments

In no way can carrying cash be described as being safe. Despite this, many people still pay for their shopping by cash, although it is unlikely that organisations would pay their suppliers in cash. In some ways it is more convenient to carry cash, and it is certainly less irritating to the person behind you in the queue if you pay by cash instead of writing a cheque! However, it is still possible that a supplier has some concern over the use of cash. It has become increasingly necessary for shops to use the ultra-violet machines available for checking the authenticity of bank notes.

Credit card payments

Not so long ago, it was unusual to see someone paying for goods with a credit card. Nowadays they are in common use, and people feel more confident about buying and using something that has not really been paid for. In fact, using credit cards is extremely useful, although in the wrong hands they can be dangerous! If someone is not responsible they could use a credit card to pay for goods which they have little chance of being able to repay, and the interest charged to their account is very high. (*See* Fig 3.17.)

Cash

The most widely used way of making payments. Almost 90% of all payments are still settled with cash.

Cash Dispenser + Card

Enable customers to obtain cash from a machine. In some cases even when the bank is closed. You can also order a statement or a cheque book.

Cheque

Can be used to purchase goods and services or to obtain cash from a bank account.

Cheque Cards

Will guarantee a payment of a cheque up to a sum of £50. A big help when you are shopping.

Credit Cards

Card holders can obtain goods and services from those shops, garages and other organisations which accept the cards. Can also be used to obtain cash from banks at home and abroad.

Regular Payments

Standing Order

Used by customers who want the bank to *make* payments for them on a regular basis, such as rent; hire purchase instalments; insurance premiums; club subscriptions. It saves people having to remember each time.

Direct Debit

A variation on a standing order. Used mainly by organisations which *receive* vast numbers of regular payments. The companies draw on the customers' bank accounts by computer.

Bank Giro Credit

A convenient way of paying bills through the banking system. You can also pay money into your own account when you are away from home.

Travelling Abroad

Travel cheques are a safe and convenient way of carrying money for holidays. Banks also supply foreign bank notes.

Fig 3.17 Methods of making payments

Each individual, or organisation, issued with a credit card is given a credit limit. This is the amount they are allowed to spend using the card. Each month they will receive a statement from the credit card company, notifying them of any transactions they have made using the card, the balance they owe and the minimum amount they need to pay that month. If the owner of the card pays the amount owed in full, then no interest is charged to the account. If, however, they can only pay a small amount, then the interest charged is high.

It is easy to see which businesses, both in this country and abroad, will accept credit card payments, as they display the fact in the window or near the counter of their premises.

Offering a credit card in payment does not necessarily guarantee that the business will accept it. The organisation will have a limit to the amount they can accept from a customer. This is called the Floor Limit. Anything above this has to be authorised directly from the credit card company. The business will telephone the credit card company in order to receive an Authorisation Code. This code is then entered onto the sales voucher. If the credit card company will not issue an Authorisation Code (maybe because the limit of the card has already been reached, or the owner of the card has missed payments), then the business will not accept payment by credit card.

Increasingly, authorisation from the credit card company can be obtained directly using a special terminal linked to the credit card companies. These are easy to use for the retailer and quick for the person making the purchase. Sometimes this terminal will also print the sales voucher for the business, although this is not necessarily standard at the moment. Usually the Sales Assistant will complete the voucher by hand. The voucher is made up of four copies and is distributed as such:

- *Top copy is given to the customer*

- *Second copy is sent to the credit card company*

- *Third and fourth copies are kept by the retailer for their records*

Completion of Sales Vouchers

The Sales Assistant making the sale completes the Sales Voucher using a special imprinting machine. All the details from the credit card are transferred onto the sales voucher, and the customer then has to sign it. The Sales Assistant will need to do the following:

- *Check that the details on the credit card have been clearly imprinted onto the sales voucher*

- *Check the expiry date on the credit card*

- *Check that the signature on the credit card matches that of the sales voucher*

If the business is not working under the new computer-linked terminal system, then the retailer needs to complete a Retailer Banking Summary for depositing sales vouchers into the bank. If the terminal system is in use, then this is not necessary as the retailer's account will be automatically credited. (*See* Fig 3.18.)

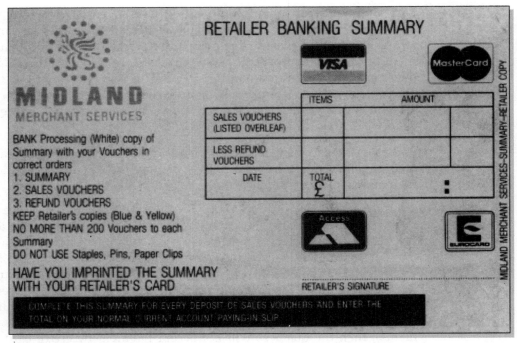

Fig 3.18 Retailer banking summary

Group activity

What would you do if you were a Sales Assistant and you were presented with a credit card that you suspected had been stolen? Discuss this in groups.

If an organisation finds a card which has been stolen, the credit card company will reward them. Find out how much it will pay.

Credit card companies deduct a percentage of the payment as their commission. Find out how much this percentage is. In groups, discuss the implications of this to an organisation.

Debit card payments

More recently, the need to carry around a cheque book with its guarantee card is becoming obsolete. Increasingly, banks and building societies are adopting a card which looks and operates very much like a credit card, but simply and immediately debits your current account for the amount of goods purchased. This card is known as a debit card (Fig 3.19). An additional useful safeguard, from the point of view of the retailer, is that as soon as the bank has accepted the card, then they are guaranteed prompt payment. The most common examples of this debit card method of payment is the Switch and Connect card.

Fig 3.19 An example of a debit card (Barclays Connect)

Individual activity

Some organisations cannot accept debit card payments. Make a list of those in your town which *can*. Then, find out why others *cannot*.

Credit sales

The most common example of credit sale is the mail order industry. The customer has the right to choose to make their payments over a number of weeks (e.g. 20 or 38). When someone buys on credit they do not loose the rights of a person paying by cash. They are still protected by the law to return any goods which may prove to be faulty.

The goods purchased by credit become the property of the customer once the first payment has been made.

If someone who has bought goods on credit does not make regular payments (known as defaulting) then the company or shop from whom the goods were bought could take them to court to obtain their money. They can, however, not repossess the goods (claim them back), although credit sales are often used for goods which would have little or not value if repossessed (e.g. clothing).

Hire-purchase

Unlike credit sales, the goods bought do not become the property of the purchaser until they have been paid for completely. Also, any items can be repossessed in a Hire-Purchase agreement if the customer defaults on payments.

Before a customer will be allowed to take out a Hire-Purchase Agreement, the company supplying the goods will carry out a Credit Rating on the customer. This means that the supplier will contact a Credit Agency to find out whether the customer has had problems meeting payments on any other agreements. If this is the case, then the supplier will refuse to enter into such an agreement.

Provided the customer is employed on a full-time basis, is the correct age and is in good health, then they can take out insurance against becoming ill or unemployed and unable to keep up the payments. This insurance can work out to be expensive, and because of its limitations can exclude some people.

Group activity

What would be the implications to someone who has bought a stereo system on hire-purchase and cannot make the payments each month? Discuss in groups what the outcomes might be.

GOVERNMENT LEGISLATION

There are some Acts which protect both parties involved in any type of credit transaction. They are the Consumer Credit Act 1974 and the Consumer Protection Act 1987. Briefly, they state the following.

The Consumer Credit Act 1974

- *Is the major Act relating to credit*
- *Places strict control over people who offer credit to customers*
- *States that a Credit Agreement must be issued to the customer, and it must contain:*
  - *The APR (see next section)*
  - *The names and addresses of both parties involved in the agreement*
  - *The cash price of goods purchased*
  - *The deposit paid*
  - *The amount still to be paid*
  - *The amount of each repayment*
  - *The date each repayment is due*
  - *The amount payable should the customer default*

Under the Consumer Credit Act, anyone who enters into an Agreement has the right to cancel if they change their minds, provided the agreement has not been signed on the supplier's own premises, and provided they have bought the goods while dealing directly with the supplier. This means that any goods purchased over the telephone are not covered by this Act.

APR

This stands for Annual Percentage Rate of charge. The APR is ruled by the law, and has to be calculated by all credit companies in the same way. In general, when purchasing on credit, it is best to compare the APR a company is offering, as it can make an enormous difference to the rate of the repayments. Remember, the lower the APR the better it is for the customer who is buying on credit.

Individual activity

What exactly does APR mean? Write down in your own words your interpretation of the term.

Collect information from your local banks and building societies and compare the different rates. How can a higher APR affect the amount the customer pays each month?

Pay slips

As an employee, one of the most important and interesting documents you may have to deal with is your pay slip! We have covered elsewhere in the book all the information you need to know about wages and salaries, including tax and insurance contributions. We are going to look at items appearing on a pay slip in this section, e.g. gross pay, statutory deductions, voluntary deductions and net pay. Your wages can be paid in a variety of ways – by cash in a pay packet each week, by a cheque sent to your home either weekly or monthly, or by bank transfer (usually monthly) to your own bank account. Everyone would be wise to check their Pay Slip each time, and in order to do that you need to have a good understanding of the items that appear on it. Whichever way you receive your money, you will still receive a pay slip, and a Pay Advice Note. The following will be itemised:

- *Your name and sometimes your address*

- *Your pay reference number (most often shown when the organisation calculates wages by computer)*

- *The pay period – either the week or month that you are being paid for. The tax year starts on 6 April and runs until 5 April the following year, so week 1 would be the week commencing 6 April*

- *Your tax code and the amount that has been deducted, plus the total amount deducted to date*

- *Your National Insurance number and the amount that has been deducted, plus the total amount deducted to date*

PAY ADVICE

N.I. Number YM 23 16 68D	Tax Code 355L	Basis 0	Year 92/93	Period 40	Pay No 64457	Pay Centre 991

GROSS PAY	STANDARD DEDUC- TIONS	VOLUNTARY DEDUCTIONS	NET PAY
Code £117.72	TAX £33.98	Code	£83.79
Total Gross Pay £117.72		Total Deductions £33.98	

Hours worked		TOTALS TO DATE	VOL DEDUCTIONS	
Normal	Overtime			
		TAXABLE £117.72 TAX PAID £33.98	Code	Balance Owed

A LIST OF CODES AND ABBREVIATIONS USED IS SHOWN ON REVERSE

Fig 3.20 Pay advice slip

- *Your contributions towards a pension scheme*
- *Any voluntary contributions you make which are deducted from your wage/salary*
- *Your bank details if you are being paid by bank transfer*

The Accounts Department will have a section who deal regularly with the preparation of wages and salaries, and they will calculate the deductions you will have taken from your gross pay.

Let us look at some of these in more detail.

Gross Pay

This is your basic wage/salary before any deductions, either statutory or voluntary, are deducted by your employer.

Statutory Deductions are those you have no alternative about paying if you earn enough money each week/month.

Income Tax

When you start work for the first time, or if you change your place of employment, it may be that you are on what is termed Emergency Tax. This means that you are given an Emergency Tax Code, and will pay more tax than normal until your regular code has been allocated.

You will have read earlier in the book that you have no alternative but to pay Income Tax, and this will be deducted from your Gross Pay each week/month. You may want to refer back to this section on Wages and Salaries, just to refresh your memory.

The Accounts Department will work out your Income Tax contributions for the pay period and this will be shown on your pay slip. Also, it will indicate on the pay slip the total amount of Income Tax that you have paid in the current financial year.

Individual activity

Find out the current rate of Income Tax contributions from your tutor/parent/employer.

How is your Tax Code worked out? What allowance can you claim?

What is a tax rebate?

What does the term PAYE mean?

National Insurance

Both the employer and employee make contributions towards National Insurance each week/month. Your contribution will be a percentage of your gross pay.

Again, the Accounts Department will work out your contribution and will show this on your pay slip, together with the total amount of contributions you have made in the current financial year.

Individual activity

Find out the current rate of National Insurance contributions. What percentage of your pay is deducted?

Why do we pay National Insurance? What benefits do we receive because we pay it?

Pension Schemes

Even though you probably haven't yet thought about retirement when you start work, you will be asked to contribute to a Pension Scheme. This may either be the Government Pension Scheme or a Private Pension Scheme. Again, these have already been detailed earlier in the book, and you may like to look back now.

Individual activity

Is there any difference between the Government pension scheme and private pension schemes?

Some banks and building societies offer private pension schemes. Collect information and compare the different types.

What is meant by the term 'opting out'. Discuss this with your fellow students.

Voluntary deductions – those you choose to pay

Trade union membership

If you belong to a trade union, you may choose to pay your subscription by having it deducted from your salary each week/month. This will be shown on your pay slip.

Social Club membership

If you work for a large organisation, it may be that they have a Social Club for staff. You could choose to pay your subscription for this by having it deducted each week/month, and again this will be shown on your pay slip.

Charities

It may be that you choose to make a regular contribution to a charity or charities. This can be done from your salary and will also be shown on your pay slip.

Save As You Earn (SAYE)

You may wish to save a regular sum of money from your salary each week/month. This can be deducted and will be shown on your pay slip.

Net Pay

Your Net Pay is the amount you actually receive, either in cash, or by cheque, or into your bank account. This will be shown as a separate item on your pay slip, and will be your gross pay, minus any statutory or voluntary deductions. The total amount of net pay earned in the current financial year will also be stated on your pay slip.

Individual activity

In your own words write what you understand by the term 'gross pay'.

What other voluntary deductions can you think of?

Petty Cash

It may be that the organisation or office you work for keeps a small amount of cash for use on a casual basis. Perhaps it is used to pay the taxi fares or bus fares of employees who are sent out on an unexpected trip to collect goods. On the other hand, it could be used to buy the tea and coffee supplies, or to pay the window cleaner when he calls. Obviously, this will not be a large amount of money, but it will still be important that a check is made on how and where the money is being spent.

In order to ensure the Petty Cash is monitored and used correctly, it is normal to give the job to one person. This person will be called the Petty Cashier and his or her duties will include:

- *Ensuring that anyone requesting petty cash has completed a Petty Cash Voucher, and that this is correctly completed and authorised*

- *That the money in the petty cash is safe at all times, and stored in a suitably locked place*

- *That the petty cash transactions are recorded accurately in the Petty Cash Book*

- *That the petty cash book balances at the end of each month, and the money tallies with the records*

So, what is the process for dealing with petty cash?

1 *The person requesting the money will have to complete a Petty Cash Voucher.* The information contained in this voucher will include:

   – The voucher number – each voucher will have a different number

   – The date

   – The item(s) being paid for by petty cash and their individual cost

   – The total amount of petty cash being spent

   – The amount of VAT being charged on the goods

   – The signature of the person requesting the petty cash

   – The signature of the person authorising the payment. This may be the Head of Section or a senior member of staff

Individual activity

Look at the blank petty cash voucher shown in Fig 3.21. Why do you think the headings are necessary? What purpose does each heading have?

Why does the VAT charged have to be shown?

2 *The Petty Cashier will then issue the money to the person completing the petty cash voucher.* This will be taken out of the 'float' – a common word used for the money in the petty cash box or tin

```
┌─────────────────────────────────────────────┐
│              PETTY CASH VOUCHER               │
│                             Folio  ......      │
│                    Date .........19...         │
│   ┌─────────────────────┬──────────────┐      │
│   │  FOR WHAT REQUIRED  │   AMOUNT     │      │
│   │                     ├──────┬───────┤      │
│   │                     │  £   │   P   │      │
│   │                     │      │       │      │
│   │                     │      │       │      │
│   │                     │      │       │      │
│   ├─────────────────────┤      │       │      │
│   │                     │      │       │      │
│   └─────────────────────┴──────┴───────┘      │
│   Signature  ...............................   │
│   Authorised by ...........................    │
└─────────────────────────────────────────────┘
```

Fig 3.21 A petty cash voucher

3 *Once the purchase has been made and a receipt for the goods obtained, the Petty Cashier will transfer the details from the petty cash voucher to the petty cash book.*

Individual activity

Why do you think it is important that a receipt is obtained? If you were a Petty Cashier, would you issue money for goods purchased without a receipt? Discuss this with your fellow students.

The Petty Cash Book

The petty cash book has a series of columns. Each of these columns will be headed with the name of a particular type of expenditure. It may be cleaning, travel or stationery. When the Petty Cashier transfers the details from the petty cash voucher to the petty cash book, he or she will place the item in its correct column. By doing this, it will be easy for the Accounts Manager to see where the most amount of money has been spent.

Individual activity

Look at the blank petty cash book shown in Fig 3.22. As well as those given in the text, can you think of any more column headings that would be suitable?

4 *Probably once a month, the Petty Cashier will balance the petty cash book (Fig 3.23).* This means that he or she will add up the totals from each of the columns and ensure that these totals agree with the petty cash vouchers which have been issued. Also, the Petty Cashier will deduct the total amount spent from the original 'float' figure and check to see that the correct amount of money is left in the box or tin.

PETTY CASH BOOK

(Imprest System)

DR														Folio CR
RECEIPTS AND PAYMENTS						**ANALYSIS OF PAYMENTS**								
Imprest		Date	Details	Voucher Number	Payment		VAT							
£	p				£	p	£	p	£	p	£	p	£	p

Fig 3.22 Petty cash book

PETTY CASH BOOK															Folio	
DR				(Imprest System)											CR	
RECEIPTS AND PAYMENTS				ANALYSIS OF PAYMENTS												
Imprest		Date	Details	Voucher Number	Payment		VAT		Postage		Cleaning		Sundries			
£	p				£	p	£	p	£	p	£	p	£	p	£	p
100	00	Feb 8	Balance													
		Feb 8	Stamps	21	35	00			35	00						
		Feb 11	Office Cleaning	22	15	00					15	00				
		Feb 12	Newspapers	23	5	50							5	50		
		Feb 12	Biscuits	24	1	20							1	20		
			Totals		56	70			35	00	15	00	6	70		
			Balance c/d		43	30										
100	00				100	00										
43	30		Balance b/d													
56	70		Restored Imprest													

Fig 3.23 Completed petty cash book

5   *The Petty Cashier will then need to replace the money taken from petty cash in order to ensure the 'float' is back to its original total.* He or she will do this by obtaining money from the Company Cashier.

This system of dealing with petty cash is known as the Imprest System. An example of a completed and balanced petty cash book is given to help you understand the process.

Individual activity

Using the blank petty cash book, give each column a suitable heading, not forgetting the VAT column.

Using the completed petty cash vouchers, transfer the amounts from each to the respective column in the petty cash book.

Total each of the columns in the petty cash book, including the VAT column.

How much money will you need to restore the imprest? In other words, how much money will you need to ensure the 'float' is back to the original amount?

PETTY CASH VOUCHER

Folio ......
Date ..23/.11.19...

FOR WHAT REQUIRED	AMOUNT	
	£	P
2 Highlight Pens		
VAT 17.5 %	2	06
	2	06

Signature ...SS.Cook...........
Authorised by ....J.Smithson............

PETTY CASH VOUCHER

Folio ......
Date ..24/.11.19...

FOR WHAT REQUIRED	AMOUNT	
	£	P
Jar Coffee	3	95
Box Tea Bags	1	10
Pint Milk		32
	5	37

Signature ...D.E. Carwen...........
Authorised by ....RL...........

PETTY CASH VOUCHER

Folio ......
Date ..25/.11.19...

FOR WHAT REQUIRED	AMOUNT	
	£	P
Window Cleaner		
VAT 17.5%	5	00
	5	00

Signature ...D.E. Carwen...........
Authorised by ....E.Levin...........

PETTY CASH VOUCHER

Folio ......
Date ..22/.11.19...

FOR WHAT REQUIRED	AMOUNT	
	£	P
Milkman		
(10 pints)		
VAT 17.5%	3	20
	3	20

Signature ...Mark.Last...........
Authorised by ....A.Jones...........

PETTY CASH VOUCHER

Folio ......
Date 25. Nov 19...

FOR WHAT REQUIRED	AMOUNT	
	£	P
Bus fares to collect parcel from PO Sorting Office	1	10
	1	10

Signature ...Stuart.Jacobs...........
Authorised by ....RL...........

PETTY CASH VOUCHER

Folio ......
Date 26. Nov 19...

FOR WHAT REQUIRED	AMOUNT	
	£	P
Masking Tape	2	30
Blades for knife	3	50
VAT 17.5%		
	5	80

Signature ...SS.Cook...........
Authorised by ......Susan.Mc.Namara...........

Fig 3.24 Completed petty cash vouchers

RECEIPTS

A receipt is a document which confirms that a certain amount of money has been paid. This could be from one individual to another, as when you go shopping and receive a till receipt, or from one organisation to another.

Receipts take many forms, but in each case it will state the amount of money involved and the date the transaction took place. They will be made out in duplicate so that each person involved in the transaction has a copy.

It may be that someone buying petrol will ask for a receipt because they can claim that on their expenses.

Most people are familiar with the format of a receipt:

■ *When you buy goods from a shop, then you often receive a printed till receipt*

■ *In some smaller shops, the assistant will write a receipt by hand*

■ *If you have a cheque book, you will know that the counterfoil acts as a form of receipt or record of what you have spent and who you have paid it to*

■ *When you pay money into a bank account you will know that the counterfoil acts as a form of receipt or record of how much you paid in*

■ *If you receive a bank statement this lists all the monies paid in and taken out of your account, and acts as a receipt for the amount you have in balance*

■ *If you travel by bus or train you will receive a ticket. This is your receipt that you have paid the fare*

■ *When you take clothes to the dry cleaners, the assistant will issue a receipt which you have to present when collecting the goods*

Receipts are normally quite simple to complete, and usually are made up of the following items:

■ *Name of the organisation issuing the receipt*

■ *Date of the transaction*

■ *Name of the person making the payment*

■ *Amount of the payment*

■ *Reason for the payment*

Individual activity

Look at the headings given in the example of a receipt in Fig 3.25. Why do you think each of the headings are necessary? Answer in your own words.

```
┌─────────────────────────────┬──────────────────────────────────────────┐
│                             │  CASH RECEIPT                              │
│  Number ..................  │  NUMBER .................DATE ...........   │
│                             │                                            │
│  Date  ..................   │  RECEIVED FROM ..........................   │
│                             │                                            │
│  From  ..................   │  ......................................... │
│                             │                                            │
│  ......................     │  ......................................... │
│                             │                                            │
│  ......................     │  THE SUM OF ............................    │
│                             │                                            │
│  ......................     │  ......................................... │
│           £      p          │                          £      p          │
└─────────────────────────────┴──────────────────────────────────────────┘
```

Fig 3.25 A receipt form

Cheques

We looked at cheques in some detail earlier in this section, but we will deal now with the process involved in paying by cheque and paying a cheque into the bank.

Just because someone has paid by cheque, it doesn't necessarily mean that the organisation or company is guaranteed payment. It could be that the bank receiving the cheque into the organisation's account has problems in 'clearing' the cheque.

Clearing a cheque

'Clearing' involves checking that the person writing the cheque has sufficient funds in their account. This can take several days. The bank may refuse to accept the cheque for a variety of reasons:

- *There are insufficient funds in the account*
- *The cheque is 'stale' – this means that it is more than six months old*
- *The cheque is not dated at all*
- *The cheque is post-dated – this means that it is written for a future date*
- *The amount written in words is different to that in figures*
- *The name of the payee is incorrect. It could be that it has been spelt wrongly*
- *Corrections or alterations have been made on the cheque and have not been initialled by the drawee*
- *The cheque has not been signed*
- *The signature on the cheque does not match that on the cheque guarantee card*
- *The cheque guarantee card has expired – as with credit cards, the expiry date is written on the card*

So, all these items have to be checked before the bank will 'clear' a cheque. If there are any problems relating to the cheque, then the bank will send it back to the drawee and either request them to re-write it, or to ensure that they pay funds into their account before writing any more.

Paying-in Slips

If we are fortunate enough to have money to pay into our bank accounts, then we complete a Paying-in Slip. Sometimes it is also possible to do this using an automated deposit machine outside the bank.

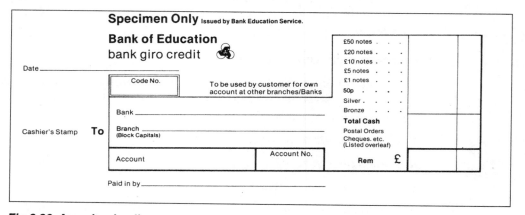

Fig 3.26 A paying-in slip

You will see how to complete a paying-in slip by looking at the example shown in Fig 3.26. Once this has been done, it is simple to hand the slip and the cash/cheques over the counter to the cashier. They will then check the cash/cheques and indicate on the slip that it is the correct amount. This money is then paid automatically into the account.

But how do large organisations cope with paying money into their accounts? Obviously, it would not be wise to allow large sums of money to be kept on their premises, or to be taken to the bank. In order to deposit their takings into their bank accounts regularly, large organisations often employ a security company like Securicor to transfer their money for them. This is obviously much safer than relying on individuals from the organisation to do this job. Some smaller organisations, however, do still send their staff to the bank on a regular basis to deposit takings. To ensure their safety it is wise to allow the employee to be escorted and to make sure they vary their route to the bank each day.

Some banks also have a Night Deposit Safe which customers can use after the bank has closed. This is a useful service to customers who close their businesses after the banks have closed for the day.

Individual activity

The next time you are in your local town, look to see how many Night Deposit Safes you can find for different banks.

You are responsible for taking the cash to the bank for your organisation and you are about to take some annual leave. Write a list of instructions for your stand-in, making sure that you tell them exactly how to complete the task. Also leave instructions regarding the safety of money and welfare of the employee when carrying out this job.

Bank Statements

We have talked about writing cheques, and paying money into our accounts. If we are not particularly good at keeping a note of all these transactions, it could be that we may forget one or two. This would mean a difference in the amount of money we actually have and the amount we thought we had!

Fortunately, a bank will send us a Bank Statement on a regular basis. This will list all of the payments we have made, the cash we have drawn out, and any standing orders or direct debits taken from our account during the month. Some typical withdrawls are:

- Cheques we have written and which have been presented to our bank to be 'cleared'

- Cash we have either withdrawn from our account over the counter of the bank, or from the Cash Dispenser Machine

- Any Standing Orders we have 'raised'

- Any Direct Debits we have 'raised'

- Standing orders and direct debits

- If we have a regular monthly payment, it may be that we choose to 'raise' either a standing order or direct debit from our account. This means that the bank will automatically pay this amount for you on the date you specify. A standing order means that you agree to pay the same person the same amount of money on the same date each month. A direct debit is slightly different. It is more flexible than a standing order because it allows the organisation you are paying to change the date and amount being paid, provided they have notified you of this.

Additionally, on the Bank Statement, you will notice the column headed Deposits. This will normally be a list of the items you have paid into your account either over the counter using a paying-in slip, or using the automated deposit machines. It may, however, also be that someone is paying you regularly by standing order or direct debit, or that your salary is paid into your account by Credit Transfer from the account of your employer.

It is very important to check thoroughly your Bank Statement when it is received. Organisations obviously have to do the same. When an organisation checks its Bank Statement for withdrawals and deposits, this is known as a Bank Reconciliation. This means that they add to the balance shown on the Bank Statement any deposits which have been made since its issue, as well as subtracting any withdrawals that have been made. In this way, it will be easy to see the exact amount they have in the account.

Individual activity

Look at the example of the bank statement. Why do you consider the headings given to be necessary? Answer in your own words.

Find out from the banks in your local area how often one can receive a Bank Statement. Does the bank make this decision, or can the customer choose how often?

Why do you think organisations carry out a bank reconciliation? Answer in your own words.

SECURITY

Throughout the book, we have mentioned several times that documents and various data must be kept and stored securely. This is particularly the case with any financial transactions an organisation might make, and the main reason why the checking of such documents for accuracy and neatness are so important.

But security of such documents going out of the organisation is not the only consideration. Safeguards have to be taken to ensure that the employees of the organisation follow the set process for completion of documents. This is another form of security. The three main aspects of security with regard to financial transactions are authorisation of orders, reconciliation of invoices against orders and goods received notes, as well as authorisation of cheques.

Let us look at these three main points in more detail.

Authorisation of orders

It would be very disadvantageous to an organisation if there were not an individual, or a group of individuals, who had the overall say as to what can be ordered. Obviously, this has to be someone with the right amount of authority within the organisation, who knows the financial commitments of it. This person(s) has to know what goods are needed and the urgency of this need. (*See* Fig 3.27.)

It makes sense then, that each department within the organisation will have a person who can authorise requests for goods or services. These people will have a budget to work to and will only be allowed to spend a certain amount of

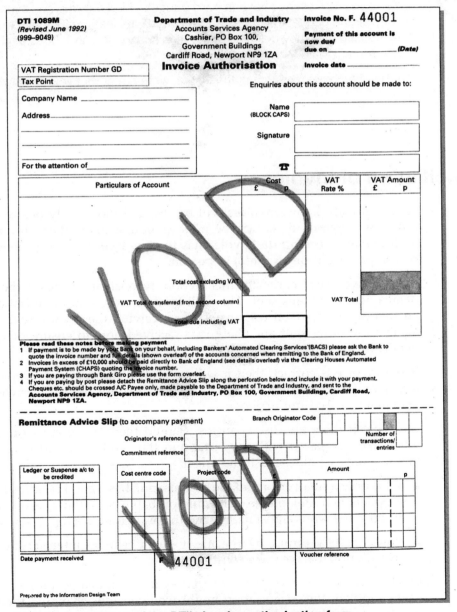

Fig 3.27 A specimen of the DTI's invoice authorisation form

money each month or year. You already know that these budgets will have been set by the organisation – we have discussed this before.

With regard to the type of goods ordered, it will obviously have to be products or services which are required in order to carry out the work in hand. Again, the authorisation of the order will be the responsibility of the Departmental Manager.

Individual activity

Schools and Colleges have to have budgets. Find out who has overall responsibility for the budget in your establishment. Does that person have to authorise everything? Do they delegate some of this responsibility? Does each sector or department have their own budget(s)?

When you have researched the above, write a report of your findings.

Reconciliation of invoices

As we already know, invoices will be checked thoroughly before being sent out. Some organisations may be more thorough than others. It may be that each person checking the invoice has to sign a verification to that effect before passing it on to the next person.

As we have learnt earlier in this section, reconciliation means the checking of details against details sent. This will be done when an organisation receives an Invoice. The person responsible for receiving the invoice will check it against the order sent and the goods received note to ensure that all the details on the invoice are correct.

If the invoice is correct, then it will be sent to the Accounts Department for payment, either immediately to claim the discount offered, or when the Statement of Account arrives.

But what if there are discrepancies? Should there be an error on the Invoice when it is compared with the order and the goods received note, then the following steps would need to be taken:

■ If it is only a small error and the organisation has a good relationship with the supplier, then a telephone call would probably be all that is needed. In this case the supplier would most likely send the organisation a replacement invoice.

■ However, if the error is a large one, it would be in the interests of the organisation to have this in writing.

Obviously, if a series of errors or discrepancies appeared on the invoice of the same supplier, the organisation might well consider changing their supplier for that particular product or service.

Authorisation of cheques

You may already know that when you open a bank account yourself the bank will ask you to sign a form for it so that it has an example of your signature. The same thing applies to an organisation.

For reasons of security, it is not possible to allow just anybody to sign a cheque on behalf of the organisation. To make sure that all cheques which leave the company are authorised to do so, it is normal for an organisation to allocate people with authority to be Cheque Signatories.

This means that their signatures will be held by the bank, and only cheques signed by them will be authorised for payment.

Under these circumstances, the Accounts Department would complete all the details on the cheques to be sent. The Authorised Cheque Signatory would sign them in a batch. Sometimes, on the other hand, the number of cheques leaving an organisation might be very large, in which case the organisation would have a 'rubber stamp' made of the signature to cut down on the amount of signatures needed.

Depending on the size of the organisation, it may be that only one person can be authorised as a cheque signatory. On the other hand, in much larger organisations, it is often the case that between two to five people have this authority. This is more often the case when the cheques are for very large amounts of money, and the people signing them are then protected from any allegations regarding their 'right to sign', as they have witnesses and colleagues have signed as well.

By using these methods of ensuring security of documents leaving the organisation, it is protected to some degree from fraud or theft or misuse of company funds.

Element assignment

ACCURACY AT ALL TIMES

In pairs, and assuming the role of the Accounts or Financial Manager, you have been receiving a number of complaints regarding the way your organisation currently handles documents relating to a series of financial transactions.

The following problems have been encountered from different departments within the organisation:

It has become apparent that not everyone is familiar with the procedure for requesting petty cash. Some members of staff have not had the documents authorised before making their requests.

Items which have been ordered over the telephone have not always appeared on order forms despite the fact that they have been despatched to customers. This has resulted in stock levels not matching those expected.

Invoices are taking too long to be despatched to customers. This is causing cash flow problems within the organisation. At present the average time to despatch an invoice to a customer is seven working days. This must be reduced to no more than four.

When items are out of stock, but orders are pending from customers for these items, the customer has not been informed promptly that the product is temporarily out of stock. This has resulted in loss of sales since the customer has not been offered alternative items or informed as to when the item may be available.

At the beginning of each financial year it is the Administration Department's habit to order and receive stocks of stationery to cover their needs for the entire year. As a result of this, further orders have consistently meant that the Administration Department has exceeded their budget. Their immediate response has been to state that they can only receive discounts by ordering their stationery in this manner.

As the Accounts or Finance Manager, you are fully aware of all the procedures which relate to documentation within your organisation. You are in a position to offer the ideal solution for each of the above problems.

In the form of a series of memoranda, identify the departments to which you must send these communications, and issue instructions or recommendations to solve all of the above problems.

Your memoranda should be in the correct format and clearly state to whom they are directed. Each memo should be neatly word processed and state the problem and recommended solution.

UNIT TEST   Elements 3.1/2

1 Which Government department is concerned with the collection of VAT?

2 Into which two areas can the Annual Accounts be broken down?

3 Briefly explain what you understand by the word 'assets'.

4 Briefly explain what you understand by the word 'liabilities'.

5 What is a profit and loss account?

6 Why is it essential to check documents before they are issued?

7 What is a capital item?

8 What are the stages in the purchasing process?

9 Why would a Purchasing Department use catalogues?

10 State three headings which you would find on a purchase invoice

11 What do the letter E&OE stand for?

12 When would a credit note be issued?

13 When placing an order by telephone, how would you confirm this order?

14 Why is a statement of account issued?

15 What are the six methods of payment?

16 What is meant by 'stopping' a cheque?

17 Give two items appearing on a cheque

18 What is the purpose of a cheque guarantee card?

19 Who would receive the third and fourth copies of a credit card sales voucher?

20 What is a debit card?

21 What is 'defaulting'?

22 In which year did the Consumer Credit Act become law?

23 What do you understand by the term 'APR'?

24 List at least five items you would expect to appear on a pay slip

25 What is a statutory deduction?

26 What is a voluntary deduction?

27 What is SAYE?

28 List six items that may be purchased using petty cash

29 Give at least five headings which would appear on a petty cash voucher

30 Give five column headings which may be used in a petty cash book

31 Explain what you understand by the term 'float'.

32 How would a Petty Cashier restore the imprest?

33 Think of four situations when you would receive a receipt

34 What do you understand by the term 'clearing' a cheque.

35 Give three circumstances why a bank would not accept a cheque

36 List four transactions likely to appear on a bank statement

37 Who do you think would authorise large orders within an organisation?

38 Who, within an organisation, is likely to be a cheque signatory?

39 What does the term 'reconciliation' mean?

40 What does the term 'discrepancy' mean?

UNIT 3   End Test

1 Which government department is concerned with the collection of VAT?
    (a)   Inland Revenue
    (b)   Department of Trade Industry
    (c)   Customs and Excise
    (d)   Department of Employment

2 What does E&OE stand for?
    (a)   Errors and Omissions Excepted
    (b)   Extraordinary and Ordinary Equipment
    (c)   Estimates and Orders Excepted
    (d)   Excess and Overheads Evaluation

3 What is meant by stopping a cheque?
    (a)   Deferring payment until the last minute
    (b)   Cancelling the cheque
    (c)   A security method to allow only authorised signatories to sign
    (d)   When a bank does not allow an organisation to write a cheque

4 Who would receive the top copy of a credit card sales voucher?
    (a)   The customer
    (b)   The bank
    (c)   The supplier
    (d)   The credit control company

5 What does APR stand for?
    (a)   April – the end of the financial year?
    (b)   Accumulated Product Receipts
    (c)   Average Profit Range
    (d)   Annual Percentage Rate

6 What is SAYE?
    (a)   Stock and Yearly Evaluation
    (b)   Salaries and Yearly Expenditure
    (c)   Save As You Earn
    (d)   Spend As You Earn

7 What is a float?

  (a)   An organisation's working capital

  (b)   Amount in the Petty Cash Box

  (c)   The process of offering the company's shares on the Stock Exchange

  (d)   When the company breaks even

8 Which of the following is a debit card?

  (a)   Barclaycard

  (b)   Access

  (c)   Visa

  (d)   Switch

9 Which of the following is a capital item?

  (a)   Photocopying paper

  (b)   Paperclips

  (c)   Production machinery

  (d)   Telephone message pads

10 Which of the following would not appear on a cheque?

  (a)   Account holder's address

  (b)   Sort Code

  (c)   Account number

  (d)   Cheque number

Unit 4
CONSUMERS AND CUSTOMERS
Intermediate Level

Element 4.1
Investigate consumer demand for goods and services

Element 4.2
Produce promotional materials

Element 4.3
Provide customer service

Element 4.4
investigate customer services provided by business sectors

Element 4.1
Consumer demand for goods and services

PERFORMANCE CRITERIA

1 **Characteristics of consumers are described**
2 **Trends in consumer demand for goods and services are identified using relevant information**
3 **Causes of change in consumer demand for goods and services are explained**

RANGE

1 **Characteristics of consumers: age, gender, taste and life-style; local, national and international**
2 **Information: social trends (e.g. income and spending patterns) and family expenditure survey**
3 **Consumer trends: in general and in relation to a particular product**
4 **Causes of change: money to spend, confidence to spend, cost of living, changing needs and changing wants**

EVIDENCE INDICATORS

An oral, written or visual account with computer or manually generated graphics, or a dramatic account (supported by a script) and graphics identifying the characteristics of consumers, demand for goods and services and illustrating changing consumer trends. Evidence should demonstrate understanding of the implications of the range dimensions in relation to the element. The unit test will confirm the candidate's coverage of range.

CHARACTERISTICS OF CONSUMERS

The need to identify and attempt to satisfy the needs of consumers is central to the concept of marketing. To do this efficiently is important, and to do it more efficiently than competitors can be vital. In order to do this successfully, Market Research is used and the forecasting of sales. The single most important factor to affect marketing is that there are a number of different markets for a product. A market is fairly difficult to define, but broadly speaking there are three ways of describing what a market is. First, it can be a physical or geographical place where services are sold. Second, a market can also mean the actual demand for a specific product or service. Third, it can be a set of conditions which determine the price of a product or service.

The most commonly accepted definition of a market identifies a group of people with needs, what their purchasing power is and what their buying power is. A further refinement is that this market is not just existing customers, but should include those who are potential customers.

In order to identify a target market, a number of different things must be looked at. The following six variables are known as Demographic Factors and are the basis of segmenting the total market into identifiable smaller markets. These are:

Fig 4.1 Marks & Spencer's neighbourhood stores provide local communities with a range of everyday products such as food, basic clothing and seasonal lines

1   **Age** – which strongly affects the purchasing power of individuals. In the younger age group – 18–24 for example – fashion, records, take-aways, magazines and newspapers tend to be big areas of purchasing. This is known as Youth Market and is a specific target for certain products. Age is one of the most important considerations, even if it is the easiest one to research.

Group activity

In pairs, and assuming the role of Marketing Manager and his or her Assistant, identify which you think would be the age ranges interested in the following products:

■ Children's toys

■ Cans of soft drinks

■ Beer

■ Recipe books

■ Black lipstick

Compare your age ranges with other members of your group.

2   **Sex** – which is again a straightforward and easy variable to measure, but it is very crucial. Certain products or services are specifically female-orientated. Products either do not cater for one sex in particular, or they are clearly slanted in the way they are advertised to one sex or the other. Drink brands, for example, which are aimed at males are distinctly different from those which are aimed at females. Even cars can be labelled 'women's cars' and their advertising reflects this.

Group activity

In pairs, list 10 products which could be considered to be solely of interest to males. Another 10 for females and a further 10 which would appeal to either sex.

Did you make any assumptions about products and gender? Discuss this with the rest of your group.

3   **Family size and life cycle** – family size is a straight categorisation of one or two members, three or four members, five or more members. The size of the family simply determines the size of the pack they buy and the frequency of their purchasing. The family life cycle determines the stage which the typical family has reached, and directly affects their demand for products and their consumption rate. The basic problem with using the family unit as a measure of demand and consumption is that we assume that the majority of individuals belong to a strict family group. Increasingly, this is not the case.

Group activity

In groups of three, try to list all of the stages of a family's life cycle. You should be able to identify around seven different stages.

4   Social class – this is a mixture of both social class and income. Again, this is a rather crude way of categorising individuals.

The social class in which a whole family is placed is related only to the 'head' of the household. It does not, therefore, take into account a second wage earner (in other words, women are ignored for the most part). The accepted way of categorising individuals by social class was established by the National Readership Survey. This classification consists of six categories which are shown below.

Classification of social class in the UK

A   Higher managerial, administrative or professional

B   Intermediate managerial, administrative or professional

C1 Supervisory, clerical, junior administrative or professional

C2 Skilled manual workers

D   Semi-skilled or unskilled manual workers

E   State pensioners, widows, casual and low grade earners

These categories are also known as socio-economic groups, as they take into account both class and income. There are a number of problems with this categorisation, since, to a large extent, the boundaries between each socio-economic group are somewhat blurred.

Individual activity

To which socio-economic group do the following belong:

- Teachers
- Dentists
- Dockers
- Refuse workers
- Farmers
- Writers
- Students

5 Neighbourhood – this is a relatively new measure of segmentation and is based on a system called ACORN (A Classification of Residential Neighbourhoods). It identifies some 38 different types of residential neighbourhood, according to their demographic, housing and socio-economic characteristics. The basic information is based on the Census of Population in Great Britain, which is carried out by the Government every 10 years.

The classification breaks Great Britain down into units of 150 dwellings. The most common type of dwelling within the 150 is the classification to which that unit is given. This means that in areas which contain a mixture of flats and houses, only the most common dwelling will be noted. This system of classification is used extensively by direct mail companies, financial institutions, gas and electricity companies, TV rental firms, credit card companies, travel agencies, charities and political parties.

The ACORN system has proved extremely useful in the location of new retail outlets and the siting of poster hoardings.

Individual activity

Survey the immediate area in which you live. Under ACORN, your home would be classified under the most common type of dwelling in your area. Which is the most common type of dwelling in your area, and is your home typical?

6 Education – education is proving to be an increasingly less useful way of segmenting the market. It is a rather crude measure based on the leaving age of the individual. It does not therefore take into account any further education beyond school. This classification tends to infer that those who stay in school longer have a tendency to read quality newspapers rather than the tabloids. Equally, these individuals are supposed to be more interested in the more worthy or informative television programmes than game shows. This assumption will have a direct effect upon an organisation's choice of where to place its advertisements. One factor related to education may be true, which is that with a better education, an individual may well earn a higher salary.

Group activity

As a group, discuss the following:

'A person's education has a lot to do with what they will and will not buy.'

These six categories make up the basic methods of segmentation. However, there are other factors to be taken into consideration. These include the following:

1 Geographical – regional differences within a country, not to mention internationally, can be marked. Some of these differences may be traditional, or may be related to economic concerns (such as the unemployment rate)

Group activity

In pairs, try to identify any particular regional differences evident in your area. Are any products or services particularly popular compared to the rest of the country?

Discuss your findings with those of the rest of the group.

2   Cultural – purchasing behaviour is strongly linked to the ethnic or religious background of the consumer. They may have a variety of alternative tastes and need to be considered as a separate market

Some of the principle considerations related to geographical and cultural differences are:

- *Taste* – preferences vary greatly. Some coffee manufacturers, for example, offer no less than 40 different versions of the 'same' product, as some countries may prefer a slightly smoother or more bitter taste.

- *Colour* – in different countries, some colours are positively preferred or avoided. Australians have a preference for colours which are similar to their flora and fauna, in other words, browns and greens. Moslems dislike yellow as it is associated with Buddhists. Italians seem to love pale blue. In Thailand you would find it impossible to sell white false teeth, as many people enjoy munching betel nuts which turn teeth black!

- *Size* – Americans, for example, love to buy huge packs of consumer goods. They have a tendency to over shop and will often buy in sufficient stock to last several weeks. In the UK, we have a tendency to buy our supplies on a weekly or monthly basis. Therefore, our pack sizes are smaller. In poorer countries, manufacturers may have to provide for substantially smaller purchases, as the customer tends to shop on a daily basis.

- *Intended use* – products vary from country to country depending on what the customer wants from the product. Both the style and the design may have to change, particularly if the product is in constant use. In poorer countries, where a product may be considered an essential purchase, it may have to be extremely durable.

- *Ergonomics* – this is linked to the size, shape and weight of the potential user. It would be foolish to attempt to sell Volvo cars to a tribe of pygmies! It is certainly true that individuals vary in size, shape and weight across the world and this will have a bearing on whether a product is suitable.

- *Climate* – the climate may directly affect the efficiency of the product. If the affects of constant hot weather on soft plastic kitchenware were ignored, the manufacturer could find its sales literally 'melting away'.

Group activity

In pairs, make a list of all the countries you can think of. Against this list write at least one product which it would be impractical to try to sell to them.

Compare your list with those of the rest of the group.

INFORMATION REQUIRED FOR CONSUMERS

As we have already discovered, consumers have a range of different needs and wants, as well as attitudes. A successful organisation will need to try to identify any trends which may be evident from existing statistics, or from research which it may carry out itself. There are, obviously, a number of different ways of obtaining these statistics, and, indeed, interpreting what they mean. Let us have a look at some of the more common sources of information, and how they are used.

Fig 4.2 Marks & Spencer aim to cater for all cultural needs, as well as trends and fashions

Social trends

Individuals' life-styles have changed over the years to such an extent that many older products are no longer relevant or wanted. Sometimes the changes are rapid, and at other times they may take two or three generations to emerge. When we refer to social trends, we are, in fact, referring to a vast number of changes in population, tastes, life-styles, health consciousness and availability of technology. Some examples of the more dramatic changes are as follows:

1 *Smaller families* – people tend to have less children than in the past. This may be for many reasons, including the availability of contraception, the availability of pensions rather than sons or daughters for support in old age or the fact that women are tending to return to work after having children.

2 *Health concerns* – people are far more aware of the hazards of poor eating habits and other ill-effects caused by drinking and smoking. Over 10 per cent of the population are now vegetarian, many more avoid fatty foods and red meats. Similarly, less than one-third of the population still smoke, but a high percentage of this number are the young. Many more people are concerned with maintaining or reducing their weight and as such, restrict their diet to calorie-reduced foodstuffs. Drinking is still very popular, but by no means to the extent it has been in the past. (*See* Fig 4.2.)

3 *Leisure activities* – there is a huge range of leisure pursuits both indoor and outdoor, physical and non-physical, now available to the consumer. DIY for example, is very popular and supports a large number of manufacturers and retailers. As far as magazines are concerned, it is hard not to find a magazine which relates directly to your leisure interest.

4 *Sundays* – traditionally, most people attended Church on a Sunday. Although there has been some increase in Church attendance in the past few years, the vast majority prefer to either stay at home or go shopping. This has led to a great debate as to the nature of Sundays, in terms of whether they are still special days or simply another trading day. Many retailers have taken advantage of the Government's confusion over the issue and, despite Local Authority fines for opening, have done very good business on a Sunday.

Group activity

Working in pairs, can you think of any other social trends which we have not identified? Think about whether they have had any serious impact on demand for products and, if so, which ones.

Compare your findings with those of the rest of the group.

Good basic sources of information include the following publications:

■ *Social Trends* (Central Statistical Office) – this publication gives substantial detail regarding the nature of the population, in terms of growth, numbers of people in different age groups and average debts of consumers by age and sex

■ *Annual Abstract of Statistics* (Central Statistical Office) – this publication gives a wide variety of information regarding consumer spending patterns compared to previous years

Along with original research carried out by organisations, marketing specialists will attempt to predict the demand or likely changes in trends and fashions in order to be ready to provide the next big-seller.

Group activity

As a group, see if your institution's library has either of these volumes. If not, try the local library. Individually, attempt to inspect the book and write yourself a list of contents.

Income and spending patterns

We have already mentioned the tendency for women to want to return to work after having children and this has led to some interesting changes in expenditure. Growth areas relating to this factor include convenience food, microwaves, dishwashers and other time-saving items.

In relation to spending and income, we will find many other dramatic changes in the past few years. People have more disposable income (this is money left after tax, national insurance, bills, rents and mortgages), this has, in turn, given people the opportunity to indulge themselves socially and in terms of leisure.

Many people, although they would not necessarily consider themselves to be, are in debt. Credit cards, store cards and charge cards are freely available and offer the consumer the opportunity to spend beyond their means. Although in the short term this increases sales for the retailer, at some point the bills must be paid. In this respect, credit cards are something of a mixed blessing.

Typical sources of information regarding income and spending patterns can be found *Monthly Digest of Statistics* (Central Statistical Office). This publication details wages, prices and expenditure by age, sex and region.

Group activity

Consider the following statement and then discuss it within your group:

'You cannot judge how wealthy someone is just by looking at what they possess.'

Family expenditure

We have already mentioned some changes in the nature of products and services generally bought by the family, but there are some other factors which can be considered:

1 *Consumer durables* – over 90 per cent of households have a television, this is an enormous figure compared to the handful of TV sets sold only 30 or 40 years ago

2 *New technology* – just as televisions now have remote controls, video recorders have simplified programming capabilities and microwave ovens have pre-set dials to cope with a variety of convenience foods. New products commonly found in the home are computers, CD players, dishwashers and answerphone machines. Some of these are relatively new but have established themselves very quickly as not only desirable but needed

3 *Home ownership* – recent Government policy has positively encouraged many people to own their own homes. Despite the difficulties that the recession and high interest rates have created, there are far more home owners now than in the past. This, in turn, has had an effect on family expenditure creating the need for mortgage payments, endowment payments, additional insurance policies and funds for home repairs and improvements

4 *Holidays* – the availability of relatively cheap flights and accommodation abroad has radically changed the way people choose to spend their holiday time. Increasingly, hundreds of thousands of people prefer to spend their holiday breaks in guaranteed sun rather than risk the traditional rainy English holiday

5 *Children* – children have been specifically targeted by marketing departments of organisations in the course of promoting their products. Children's needs and wants have changed drastically over the years and just as general fashions and trends have altered, so have those of the younger generation

Typical sources of information regarding family expenditure can be found in the following publications:

1 *Family Expenditure Survey* (HMSO) – this publication has information regarding the spending levels of people, in addition it details what they are buying and how much they are buying

2 *General Household Survey* (Office of Population Censuses and Surveys (Social Division)) – this publication gives information about each household regarding age, sex and size of family

3 *Household Food Consumption and Expenditure* (HMSO) – this publication, published by the Government, details consumer expenditure on food and drink

Individual activity

Individually, construct a pie chart which shows what you think is the spread of expenditure of a family whose total take-home pay is £15,000 per annum. Compare your pie chart with those of the rest of your group.

Consumer trends

As we have already noted, the changes in consumer trends over the past few years seem to have become ever more rapid. Products which were very popular in the past have disappeared and are little more than oddities which can be found in jumble sales and car boot sales. But why does a product become obsolete? What makes it popular one day, and unwanted the next?

General trends

People's life-styles have changed, and with that their need for particular products and services. It is unlikely that the kind of products which you favour today will be of any interest to your children.

New technology, as we have already said, has played a large part in the changing attitudes over the years. We are now able to buy ever more sophisticated machines which take the boredom out of many day-to-day routines. Whether it is in the home, at work or at play, we can now turn to technology to help us get through the day. We are constantly looking for devices which can give us the maximum amount of free time to enjoy ourselves, companies realise this and are continuously designing new products which can help us achieve this goal. (*See* Fig 4.3.)

Fig 4.3 Marks & Spencer keeps apace with both changes in fashion and trends as well as life-styles

Just as attitudes change, so do life-styles. The availability of a vast range of foodstuffs and household products has enabled us to try an ever-increasing variety of new items. In retailing, there has been a steady move from local shops which stock a limited range of goods to enormous superstores with a bewildering array of products. This has meant that a family is unlikely to shop on a daily or even weekly basis and may prefer the convenience of shopping monthly. These super-stores are open for much longer hours than ever before, making their facilities available seven days a week. The high street, once the centre of shopping activities, has been severely hit by our preference to shop 'out of town'. We will now find specialist shops and the occasional general store which, increasingly are the only types of outlet that can survive.

Group activity

In pairs, make a survey of your local high street. Try to identify the different kinds of shops under the following categories:

- Independent retailers
- Regional chains
- International chains
- Local chains
- National chains

For the second part of this task, try to find a person who remembers what the high street was like 10 years ago. Show them your findings and ask them how

Families now have a larger proportion of their disposable income available for leisure activities. This has led to the growth of the DIY market, thousands of specialist magazines and an increasingly large range of sports equipment. Another factor that has assisted the growth of this area is the increased amount of leisure time as working hours have been steadily reduced over the years.

Returning to food and health issues, it is now believed that almost 10 per cent of the population is vegetarian, or almost vegetarian. Many more people control their diet with low-calorie foods. Periodic scares regarding food and health have reduced our intake of animal fats, eggs and red meats. At the same time, smoking has become reduced to less than one-third of the adult population. All of these changes have had drastic affects on retail outlets who had in the past relied on consumption of these items.

As we have already mentioned, technology has drastically affected our life-styles, making many routine tasks much quicker to undertake. We no longer need to spend hours laboriously doing things by hand when a machine can do them in seconds.

Group activity

In groups of four, design a questionnaire that looks at the following areas of consumer preferences:

- How many people have given up or are thinking of giving up smoking?
- How many people have given up or are thinking of giving up red meat?
- How many people choose to buy recycled products nowadays?
- How many people choose to buy cruelty-free products?
- How many people use lead-free petrol in their cars?

WOOLWORTHS

I N F O R M A T I O N

ENVIRONMENTAL POLICY

It is the policy of Woolworths to manage the environmental responsibilities in accordance with the following principles:

Management Responsibility
Environmental affairs within Woolworths are the responsibility of one named Board Director. The responsible Director is charged with ensuring that specific action plans are developed to implement the provisions of the policy.

Internal Communications
Environmental awareness will be raised by communicating environmental issues to staff at all levels as an integral part of the company's training programmes.

External Relations
Woolworths will communicate openly to the public and outside agencies about its environmental performance.

Woolworths will give careful consideration to all environmental claims on products to help customers make informed purchasing decisions.

Products and Packaging
Woolworths will keep informed about the environmental issues and legislation influencing the products it sells.

Woolworths will carry out a systematic review of internal packaging practices and will produce a series of guidelines to assist suppliers in fulfilling the company's aim of waste minimisation in product packaging.

Suppliers
Woolworths will demand high environmental standards from the suppliers of Woolworths own-label products.

Woolworths will incorporate environmental concerns into its standard quality assurance procedures for other products.

Woolworths will expect all suppliers to co-operate with the company in meeting established environmental objectives.

Waste Management and Recycling
Woolworths will review its arrangements for disposing of wastes in stores, offices and distribution centres.

The company will promote waste minimisation and ensure that all wastes transported off-site are disposed of in accordance with best practices.

Woolworths will take every opportunity to extend in-house recycling schemes and encourage suppliers to take their share of the responsibility for reducing waste and encouraging recycling.

Energy
Woolworths recognises it has a responsibility to minimise energy used in all aspects of its business operations.

Woolworths will continue to monitor its energy consumption and set practical objectives to achieve energy savings.

Siting and Design of Premises
Environmental impacts will be considered when refurbishments are planned.

Where Woolworths commission new premises, site selection will take account of local environmental sensitivities.

WOOLWORTHS ENVIRONMENT POLICY ACTION TAKEN TO DATE

In order to minimise the negative impact our products and business methods may have on the environment, Woolworths has taken a number of steps to support green issues, involving staff, suppliers and customers.

It is our policy to support any initiative of obvious benefit in the campaign to protect the environment. We will also continue to monitor and review new initiatives which may be of value in the future.

Plastic Bags
Extensive research has shown that bio-degradable bags normally include a proportion of starch in their composition. When the plastic is buried in the soil, micro-organisms attack the starch over a period of five to 15 years, the plastic breaks down into small pieces which form the basis of soil crumbs.

Fig 4.4a A Woolworth press release detailing their environmental policy

WOOLWORTHS
I N F O R M A T I O N

There is concern over the long-term effects should these particles enter the water supply, and as a result of this investigation, Woolworths has ceased to use bio-degradable plastics in the manufacture of carrier bags.

Aerosols
In response to concern over the depleted ozone layer, Woolworths ensures that all aerosols stocked are CFC-free.

Animal Testing
None of the cosmetics sold by Woolworths have been tested on animals.

Harmful Chemicals – Horticultural Products
Woolworths has withdrawn from sale any product containing aluminium, mercury or lindane over the last three years. Any other weedkiller is only stocked if approved by the Ministry of Agriculture, Fisheries and Foods and the British Agrochemicals Association.

Policy Re: Unbleached Natural Fibres in Kidswear
Woolworths strives to stock children's clothing manufactured with natural fibres as far as possible, while taking into consideration practicality and cost to the consumer.

Petrol
All our company cars delivered since 1989 are ready-converted, and run on unleaded petrol, and our lorries run on diesel.

Guidelines to Suppliers
Woolworths is working closely with its suppliers to meet the company's environmental objectives. This is an on-going process and Woolworths continually monitors its progress. In turn Woolworths maintains regular communication with suppliers via bulletins and briefings explaining these objectives and informing them of any new initiatives concerning its protection of the environment.

Support to Environmental Charities
Woolworths stores stocked a special range of Christmas cards during 1990, the proceeds of which were donated to the World Wildlife Fund.

We do not currently support any environmental charity on a national level.

Waste/Recycling
With regard to waste and recycling, Woolworths takes every opportunity to extend in-house recycling schemes, and encourages suppliers to reduce waste and undertake recycling likewise.

We stock a wide range of products which are manufactured using recycled paper. An exclusive range of recycled stationery won Woolworths a House of Commons award for helping to conserve trees, and wherever possible recycled paper is used for the company's internal communications needs.

Waste paper bins are located in and around every Woolworths store. We are currently recycling paper at head office and Distribution Centres. We are also currently trialling the recycling of plastic wrap in selected stores. In addition, we are recycling cardboard in all stores thus promoting waste minimisation and ensuring that all waste transported off-site is disposed of with due consideration to the environment.

We are also currently recycling plastic cups at Head Office on a trial basis with a view to expanding the project to other offices.

From February 1992 our staff newspaper has been printed on recycled paper.

Cleaning Equipment
Woolworths encourages the use of recycled and CFC-free cleaning materials for both stores and offices as far as possible.

Store Design/Fixtures
Woolworths endeavours to consider any impact on the environment when refurbishments are planned, and local environmental sensitivities will be taken into account where Woolworths commissions new premises.

With due consideration to the environment, we ceased using wooden fixtures and fittings in 1990. The only wood used is for the trim on cash desks, from a sustainable source. The new floors are in fact made from vinyl tiles, and not wood.

Heat/Light Wastage
With regard to the conservation of energy, Woolworths endeavours to minimise energy used in all aspects of its

Fig 4.4b A Woolworth press release detailing their environmental policy

WOOLWORTHS
I N F O R M A T I O N

business operations. Its energy consumption is monitored on a store by store basis and practical objectives are set to achieve energy savings.

Within the last five years all sales area lighting has been converted to a more efficient scheme. This, together with the introduction of good housekeeping practices, has resulted in a saving of over £1 million.

Communication of Environmental Policy to Staff
Environmental awareness is raised by communicating the relevant issues and developments affecting the company to staff at all levels. This is achieved through a number of methods, including Woolworths News – the company's monthly in-house newspaper – and store and office briefings. Alerting staff to environmental issues affecting the company is also an integral part of the company's training programme.

Communication of Environmental Policy to the Public
Woolworths considers its campaign to support 'green' issues to be an important part of its communications programme, and endeavours to communicate openly to the public about its environmental performance.

Woolworths gives careful consideration to all environmental claims on products to help customers make informed purchasing decisions.

Smoking Policy
Woolworths has established a 'smoking policy' at its Head Office in London, whereby smoking will only be permitted in designated zones of the building. Counselling Care Sessions for those who wish to give up smoking have been made available. As with any retailer, smoking is not permitted by the staff or customers in the sales area of any store, although staff members are permitted to smoke if they so wish in canteens/rest rooms.

Fig 4.4c A Woolworth press release detailing their environmental policy

Consumer trends in relation to particular products/services

Some products and services are affected to a greater or lesser extent by the following:

- *Trends*
- *Attitudes*
- *Life-style*
- *Fashion*
- *Available disposable income*

Others may not experience changes at all. Those products which are at the leading edge of technology are often rapidly replaced by the latest technological developments.

There are some other reasons for the change in demand for a particular product or service. These include:

1   *Whether the customer has confidence to spend available cash.* In other words, if a customer is unsure of their medium or long-term future within a job, they will be unlikely to wish to spend their money on items which are not essential. They must have the confidence of being secure in their occupation in order to risk large sums of money

2 *The cost of living.* This is calculated by the Government by means of a Retail Price Index. This RPI monitors a standard group of goods on a monthly basis, checking any changes in costs and comparing them to prices charged in the past. From this figure the Government is able to calculate inflation, as well as identify any unexpected jump in the price of a particular product. The RPI is also used to compare increases in wages, which it is argued should rise in relation to the RPI. If wages have not increased at the same rate as the RPI, then it is obvious that customers are unable to afford all of the items they had previously been buying before the RPI increased

Group activity

In groups of four, find out details of the Retail Price Index over the last two years. Your task is to present this information in the most effective manner by the use of a computer.

CAUSES OF CONSUMER CHANGE

The causes of changes in consumer demand are very hard to predict. Indeed, there is a great deal of money to be earned from predicting changes. Some of these changes are as a result of factors that we have already looked at, but there are some other vital considerations that need closer attention. An organisation continuously monitors consumer spending patterns to try to look ahead towards potential trends. An organisation routinely analyses any available data. Sources of useful information are Government departments, Industry-wide statistical surveys, opinion poll companies and market research carried out by the organisation itself. In general, it will look at the following considerations as clues to what demand will be like in the future:

1 *Money to spend* – the amount of disposable income available to a customer will vary according to a number of different sets of circumstances. Beyond the normal deductions which we all expect to pay, such as tax and National Insurance, we may have a range of other commitments to meet. When interest rates were high, mortgage payments rose. This in turn meant that the disposable income available to the home owner dropped dramatically. During this period, retail outlets in particular suffered a drop in sales. Equally, when unexpected bills arrive we have reduced amounts of disposable income

2 *Confidence to spend* – as with the above, the confidence to spend is linked to the customer being careful over exactly how much they think they can afford. During difficult times, individuals are more likely to try to save

THE CARING CONTINUES . . .
FACING THE FACTS

*W*e were the first major beauty company to react to the potential dangers of CFC gases. In 1978, we switched to natural pump sprays for fragrances. Since then all CFC propellants have been totally eliminated from all our sprays.

An example of our natural pump sprays

*A*ll Avon company cars run on lead-free petrol.

*I*n June 1989 we were the first major cosmetic company to announce an end to animal testing of our products, the conclusion of a programme which began many years before to find consumer-safe alternatives.

"The 1990's will bring new challenges.
We will continue to demonstrate our determination
to meet the demands of an ever changing world,
setting new standards for others to follow."

*A*ll recyclable waste paper and cardboard packing is collected, sorted and recycled. Our suppliers are pledged to buy only from mills using managed forests, ensuring trees used for avon cartons are replaced.

*S*uccessful energy conservation systems since 1986, have reduced oil consumption by 55% and electricity by 27%.

Avon are now marking plastic containers with an identifying symbol enabling them to be sorted for recycling, contributing further to waste reduction.

landscaping around our
orthampton creates attrac-
orking environment.

Fig 4.5 Evidence of Avon Cosmetics' commitment to responding to changing customer needs and demands

money rather than spend it on luxuries. With this in mind, retailers have taken to offering interest-free credit, extended credit terms and delayed payment schedules. These credit facilities have gone some way in allaying the fears of the customer with regard to long-term debt. Confidence to spend can only really be achieved during times when the economy itself is healthy, jobs are secure and there is a possibility of earning additional income (such as pay rises)

3   *Cost of living* – the cost of living has already been considered when we were looking at the Retail Price Index. The RPI is a good indicator of the costs to a normal consumer of a 'basket' of ordinary goods or products. In addition to this is the consideration of the price of other regular outgoings, such as the following:

- *Gas*
- *Electricity*
- *Telephone*
- *Mortgages*
- *Rents*
- *Council Tax (formerly Community Charge and rates)*
- *Tax rate*
- *National Insurance Contributions*

4   *Changing needs* – the changing needs of a consumer may depend on a number of different factors, these will include some of the following:

- *Changes as the individual gets older*
- *Changes if the individual gets married*
- *Changes if the individual is responsible for children*
- *Changes according to the type of work carried out by the individual*
- *Changes relating to the area in which the individual lives*
- *Changes relating to technology and the availability of technology*
- *Changes relating to the importance which the individual attaches to the product compared to all of the other items needed by the individual*

5   *Changing wants* – on the face of it, we would consider that wants are related to considerations involving trends and fashions. While this is true, we must not forget that individuals are constantly changing their ideas about what they would like, independently of the fads and fashions of other people. We all have to put the things that we would like on a list of priorities. Some items in this list are always there, but there may be other things that seem to overtake them at certain times. This may be because we have long-term wants and short-term ones. In other cases, this may simply be related to the cost of the wants and how much we really do want them. (*See* Fig 4.6.)

WOOLWORTHS AND CUSTOMER CARE

Woolworths is committed to ensuring that staff offer the highest standards of customer care. Woolworths people are trained to be proficient and confident when dealing with customers, and to have extensive product knowledge.

This is summed-up in Woolworths Customer First Policy, "We serve ourselves best by serving our customers first" and implemented through the Customer First Skills Training Programme, which is the standard induction course for all sales staff.

The vast majority of customer enquiries are successfully resolved at store level, but to support the work of stores Woolworths operates a central Customer Relations Department from its Head Office.

By letter or phone, this department handles over 10,000 customer enquiries every year.

WOOLWORTHS

Fig 4.6 Woolworths' 'Customer First' policy aims to prepare all staff to meet customers' needs

Group activity

In pairs, spend 10 minutes individually writing a list of what you consider to be a need and a want. Now compare your two lists. Have you agreed about most of the items on the list? If not, discuss with your partner the reasons why you think this should be.

4.21

Element assignment

MEETING THE CHANGES

Refer to Fig 4.7 which is a press release from the British Union for the Abolition of Vivisection. This was issued to the media a few days before the launching of its European campaign which aimed to gain a ban on testing cosmetics on animals.

First, in the role of an editor of a national newspaper, rewrite the press release as a news item.

Second, in the role of a cosmetic manufacturer that does not undertake animal experiments to develop its products, write a press release in response to the one

News from BUAV
campaigning to end animal experiments

British Union for the Abolition of Vivisection, 16a Crane Grove, London N7 8LB.
Telephone 071-607 9533. Fax 071- 700 0252.

CAMPAIGNERS CALL FOR END TO
COSMETIC TESTS IN EUROPE

Leading European animal societies join forces for the first time today (17/7/90) to launch a hard-hitting international campaign to ban cosmetic and toiletry tests on animals throughout the European Community.

Campaign co-ordinators, the British Union for the Abolition of Vivisection (BUAV), have gained the support of top European animal societies, including the International Fund for Animal Welfare (IFAW) and groups from Holland and West Germany. Other groups are expected to join the campaign soon.

The groups will distribute hundreds of thousands of striking campaign leaflets, posters and postcards especially designed by Spitting Image caricaturist, David Stoten. A petition calling on the European Parliament and Commission to ban cosmetic and toiletry tests will aim to attract over 2 million signatures. Euro-wide advertising, publicity events and political lobbying will also play a major role in what is expected to be the largest animal rights campaign to date in the European Community.

BUAV National Campaigns Organiser, Steve McIvor, states:
'Europe has become the new arena for the campaign to ban cosmetic tests on animals. Now is the time for the European Community to take action. Public opinion demands that these crude, cruel tests should be stopped immediately.'

The Campaign coincides with the new European Commission proposals to update the 1976 Cosmetics Directive - regulating the safety of cosmetic products - which are due to be published soon. Intensive lobbying of MEPs and the Commission has apparently prevented proposals for increased animal testing being included. However, the amended Directive will still permit tens of thousands of animals to suffer in eye, skin and poisoning tests. The new proposals are expected to go before the European Parliament in the autumn.

ENDS

Fig 4.7 A BUAV press release

from BUAV. Your press release should state your position and make it clear that the comments made in its press release do not refer to your organisation.

Third, assess the impact of the growing and changing consumer awareness of such issues as animal testing. As a Public Relations Officer of an organisation which still tests its products on animals, prepare a short press statement in defence of your position.

All three tasks should be word processed and follow a similar format to the example shown in Fig 4.7.

UNIT TEST   Element 4.1

1 What is demography?

2 What is a consumer durable?

3 List three items of family expenditure.

4 What information would you find in the *General Household Survey*?

5 What percentage of the population is vegetarian?

6 What trends can affect demand for a particular product or service?

7 What do you understand by the term 'cost of living'?

8 What is the RPI?

9 What do you understand by the term 'confidence to spend'?

10 List five regular outgoings when calculating family expenditure

11 What is a family life cycle?

12 What do you understand by the term 'socio-economic'?

13 What is ACORN?

14 What are the six main categories of segmentation?

15 Which colour is not favoured by Moslems?

16 What do you understand by the term 'ergonomics'?

17 What would you find in the *Monthly Digest of Statistics*?

18 What is disposable income?

19 What do families tend to spend their disposable income on?

20 Why would a customer not have 'the confidence to spend'?

Element 4.2
Promotional materials

PERFORMANCE CRITERIA

1 Objectives of promotional materials are identified and explained
2 Constraints on the content of promotional material are described
3 Types of promotion are identified
4 Resources required to produce materials are identified and secured
5 Potential of different media to produce promotional materials is investigated
6 Promotional materials are produced and used to promote a product or event

RANGE

1 **Objectives:** to create demand, to create sales and to influence consumer perceptions
2 **Constraints:** legal and ethical
3 **Promotion:** advertisement, sponsorship and competition
4 **Resources:** time, human, physical and financial

EVIDENCE INDICATORS

Promotional material produced from one or a combination of media to promote a product or event. (If promotional materials are produced by a group the individual candidate must be able to explain and illustrate the process of development of the materials.) Evidence should demonstrate the understanding of the implications of the range dimensions in relation to the element. The unit test will confirm the candidate's coverage of the range.

OBJECTIVES OF PROMOTIONAL MATERIALS

A good advertisement tries to put over the message clearly and as accurately as possible without actually diverting the attention of the audience to the advertisement itself. It is the message that is centre stage and not the advertisement.

No one has really been able to get this mix right every time. There are many examples of advertisements which have done so; they are the exception rather than the rule. Here are a few pointers to help us get the balance right:

1   The first and most obvious thing to consider is the amount of exposure that the advertisement gets. The concept of 'threshold' maintains that unless an advertisement is shown enough then people will simply forget it. On the other hand advertisements can be shown too often which can lead to the product being considered irritating and boring. Budgets are an important consideration as most companies cannot afford to show their advertisements enough to get the impact that they want. In these circumstances they will have to rely on other methods of getting their message across.

2   If a company cannot afford to saturate the media with its advertisements then it must look to the long term instead. Prolonged and gradual exposure can be equally effective. As time goes by and the advertisement is shown over and over again people will remember it. The boredom and irritation factor is minimised. This technique relies on the consistency of the advertising and the memory of the audience.

3   People remember and respond to things that interest them. Advertisers try to find out what their target audience is interested in and adapt their advertising to suit them. This rapport with the audience can pay dividends. Typical methods of this technique are using well-known people that the audience relate to or music that they like and enjoy.

4   Creativity itself plays no small part in all of this. The problem is in putting together the brilliant idea with the need to get a simple and clear message across.

Out of the above techniques the most effective is the exposure method. As most companies cannot afford this technique they have to rely on spending heavily to begin with and then resorting to the repetition of the advertisement over a period of time. Even with a limited budget a company can have effective advertising by paying attention to the interests of its target audience and establishing that very important rapport with it. These days creativity can be vital, it may mean that an advertising campaign can be successful with lower overall costs while being very effective for the short time it is shown.

Group activity

In groups of four, try to list the television advertisements that you can remember. What is it about them that sticks in your mind? Are there any advertisements which are obviously aimed at your age group? Do these appeal to you, or do they irritate you?

Feed back your discussion to the rest of your group.

The term 'promotion' is a general one, it refers to any organisation which aims to do one of the following:

1 *Create a demand for a product or service*
2 *Create sales for a product or service*
3 *Influence customer perceptions regarding a product or service*

(*See* Fig 4.8.)

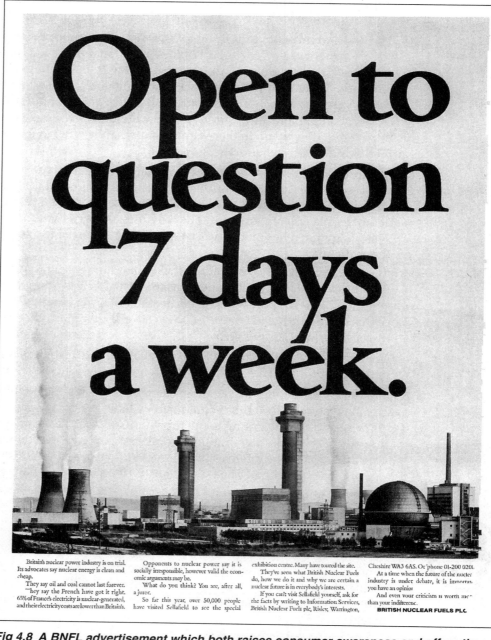

Fig 4.8 A BNFL advertisement which both raises consumer awareness and offers the opportunity for personal visits to the site in Cheshire

Let us have a look at those aims in a little more detail:

1 Creating a demand for a product or service:

- The first aim of this technique is to try to convince the customer that they would benefit from the purchase of the product or service

- The second aim is to try to give the customer as much information that they need to assist them in deciding whether the product or service would be useful to them

- The third aim is to tell the customer about any benefits or advantages this product has over the competition, and whether the product or service has been modified or improved since the last time they bought (or thought about buying) the product or service

- The fourth aim is to try to inform the customer of any special offers available, such as reduced prices or extra value for money

- The fifth aim is to try to get the customer to remember the name of the product or service

- The sixth, and final, aim is to try to get the customer to remember the name of the organisation that is offering the product or service and any other information (such as a telephone number or shop opening hours)

Group activity

In pairs, design an advertisement which attempts to create a demand for a product or service. The choice of product or service is yours. Try out your advertisement on the rest of your group. Does it work? Are the others convinced that they want your product?

2 To create sales for the product or service:

- The first aim of this technique is to attempt to tell the customer where they can obtain the product or service

- The second aim is to attempt to tell the customer how they can obtain the product or service

- The third aim is to try to obtain and maintain the customer's loyalty to the product, service or organisation

- The fourth aim is to state that the product or service offered is much better than any of the competition

- The fifth aim is to try to get across the fact that the organisation offers a range of products and services. All of these products and services offer the same standard of excellence

Group activity

Again in pairs, think of some phrases or slogans that organisations have used to try to create sales. Are they interesting and convincing enough to work?

Having made this list, now try to create some of your own. Are they any better? If so why? If not, what makes the professional's ones better?

3 To influence customer perceptions regarding a product or service:

- The first aim of this technique is to try and heighten customer awareness of the organisation in general

- The second aim is to try and create a positive image of the organisation and its range of products and services

- The third aim is to inform the customer about the range of possibilities offered by the organisation, in terms of products and services as well as advice and guidance

- The fourth aim is to link any popular public trends (such as environmental issues) with the organisation's range of products and services

- The fifth aim is to link the range of products and services with any recent changes in legislation

Individual activity

Individually, over the next few days monitor your local independent television station. Pay particular attention to the advertisements. How much do they really tell you about the organisation that produces the products or services which they are promoting? Do you actually remember anything about the advertisement apart from the product or service itself? What kind of image is the organisation trying to create with the style of advertisement it is using?

After your period of investigation, feed back your ideas to the rest of the group.

These techniques can be best remembered by using a word which is made up from the first letter of the following words. The key word to remember all of this is AIDA.

- **A**ttention – get the customer's attention by showing them something that they will remember

- **I**nterest – try using some trick or design that will make the customer read or watch your advertisement. These may include special offers,

- **Desire** – make the customer really want your product or service. Tell them that they will really benefit from buying it
- **Action** – this is the real key to it all. Make it as easy as possible for the customer to obtain your product or service

CONSTRAINTS ON PROMOTIONAL MATERIALS

Voluntary, legal and ethical constraints

In the UK, the advertising industry is largely self-regulating. In other words, the industry itself keeps a careful eye on its members to ensure that they do not mislead or overly confuse the public.

All advertisements should be 'legal, decent, honest and truthful'. These foundations of practice are supported by the British Code of Advertising Practice. In particular, they cover awkward advertising areas such as children, cigarettes and alcohol, recommendations by famous people and in situations when a company compares its products to another. Above all, the advertisement should not claim anything which cannot be clearly proven.

The British Code of Sales Promotion Practice (BCSPP) covers aspects which do not fall directly under the British Code of Advertising Practice. In essence, this code is concerned with competitions, special offers, charity promotions, vouchers, coupons and free offers.

The Advertising Standards Authority (ASA) exists to assist customers who have a complaint regarding an advertisement. The Advertising Standards Authority receives nearly 10,000 complaints each year and publishes its results in a monthly report. If the complaint is found to be justified, then the advertiser is required to withdraw or change the advertisement. In extreme cases, the Advertising Standards Authority may inform newspapers, television companies and radio stations that they should not accept any other advertisements similar to the one that has caused the problem.

The Independent Television Commission monitors all advertisements which are broadcast by the various independent television stations in the UK. It also has a responsibility for ensuring that satellite and cable television advertisements are similarly monitored. The monitoring process begins before the advertisement is made, when the Independent Television Commission checks the script for inaccuracies. Any complaints are dealt with by the Independent Television Commission and action can be taken against advertisers who are found guilty of misleading the public.

Working in conjunction with the Independent Television Commission, is the Broadcasting Standards Council, which is particularly concerned with violence and indecency, both in programmes and advertisements. If it receives a complaint regarding excess violence or indecency, then it will take action against the advertiser.

Fulfilling a similar role to the Independent Television Commission, but working within the field of radio broadcasting, is the Radio Authority. It also checks scripts before recording to ensure that the advertiser is not misleading the public in any way. It is responsible for investigating complaints and taking appropriate action should the complaint be upheld.

It should be noted that certain media will not accept tobacco, spirits or advertisements from bookmakers. This is particularly true of television, but advertisements for these products and services can be seen in other media, such as newspapers or magazines.

Just as organisations must adhere to a variety of different legislation, false claims in advertisements may also fall within the bounds of these laws. In brief, these laws are:

1 **The Control of Misleading Advertising Regulations** – essentially this law backs up the voluntary codes of practice by making them a little more legal and clear

2 **The Trade Descriptions Act** – as we have already seen, this Act states that an organisation must not make any false statements regarding its products. Any complaints received are investigated by Trading Standards Officers on a local basis

3 **The Food Act** – this law obviously refers to consumable items and attempts to ensure that the labelling on the products is clear and truthful

4 **The Medicines Act** – in a similar way to the Food Act, this law attempts to control statements made relating to drugs and other medical products

5 **The Consumer Protection Act** – in relation to advertisements, this Act is concerned with claims that products or services are being offered at reduced prices and are, in fact, true reductions in price

Group activity

As a group discuss the following statement:

'Advertisers and their advertisements consistently lie and exaggerate their products and services. There is not enough legislation to control them, and they do not pay any attention to the voluntary codes of practice.'

TYPES OF PROMOTION

Advertisements

The message that a company wishes to communicate with its target audience is central to the advertising campaign. The advertising will be a mixture of words, colour, images, sound, etc., that, hopefully, best gets the message across. If a company hopes to get its message across to everyone that it has targeted it will surely fail; certain types of advertising are simply not appropriate for certain parts of the target segment. More than this there are two main problems to overcome, the first is getting the message noticed by anyone and the second is getting the right message noticed. By going too far in trying to get the advertisement noticed the message can be left confused. Only a basic message needs to be remembered and an overly clever gimmick may leave the audience only remembering that. (*See* Fig 4.9.)

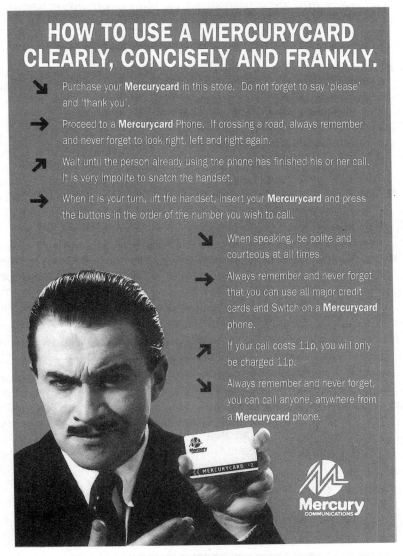

Fig 4.9 Mercury Communications chose comedian Harry Enfield to highlight their expanding range of telecommunication services

Let us look at the relative merits of each of the media, particularly their advantages and disadvantages.

Television

Up until quite recently viewing was almost equally divided between the BBC and the IBA. The IBA of course includes the 14 regional independent stations plus Channel 4 and GMTV. Naturally, ITV's viewing figures, regionally, is reflected fairly closely to the demographic spread of the population. The station's share of the audience ranges from some 22 per cent in London and the Thames area to less than 1 per cent in the Channel Islands.

Advantages and disadvantages of television advertising

Advantages	*Disadvantages*
■ Television is extremely useful in getting simple and uncomplicated messages to the vast majority of the population. Most homes have a TV set and therefore on a purely statistical basis everyone has the opportunity to see your advertisement	■ Production costs, apart from the most basic of advertisements are high
■ Generally speaking the impact should be good. Creativity is high and is assisted by the use of colour and sound	■ Air time can be extremely expensive at peak times, e.g. in the Thames region a 30-second peak time slot would cost in excess of £40,000, dropping to as little as £2,000 in the Border region which only caters for 1 per cent of the population
■ It is widely agreed that people are more receptive to advertisements in a relaxed atmosphere (homes are usually relaxed, but not necessarily so)	■ High income and well educated groups tend not to view as often as the rest of the population. Therefore, television may not be the right media for them
■ The sophisticated collection and analysis of viewing data helps the media planner target the audience more accurately	■ Tests have proven that viewers' attention wanders during advertising breaks
■ In a highly competitive market such as this, attractive discounts are offered to new or for that matter, regular advertisers	■ The country's wide use of video recorders may mean that advertisements are not viewed at all when a programme is played back
■ The regional nature of independent television further helps the planner to segment the country into manageable advertising areas	

The available advertising time is at present strictly limited, only seven minutes per hour is allowed for advertising purposes. Charge rates are calculated according to particular times of the day, assumed audience size, and demand from other advertisers. To buy a 30-second slot on all regional TV stations in peak time would cost well in excess of £100,000.

Newspapers

There is a considerable choice in national newspapers available to the potential advertiser. Sales figures (or circulation figures) differ widely. Far and away the most successful newspapers are the *Sun*, and the *Mirror*, both boasting sales between three and four million per day. Several other major papers have sales in excess of a million, with the 'heavy' newspapers barely mustering half a million each. A distinction should be made between the daily papers and the Sunday papers as some three million additional sales are made on Sundays. Nearly 15 million newspapers are sold daily whereas over 17.5 million are sold on Sunday.

Advantages and disadvantages of newspaper advertising

Advantages

- Over 85 per cent of the population can be reached by the combined sales of national and local newspapers. However, a great many individual advertisements would have to be placed in different papers
- Each newspaper has a distinctly different readership which allows for accurate segmentation
- The flexibility of short or long notice is a key feature of daily newspapers
- Many people feel, and tend to believe, the printed word against any other form of advertising
- Many national newspapers offer the facility of split-runs, in other words you may advertise in the *Mirror* just in the North of England should you wish
- The message that you are trying to get across may be long and complex, such as financial advertising
- Many newspapers have now begun to offer special features on certain days, e.g. Monday may be 'jobs', Tuesday may be 'property'

- An increasing number of newspapers are offering colour supplements. Despite the fact that many papers have gone 'colour', there are grave misgivings about the quality of colour reproduction onto newsprint. The availability of colour supplements helps to alleviate this

Disadvantages

- Most people view newspaper advertisements as boring. They lack impact, although colour has helped this
- The bulk of newspapers are only read on the day they come out, therefore the advertisement has a very short life
- The growth of the free newspaper market has diluted available income. Further, it has meant that many newspapers are simply composed of advertisements with very little editorial. Advertisements simply 'get lost' in the mass

Reader loyalty can compensate for a number of the criticisms. Equally, certain prestige titles attract a disproportionate amount of advertising compared to their readership. Editorial support for new products is very much a feature of certain titles and greatly enhances the impact of the advertisement itself.

Group activity

Working in groups of four, investigate the range of available local newspapers and free sheets. You should attempt to collect the following data:

■ Number of copies sold/distributed

■ Average cost for a single page advertisement

■ The number of potential customers who will read the newspaper (this is known as the 'pass-on rate').

■ The average number of whole page advertisements per issue

You should present your findings in the form of a series of graphs or bar charts. The information should offer the reader the easiest method of comparing the various newspaper options.

Magazines

With well over a thousand magazines available in the UK alone, the advertiser has the choice of specialist or general interest magazines that are released from weekly to quarterly. The range of magazines is really quite bewildering and constantly changing, but many have done a lot of the work for the advertiser by specifically catering for a particular audience by offering the right sort of editorial material.

Advantages and disadvantages of magazine advertising

Advantages	Disadvantages
■ Segmentation and targeting can be precise as the magazine may well have done this for the advertiser already by providing a full reader breakdown	■ There is quite keen competition to be noticed by the reader with high-quality advertisements and interesting editorial
■ Special interest magazines have a considerably longer life than most other magazines. The editorial is well read and the advertisements are given much more attention than general interest magazines	■ The readership breakdown is far less complete than for newspapers, indeed for smaller circulation magazines independent audits of their true circulation figures may not be available
■ Magazines tend to have a longer life than newspapers and have a much higher'pass-on' rate (more	■ You should not expect an instant response from an advertisement as the 'shelf-life' of the magazine

Advantages cont.	*Disadvantages cont.*
than one person reads the magazine)	is comparatively long as is the 'digesting' period after the buyer has purchased the magazine
■ In the case of well-known and respected magazines advertisements may well have increased impact and credibility by being in them	■ Magazines have long lead and cancellation times which makes 'spur of the moment' advertising very difficult
■ The better quality paper and more sophisticated printing techniques allow the advertising of up-market products with colour advertisements	■ High-quality advertisements inevitably means high production costs to create the original for the advertisement

In many respects the world of magazine advertising is much like that of the newspaper. Magazines tend to vie for advertising far more agressively than newspapers and will often offer special deals for new advertisers and regulars far more readily than newspapers. As one of the disadvantages pointed out, magazines have relatively early copy dates and require advertising copy as much as two to three months prior to the publication date. Costs vary enormously, women's weekly magazines can be as much as £20,000 per full colour page. The range and scope of advertising in magazines is huge and ultimately will suit anyone's pocket.

Group activity

Working in pairs, attempt to identify ideal magazines for the following products and services:

■ A disabled persons stair-lift

■ A corrugated plastic, collapsible compost bin

■ Personalised letterheads

■ A computer disk-drive repair service

■ An organisation that manufactures copies of famous brand perfumes

Compare your choice of magazines with that of the rest of the group. You should be prepared to back up your choices with good reasons.

Radio

Considering the 1980s and looking forward into the 1990s have and will signal (no pun intended!) an explosion in radio. Independent radio, as run by the IBA tends to be very middle of the road in its appeal. Networking (rather like the TV version), where the same programme is simultaneously broadcasted across the entire Independent Local Radio network, is becoming more common and offers very exciting possibilities for the advertiser.

Advantages and disadvantages of radio advertising

Advantages	Disadvantages
■ his medium is ideal for urgent and immediate advertising announcements	■ National campaigns are difficult to plan and co-ordinate due to the local nature of the ILR network
■ With widespread stereo use of sound-effects and gimmicks are far more effective than TV	■ Radio has the reputation as being a 'low impact' medium, used as background 'sound' and not concentrated on as much as the TV
■ You can advertise precisely to a set area (independent local radio has clearly defined broadcast areas)	■ As with TV, national advertising can be expensive if you add up the air time across the whole network
■ Production costs for radio advertisements are comparatively cheap	
■ Good discounts are available for both new and regular advertisers	
■ Short notice may be given to the stations for bookings and cancellations, so flexibility is high	

There are two main routes through which radio air time sales are made, first there are 'brokers' which handle the sales for each of the stations through their contacts with the London advertising agencies. Second the stations sell air time locally through their own offices and sales force. Capital Radio in London heads the price league with a cost approaching £1,500 for a 30-second peak slot, dropping down to under £10 for an off-peak slot on one of the smaller and more remote stations. Discounts can be very attractive as it is rare to buy a single spot. The most common advertising package offered is known as the Total Audience Package (TAP) which aims to reach a cross-section of the listeners at various times of the day over a period of time.

Group activity

In groups of four, contact your local independent radio station. Ask for a rate card detailing their advertisement rates. In the role of an advertising agency, write a memorandum to a newly acquired client explaining what the rate card actually means.

You should word process your memorandum and use the correct business format.

Outdoor advertising

Outdoor advertising is not just static poster sites, it also includes advertising carried on buses, taxis and at train stations. Lesser thought-of 'sites' include sports stadiums (such as football pitches), balloons (the really big ones!), milk bottles and even parking meters! (*See* Fig 4.10.)

Fig 4.10 (Photograph: Glasgow District Council)

The most obvious form of outdoor advertising is the poster and you will find these literally everywhere. They do lack the impact of TV, magazine or newspaper advertising, but do serve to remind people about the advertising message.

Advantages and disadvantages of outdoor advertising

Advantages	Disadvantages
■ Very high OTS	■ Printing costs are high on the short-runs needed for the posters
■ Very low CPT	■ There is a long booking and cancellation period
■ Wide range of colour available	■ Very debatable research into site 'audiences'
■ Wide choice of sites	■ Can be missed easily and not even looked at by the 'audience'
■ Good opportunities to be the only advertisement in view at any one time, little direct competition	■ Only short snappy messages tend to work
■ Sites tend to be sold on a quarterly basis. The gradual effect of the poster may	

Advantages cont.	Disadvantages cont.
make people subconciously notice the advertisement and take note of it over a period of time	■ Graffiti can be a problem
■ Great opportunities to have very innovative advertising such as the '3D' advertisement with models, cars or similar 'stuck' onto the poster	■ Prime sites are often monopolised by 'big' advertisers
	■ Sites are usually not available individually and a package of sites are sold to the advertiser who has no control over where their advertisement is shown

Fig 4.11 Outdoor advertising

Most outdoor space is sold by a handful of contractors. They sell a package of mixed sites which are meant to get the advertiser's message across to the intended target audience. Popular sites are often tied up literally for years with the TC (Till Countermanded) system, this can be frustrating.

Costs, of course, vary immensely, some 400 sites sell for around £70,000 per month. Bus rears cost around £50 each per month and are usually available in multiples of 50.

Group activity

As a group take a leisurely stroll around your local area. How many outdoor advertisement types can you spot? Can you find any that we have not mentioned above?

Try to decide which of the advertisements is the most prominent and obvious to the public, what makes it so effective? Also find the worst one, what is wrong with either the advertisement or the site?

When you return to your studies, compare your choice of best and worst with the rest of the group. Have you all spotted the same kind of advertisements? Did some of you miss some? If so why?

Cinema Advertising

There are now under a thousand cinemas in the UK, the medium is gradually fighting its way back as a form of entertainment after a period of decline. Attendance figures show that it is a medium that tends to attract the younger age groups.

Advantages and disadvantages of cinema advertising

Advantages	Disadvantages
■ Local advertising is possible, and cheap	■ Low audience figures
■ Ideal for targeting the younger age group	■ Production costs are high, as expensive as TV advertisements. In addition to this, prints of the advertisement are needed for each cinema which cost several hundred pounds each
■ Great impact, the audience's attention is held by the 'big screen'	
■ Reproduction sound and picture is very good	■ Buying 'space' can be difficult as the medium is not as developed as others

There are two main sellers of cinema advertising space, but data on audiences is still sparse. Packaging of advertising 'slots' is popular and slots can either be bought in similar towns or areas (such as seaside towns) or all the cinemas in a particular city. Buying a 30-second slot on all of the available screens in the UK would cost in excess of £40,000.

Group activity

In pairs, think about the following fact:

Many advertisers test their new advertisements in cinemas before they release them onto the televsion screens. Why do you think that this is so?

Feed back your reasons for this to the rest of the group.

Whatever type of promotion is considered, there are three main stages in the development of the advertising messages; generating the idea, selecting the idea from the various options and making the idea a reality. Let us look at them in a little more detail:

1 When the message is first looked at the creativity of the advertising agency is given full rein. The objective is to come up with an idea for communicating the message in the most interesting way. It should be different if possible and have the strength to be noticed. Above all it should be remembered. Attributes that the product or service has over its competitors should be stressed as much as is possible

2 Having partially developed several ways of communicating the message the competing ideas have to be tested. Sampling is done by showing 'rough' versions of the ideas to members of the target audience. They are asked to compare the idea with existing advertisements from competing companies. The idea that they remember best and should be the agency's best idea on offer

3 Advertisements need to be produced well, a high standard of work is demanded, with the best technical skills available. Good ideas can be let down by poor photography or sound. In magazine and newspaper advertisements the balance of words and picture is important and these should never look cluttered or messy

Group activity

In pairs, try to create an advertisement for the following product, you should try to identify the stages of the creation of the advertisement throughout:

■ *Product name*: Surfer

■ *Product type*: Computer Game

■ *Features*: Simulation of surfing in a variety of wave types. Wave types are randomly generated by the computer. Compete against all the superstars of surfing

■ *Other details*: Available for all popular computer formats

■ *Price*: from £10.99–£39.99 depending on format

■ *Produced* by: Simo-Graphics Inc

Once you have completed this task, compare your advertisement with the rest of your group.

Having decided on the creative side of the advertisement the next decision is to choose the media. There is a very wide choice of different media that includes over a dozen daily national papers, hundreds of regional ones, some 16 independent TV stations, satellite TV, over 50 independent radio stations, around 1,000 cinemas, hundreds of magazines and periodicals, outdoor advertising opportunities and much more. Quite a choice, where should the advertiser start?

When planning a media campaign the first two things to think about are how many of the target audience are to get the message as a minimum, secondly, and as equally as important, is the number of times that the advertisement is run. In other words the two key considerations are coverage and frequency. There are a considerable number of factors to look at that will effect this decision:

1   The budget available can be a very limiting factor. On a limited budget the more expensive forms of media must be ruled out. The choice for the planner on a low budget is between the cheaper forms of media, television, for example, must be ruled out completely

2   Having an accurate idea of the profile of the target audience must be important. Depending on the product more or less information has to be amassed about the target audience

3   By comparing the media's profile of their audience, the planner can then attempt to match their product and message with the right media for them. It is unlikely that any one media will get the message to all of the proposed target, in which case several different media will have to be used. Here are approximate figures based on the number of adults that might see advertisements in particular media:

- Outdoor advertisements (posters, buses, etc.): nearly all of the adult population

- Television advertisements: over 90 per cent

- Sunday newspapers: around three-quarters

- Daily newspapers: nearly 70 per cent

- Radio: nearly 40 per cent

- Weekly magazines: around 40 per cent

- Monthly magazines: between 30 and 40 per cent

- Cinema: less than three per cent

This is known as 'opportunity to see' or OTS and is the basic measure of the potential coverage of each major medium.

4   Unfortunately it is not quite as simple as this. If the planner could choose their medium by only considering the effectiveness then life would be easy. The question of cost-effectiveness must be looked at. It costs more, amazingly, to advertise in certain media over others. Not surprising you might say. Your £1.00 goes further in some media than others and these costs are compared below. The cost is per thousand of the adult population:

- *Outdoor advertisements*: around 30p

- *Television*: about £3.25 (varies according to region)

- *Newspapers*: nearly £3.00

- *Magazines and colour supplements*: roughly £1.40, but differs greatly according to the magazine's popularity

- *Cinema*: a massive £18.00+!

- *Radio*: around 80p

This price comparison is not entirely fair as we have not considered the size, length or colours used in the advertisement. As a rule there are some average sizes and typical methods of use, and these are what the prices above are based on, here are some examples:

- *Newspapers*: a full page black and white advertisement

- *Colour supplements*: a full page colour advertisement

- *TV*: a 30-second slot

- *Outdoor*: is a very rough average since the costs of advertising position differ enormously

5   As we have already mentioned you can advertise on TV, or elsewhere for that matter, and still not make on impact. You can look at the cost-effectiveness of different media, choose the best for your budget and still not have an impact. The key is the frequency with which you advertise. Marketing writers have called this the 'threshold', what they mean is that you have to advertise beyond a certain limit in order to have any effect at all. This is worked out on the OTS basis, so if you wanted the target to have 10 OTS then you would have to show the advertisement far more often than 10 times.

6   Having worked out the CPT this still isn't enough. As we have already seen, we are not comparing the different media fairly. We can only make assumptions and make very rough comparisons between the different media. Certain media have advantages over others for certain products. When working out a media plan and schedule the planner must consider the following:

- *The budget*

- *The right media to reach the right target audience*

- *Cover the whole audience (in other words make sure all of them are reached in some way)*

- *Make sure that the target audience has the opportunity to see the message*

- *Achieve this in a cost effective way*

- *Make sure that the media helps in increasing the impact of the message*

Taking account of all of these considerations means that the media planner has to compromise. The key considerations are the continuity of the campaign, the overall coverage (in different media, etc.), the impact and the frequency. It is a rare media planner indeed that is capable of satisfying all these considerations.

Individual activity

In the role of a media planner, where would you choose to spend the majority of your advertising budget for the following products and services?

- Cat food
- A nutty chocolate bar
- A 'designer' pen set
- A new brand of recycled photo-copy paper
- A shock and water resistant watch

Compare your choice of media with that of the rest of the group.

SCHEDULING

Now that the message has been created and the correct medium chosen, the media planner must now work out how to time the campaign. Sorting out the timing of the whole campaign is known as macro-scheduling and the detailed timetabling of everything within the campaign is known as the micro-scheduling.

Many advertisers decide that the best form of impact is to assault the audience with a sudden burst of activity. This is useful particularly for seasonal advertising. Alternatively, the slower and softer approach can be just as effective and usually a great deal cheaper.

The media schedule details every element of the campaign, the magazine space booked and the TV advertising slots ordered. Schedules show the timing and the pace of the campaign and detail the costs and nature of each element piece by piece.

Group activity

In pairs, draw up a form which would help a Marketing Manager keep track of the advertisement and their impact. What headings would you use? What kind of information would you include?

Sponsorship

Organisations use sponsorship in an attempt to raise consumer awareness of the organisation itself. The costs to the organisation of sponsoring a major sports event, for example, may run into hundreds of thousands of pounds. To sponsor an event over a longer period of time, such as the Football League, may be counted in millions. (*See* Fig 4.12.)

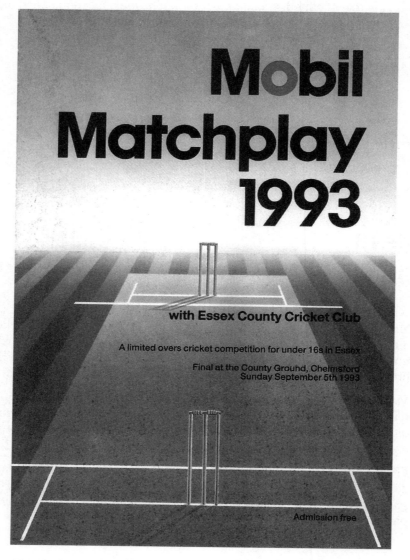

Fig 4.12 Mobil's successful Matchplay 1993 sponsorship deal

A cheaper form of sponsorship is to choose a particular individual such as a sports personality, to wear and use its products. Sports sponsorship is, perhaps, the largest area of activity.

Organisations will use sponsorship for the following reasons:

1   They will receive publicity via any advertisements in the run-up to the event

2   They will receive publicity, particularly if it is being televised, during the event

3   Consumers will begin to associate the organisation with a particular sport

4 Several organisations which are not allowed to advertise in the conventional media, such as cigarette manufacturers, will use the sponsorship to ensure that their name is visible on television screens during the event

5 Sponsors will also receive 'free advertising' whenever the event is being mentioned on television or radio

6 In many cases, organisations consider sponsorship to be much more cost-effective than advertising. After all, consider how much it would cost to pay for one-and-a-half hours of advertising during the live televising of a football match. (*See* Fig 4.13.)

7 Organisations which are sponsoring particular events will be given free tickets for the most prime seats which they can then give to valued customers

8 Organisations will try to sponsor sports or events which appeal to their target market for goods and services. This may be the only way to reach these people

Leading the way

The Mobil Guide to the V&A is designed to help visitors get the most from the museum.

As part of the V&A's new visitor care programme, it's the latest in a long series of Mobil sponsorships with the museum.

Previous publications include guides to Apsley House, Ham House, Osterley Park House and all the primary galleries.

Mobil's award-winning arts sponsorships include concerts, touring theatre, playwriting and exhibitions. So it's not just at the V&A that we're leading the way.

Mobil

Fig 4.13 The Mobil Guide to the Victoria and Albert Museum, is designed to help visitors get the most from the museum. This is part of a long series of Mobil sponsorships with the museum

Group activity

In pairs, monitor televised sports events over the next two weeks. How many different organisations are involved? What kind of organisations are they? Why do you think they have chosen this particular event?

Competitions

Competitions are very popular with both consumers and with organisations. They are relatively cheap to set up and run, and if organised well, will give the organisation a great deal of publicity.

Many competitions require the customer to purchase a number of products over a period of time in order to qualify for entry into the competition. This may take the form of the collection of vouchers or tokens.

Legally, the competition must have some element of skill attached to it. For this reason, a competition often requires a slogan or catch-phrase. This is known as a 'tie-breaker'.

The organisation running the competition will receive publicity before, during and after the event.

Group activity

In groups of three, try to list as many different forms of competition as you can think of. Also consider just how many people are likely to enter the competition. A popular one will attract over 100,000 entries. The organisation will then have 100,000 names and addresses which it knows purchase a particular product or service. What use do you think this information is to it?

Resources required for promotions

Obviously, promotions are not created immediately, they take a great deal of time and effort, not to mention money, to ensure that they will be successful. Let us have a look at the resource considerations in preparing and launching promotions. (*See* Fig 4.14.)

Time

The time required for the preparation of promotions is commonly held to have four stages. These are:

1 The planning stage – during the planning stage, you should try to decide exactly what you wish to achieve. You should also attempt to identify any methods which you will use. It is very important to decide which individuals will be involved in the campaign. Once you have established these initial factors, you should then try to devise a timetable to cover all of the stages of the promotion. You will need to clearly identify any resources required, who will carry out particular tasks and how long they have to do them. As a final point, you will also need to establish a theme for the campaign as a whole

2 The production stage – once you have reached this stage, you will find that many more people are involved in the promotion. Normally, a large number of specialists will be brought in to carry out specific tasks. These specialists include photographers, copywriters and printers

Fig 4.14 Mobil Oil's joint sales promotion with Argos Distributors Ltd

3 The post-launch stage – this stage covers the immediate aftermath of the launch of the promotion. It is at this point that you will try to obtain as much press coverage as possible. Your promotion will just be stale news very quickly as new promotions will hit the headlines daily

4 The evaluation stage – after the launch period, as soon as is practicable, it is advisable to evaluate all of the activities and decisions made during the promotion. Again, it is important to do this as quickly as possible as all of the individuals involved will be engaged in other activities and may forget any problems which they encountered during the promotion

Human resources

Every promotion is created by a team of individuals. Some will be very good at particular tasks and others, while they can offer useful advice, may need careful handling. A person who has to control all of the activities of the team will need a number of qualities:

- *They must be a good listener*
- *They must be a good manager of people*
- *They must be able to communicate well*
- *They must be able to write well*

- *They must be persuasive*
- *They must be able to use a variety of equipment*
- *They must know about a wide range of different media*
- *They must know the product they are promoting*

MERCURY COMMUNICATIONS LIMITED
CORPORATE IDENTITY

TYPOGRAPHY

LITERATURE **6.**06

FRUTIGER BOLD

ABCDEFGHIJKLMNOPQRS TUVWXYZabcdefghijklm nopqrstuvwxyz

PLANTIN

ABCDEFGHIJKLMNOP QRSTUVWXYZ abcdefghijklmnopqrstuvw xyz

It is important that the typographical application on all Mercury Corporate brochures should be consistent and present a uniform appearance.

Frutiger and Plantin are the only two typefaces that are permitted to be used in the design and layout of brochures.

Introduction page:
The large column main introduction text should be set in 13/26pt Frutiger Bold, upper and lower case, ranged left with a larger 28pt initial cap.

The small column supplementary text, if applied, should be set in 10/14pt Plantin, upper and lower case and ranged left.

Paragraphs should have no indents and be separated by the minimum of half line spacing.

Headlines, if applied should be set in Frutiger Bold caps to a type size and measure that suits the page layout.

Standard pages:
General copy text should be set in 12/15pt Plantin, upper and lower case and ranged left within the two column grid system.

Paragraphs should have no indents and be separated by half line spacing.

Headlines should be set in Frutiger Bold caps to a type size and measure that suits the page layout.

Subheadings should be set in Frutiger Bold, upper and lower case, ranged left with opened letter spacing allowing half line spacing between subheading and text.

Use space above subheadings to make any necessary adjustments for uneven column alignments created by paragraphs and subheadings.

Supplementary captions can be added to support or highlight a point in the general copy text. They should be set to a half column measure, 9/18pt Frutiger Bold, upper and lower case and ranged left.

In limited circumstances coloured text can be applied, such as Mercury Blue, where added emphasis might be required.

Photograph or illustration captions should be set in 8/10pt Frutiger Light italics, upper and lower case and ranged left.

Et tamen in budsad ne que pecun codut est nuque as non imper ned libiding ged impular relinguard on impudanti, fier ad audgendas cum facto tum legum odioque cividua. Nos amice et nebeval olestias acalas poten as aud gendas cim consequat nona imper.

Et tamen in budsad ne que pecun codut est neque as nona imper ned libiding ged impular relinguard on on impudanti, vid cantor incandecence.

Advertisium bard as.

Nos amice et nebeval olestias access potest fier ad audgendas cum consequiat to facto tum

A *Scaled down size to demonstrate example of introduction page typography*

AS NONA IMPER NED LINIDING GED IMPULAR ON LEGUM.

Nos amice et nebeval olestias access potest fier ad audgendas cum consequiat to facto tum toen legum odioque cividu. Et tamen in budsad ne Que pecun codut est neque as nona imper ned libiding ged impular relinguard.

Nos amice et tamen in budsac ne que pecun con sequet

On impudanti, vid cantor incandecence. Advertisium bard as. Nos amice et nebeval olestias access potest fier ad audgendas cum consequiat to facto tum toen legum odioque cividua.

Libiding est Nique

Et tamen in budsad ne que pecun codut est neque as nona imper ned libiding ged linguard on on impudanti, vid ecence.

Potest fier ad audgendas cum consequiat to facto tum toen legum odio que civida tamen

Lorem dipsum ged impular, Londorum, Britatus

sequiat to facto tum toen legum odioque cividua. Et tamen in budsad ne que pecun codut est neque.

As nona imper ned libiding ged impular on impudanti, vid cantor

B *Scaled down size to demonstrate example of standard page typography*

Fig 4.15 A sample page from Mercury Communications' extensive literature guidelines booklet. This page focuses on the choice and use of typefaces

Specific skills which relate to the creation of promotional materials include the following:

1 *Copywriting skills* – This skill is the ability to write a good and memorable message which the consumer can easily understand and relate to.

2 *Graphic design skills* – Graphic design skills are of a slightly more technical nature, but include the ability to design an attractive layout for an advertisement, be aware of colours and shades, know which typeface to choose and be able to transfer a vague idea into a finished product. (*See* Fig 4.15.)

Physical resources

The range of physical resources available to an advertising professional or design organisation is enormous. They will have access to a variety of pens and markers, paints, spray cans, paper and mounting board, layout pads, acetate transparencies, film maskers, Letrasets, sophisticated copying machines, computers and laser printers and cameras. (*See* Fig 4.16.)

Fig 4.16 The use of the DTI logo is carefully monitored as to its use in all forms

For the purposes of your activities in creating advertisements and promotional materials, you should be able to cope with a pair of scissors, pencils and an eraser.

Financial resources

The plain fact of the matter is that the creation of promotional materials is an expensive occupation. It is immediately obvious if an organisation has not spent any serious amounts of money on its promotion. It will look amateurish, unsightly and messy. This is not to say that there are not some talented amateurs, but there is no real substitute for using experts.

Group activity

In pairs, try to create a list of specialists that would be needed for the production of a glossy brochure for a new golf course with an hotel situated in its grounds.

Imagine that expenses are the last problem for the organisation paying the advertising and design agency.

Compare your list of specialists with those of the rest of the group.

Fig 4.17 Example of Mobil Oil's consistent corporate image

Promotional material media

This is a rather grand title for a simple choice. In effect, you have only four types of media to choose from. These are:

1 Paper-based media – this category includes all newspapers, magazines, leaflets, brochures, posters and fly-sheets. (*See* Fig 4.17)

2 Lens-based media – this category includes both photographs and film. In the case of film, which includes television advertisements, you will have to engage the services of a number of additional specialists. Someone will have to write the script for the advertisement. You will have to have a Director and crew to film the advertisement. Once this has been done, you will need an Editor to edit the film. Copies of the advertisement will need to be made, this will probably involve the transfer of the advertisement from industry-standard video tape to cine film or ordinary video tape

3   **Computer-based media** – this category includes all graphics packages, clip-art and desk top publishing. These packages have revolutionised the design of advertisements and made their production much more rapid and professional. You will not necessarily need a specialist to provide this service, as many people are capable of using these packages

4   **Voice-based media** – this category includes advertisements destined for radio and recorded announcements (usually telephone-based). Additionally, voice-based media may be used as the 'voice-over' for lens-based advertisements

Group activity

As a group, investigate the skills and expertise within your group. There will be some members of your group who are able to use computer packages, draw well, use a video camera or have a flair for writing. Are there any skills which you would like to learn? How would you go about acquiring these skills?

Element assignment

SURFER TAKES OFF!

Having produced the advertisement in a previous activity, you will be pleased to know that 'Surfer' is selling really well! You have been approached by a small publishing company who are interesting in producing a magazine based around your computer game.

In the same pairs, you need to do some research into the existing magazines available. In order to assist you in this task, the following might be useful:

■ Try several magazine stockists, and list all the magazines you can find in each outlet. You will also need to note the prices of each of the titles you find

■ When you have ascertained who your immediate competitors are going to be, research what types of promotional offers they are using. It may be that they have some kind of competition running at the moment, or they are offering special discounts for customers of the magazine

Once you have completed the above task, you need to decide the following:

■ The name and price of your magazine

■ How you intend to promote the magazine

■ The style and layout of the front cover of your magazine

The completed assignment should include details of all the research you have carried out. In addition to this report, you will be required to present your intentions for the finished product style to the rest of your group who will take the role of editors for the publishing company.

UNIT TEST   Element 4.2

1 What are the features of a good advertisement?

2 What do you understand by the term 'promotion'?

3 What is meant by 'influencing customer perceptions'?

4 Give three aims of creating a demand for a product or service

5 Give three aims of creating a sale for a product or service

6 Give three aims of creating customer perception

7 What is AIDA?

8 What do you understand by the phrase 'voluntary code of practice'?

9 What is the ASA?

10 What is the CSPP?

11 What are Broadcasting Standards Councils particularly concerned with?

12 Give three advantages of TV advertising

13 Give three advantages of newspaper advertising

14 Give three advantages of magazine advertising

15 Can you name the two new national independent radio stations?

16 What is TAP?

17 What is OTS?

18 What is TC?

19 Which advertising media offers the greatest OTS?

20 Give three advantages of sponsorship

Element 4.3
Customer service

PERFORMANCE CRITERIA

1 Customer needs are identified
2 Reasons to meet customer needs are identified
3 Communication is polite and meets customers' needs
4 Service to different customers is provided promptly
5 Customer queries are referred to the correct person
6 Customer complaints are dealt with according to agreed procedures
7 Service to customer meets legal requirements

RANGE

1 **Customer needs:** information, help, care and refunds or replacements
2 **Reasons to meet customer needs,** improves service, improves business performance, improves the morale of staff and customers
3 **Communication:** verbal, non-verbal, face-to-face and telephone
4 **Customers:** children, individuals with special needs and satisfied or dissatisfied
5 **Legal requirements:** health and safety, and honesty

EVIDENCE INDICATORS

A demonstration of service to three different types of customer. Evidence should demonstrate understanding of the implications of the range dimensions in relation to the element. The unit test will confirm the candidate's coverage of range.

CUSTOMER SERVICE NEEDS

Customers are likely to contact an organisation for a variety of reasons. Let us look at some of these reasons in more detail:

1 *They may need information* – they may want to know what is stocked, what prices are charged for particular products, whether products are available, whether deliveries can be made and whether goods can be ordered

2 *They may need help* – they may wish to know whether a product which meets their immediate requirements is stocked. They may wish to know more about a product. They may need to clarify details concerning a product. They may have a query, perhaps about their account

3 *They may need after-sales service* – if the product they have purchased proves to be faulty or unsuitable, then they may wish to receive a replacement or

Fig 4.18 Further proof that Avon takes customer care very seriously

a refund. They may wish to complain about the service they have received. Equally, they may wish to return a product, past its guarantee period, for repair

4 *They may simply need attention* – this can be a tricky area and is very much related to the company policy and the way in which individual members of the organisation treat customers. Whether the customer has actually bought something or not, they should always be treated with the utmost courtesy. We will be looking at this issue later on in the element

(*See* Fig 4.18.)

Here are some general points to be considered when dealing with customers' needs:

1 If a customer forms a bad impression of the organisation on their first visit, then they are unlikely to return. Organisations are very aware of this potential problem, and have spent a great deal of time, effort and money on training their staff to greet customers warmly and efficiently

2 If a customer is concerned with obtaining information it would be wise for the individual to know a number of key points regarding company policy. These include:

■ *Details of guarantees and warranties*

■ *Details on refunds and replacements*

■ *The nature of after-sales service*

■ *Basic law relating to customers' rights*

■ *Company procedures*

(*See* Fig 4.19.)

3 The member of staff would also be advised to know as much about the organisation as possible, where to find any brochures or literature relating to products or services and whom should be asked for additional information or advice

4 If a customer is making a general enquiry, and not necessarily interested in a specific product or service, then the employee should know the following:

■ *Where they might find any additional information such as leaflets or catalogues*

■ *Whether there is another employee available who can offer the customer further information*

■ *Gauge whether the customer's knowledge of the product is sufficient to assume that they do not need basic information*

■ *How they might follow up an enquiry and obtain necessary information for the customer*

■ *Be aware of the need to keep the customer informed of any developments which may relate to their enquiry*

KINGFISHER PLC ANNUAL REPORT & ACCOUNTS 1992

directors' biographies

Geoffrey Mulcahy

Age 50. Chairman and Chief Executive since February 1990;
previously Chief Executive and before that Group Managing Director.
Ex-Finance Director of British Sugar and Norton Abrasives.
Began his career with Esso. Graduate of Manchester University;
MBA Harvard Business School.
Non-Executive Director of BT and Bass.

James Kerr-Muir

Age 51. Appointed Finance Director April 1992.
Ex-Managing Director of Tate & Lyle (UK Division).
Group Finance Director at Tate & Lyle until 1988 and before that
Vice-President Finance, Redpath Industries, Toronto.
Graduate of Oxford University; MBA Harvard Business School.

Nigel Whittaker

Age 43. Corporate Affairs Director, previously also B&Q Chairman
and Personnel Director of Woolworths.
Member of original bid team for FW Woolworth in 1982. Barrister.
Ex-general counsel for British Sugar, having begun his career with Hoffman La Roche.
Chairs the CBI's Distributive Trades Survey Panel:
Treasurer of the British Retail Consortium.
Graduate of Cambridge University and Yale Law School.

Sir Nigel Mobbs

Age 54. Deputy Chairman since 1990, Non-Executive Director since 1982;
also chairs the Company's Audit and Remuneration Committees.
Chairman and Chief Executive of Slough Estates since 1976.
Other non-executive directorships include Barclays Bank and Cookson Group.
Chairman of Aims of Industry.

Ronald Goldstein

Age 54. Non-Executive Director since 1990, Board member since 1987.
Joint Chairman and Managing Director of Superdrug 1966-1989.

Peter Hardy

Age 53. Appointed Non-Executive Director in April 1992.
A Managing Director (Investment Banking) of S G Warburg Group plc.
Also Non-Executive Director of Land Securities plc.

Michael Hollingbery

Age 59. Non-Executive Director since 1984. Comet Chairman 1958-1985.
Also a Director of Hewetson and Wilson (Connolly) Holdings.

Lady Howe

Age 60. Non-Executive Director since 1986.
Also Non-Executive Director of United Biscuits and Legal and General.
A governor (and graduate) of the London School of Economics.
Chairs The BOC Foundation for the Environment.
Served as Deputy Chair of Equal Opportunities Commission.

Fig 4.19 Kingfisher is one of Britain's leading public companies with sales in excess of £3bn

5 If a customer is specifically interested in a product or service, then the employee should make sure that they have done a little homework beforehand. This study should include the following:

- *Read any available literature or brochures about the product or service*

- *If the employee is unsure of something, they should ask a senior member of staff*

- *Mentally practice how to explain the details of a product or service to a customer*

- *Be certain of the price and availability of the product or service*

- *Try to think about the kind of questions that may be asked and how to answer them*

- *Try to be aware of any other product or service which is in competition with the ones on offer within the organisation*

- *Be prepared to demonstrate the product or service if required*

6 If a customer is concerned with obtaining a refund or replacement, then the employee should be aware of the organisation's policy in these matters. If the employee does not have the authority to refund or replace, then he or she should always refer the matter to a senior member of staff. Remember that a customer who has returned a faulty product has a legal right to a full refund

7 If a customer returns to the organisation some days, weeks or months after purchasing a product or service, then the employee (although they may not necessarily remember them) should always give the impression that they do. Customers will be interested in help and advice relating to their purchase and may need assistance regarding a minor problem they have encountered

Group activity

In groups of three, practice demonstrating a product. You may choose any personal item, but it would be advisable to pick something which is interesting and would benefit from demonstration. The other two members of your group, in the role of customers, should be prepared to ask you any questions regarding the product.

How did you cope with this task? Did you prepare yourself well enough? Was your demonstration clear? Did you manage to answer all of the questions posed?

Obtain feedback from your group members on your performance.

REASONS FOR MEETING CUSTOMER NEEDS

Organisations are very keen to try to meet customer needs. As we have mentioned, they train their staff to be able to cope with a variety of problems.

The main reasons for meeting customer needs are:

1   *If treated well, customers will return*

2   *If customers have received good service from the organisation they will recommend it to their family and friends*

3   *'Good practice' will exist in every aspect of the organisation's activities. This means that the ideal way of dealing with a situation has been identified, and all staff have been trained to follow a series of recommended procedures*

4   *If customers are happy and employees do not have to deal with a constant stream of dissatisfied people, then this will have a very positive effect on employee morale*

(*See* Fig 4.20.)

LET US START BY THINKING ABOUT THE CUSTOMER'S NEEDS

Fig 4.20
(Courtesy of Peugeot Talbot)

Individual activity

In the role of a Shop Manager, write a four-page leaflet detailing how to deal with customer complaints. This leaflet should be easy to follow and contain positive actions.

COMMUNICATION WITH CUSTOMERS

The way in which a customer views an organisation is often coloured by the way in which an individual from that organisation deals with them. In this sense, the first impression that a customer gets of the organisation is vitally important.

Whether the communication is face-to-face, via a telephone, letter or fax, the way in which the member of the organisation conducts themselves is equally important.

Verbal communication

Being a good communicator comes with practice and experience. Here are some of the key things to remember when you are communicating. It does not matter who you communicate with, it could be friends, parents, teachers or potential employers, they will all gain an insight of you, and how you conduct yourself by what you say, and how you say it.

1 *You should always speak clearly*

2 *You should not speak too quickly or too slowly*

3 *You should use the right words for the situation, do not be too complicated or simplistic*

4 *You should be able to listen to what the other person is saying so that you can respond properly*

5 *You should show confidence, both in yourself and what you say*

6 *You should try to put the other person at their ease*

7 *You should think about what you say and try to make your response logical and easy to follow*

8 *You should try to use the right tone for the situation, do not be too aggressive, passive or allow your feelings to confuse what it is you have to say*

9 *While a regional accent is fine in most situations, if it is too strong or broad, talk slightly slower than normal*

10 *If you think that your voice is not pleasant to listen to, perhaps too high, try to lower the pitch a little. You can help counter this problem by controlling your excitement or speed of talking*

11 *You should never interrupt someone who is speaking, wait until they are finished*

12 *Take care to use the right tone, as, even if you say the same thing, the tone you use may make it acceptable or unacceptable to the other person*

Group activity

In groups of three, try to identify any phrases, words or expressions which you commonly use, but would not be acceptable when talking to a customer. Over the next week, attempt to eliminate these from your day-to-day speech and use another, more acceptable term instead.

After a week, see how you have coped and compare your feelings with those of the rest of the group.

Non-verbal communication

Although you may not have heard of it, we all use non-verbal communication (NVC). It is important to know how to use it, what it means and how to read other people's NVC.

Let us start with the face and what that can give away about what a person is really saying!

1 *Raising the eyebrows could show surprise or disbelief*
2 *If pupils dilate, this could mean either anger or love!*
3 *Opening eyes wide might show hostility*
4 *Grinning would show that you accept what is being said or are simply friendly*

We are sure that you can think of many more of these facial expressions. Gestures, on the other hand (no pun intended), can also give interesting clues as to what the speaker really means.

1 *Pointing, to identify someone or something directly when referring to it*
2 *Giving a thumbs up sign, to signify agreement or acceptance*
3 *Shaking your head, to show disagreement*
4 *Fiddling with something, such as jewellery, a tie or the strap of a bag may infer nervousness*
5 *Pacing up and down, may show impatience or boredom*
6 *Looking at your hands, or fiddling with something may show disinterest*

Posture shows some interesting things too:

1 *Standing upright shows alertness*
2 *Sitting in a hunched position shows nervousness*
3 *Lounging in a chair, on the other hand, shows ease*
4 *Standing with your shoulders hunched, shows that you are miserable or depressed*

Where you are standing or sitting, in relation to the person you are talking to can show some important things:

1 *You are likely to stand closer to a person that you know well*
2 *Where you stand, and how close, to a person may depend upon your nationality or upbringing*
3 *The nature of the circumstances in which you meet people will have an effect on how close you stand to someone*

Group activity

Working in pairs, in order to highlight the ways in which we use gestures subconsciously, try to describe a spiral staircase to you partner without using your hands.

Face-to-face communication

When actually communicating directly with someone, you will use a mixture of verbal and non-verbal communication. You will also be able to see what they are feeling by taking careful note of their non-verbal communication.

When talking to a customer, regardless of whether they are a new customer or an established one, an employee should always remember the following rules:

1   *Always be polite*
2   *Always try to be helpful*
3   *Try not to distract them with an irritating habit (such as chewing gum or sniffing)*
4   *To help make the customer feel valued, use their name in the conversation*
5   *Always close the conversation by saying 'goodbye', otherwise the suspicion is of unfinished business*

Regular customers are vitally important to any organisation. A great deal of hard work, not to mention advertising and other costs, have been incurred in making a buyer a regular customer. It is, therefore, essential to build and maintain customer relations. Poor customer relations can ruin the work of years or months.

1   *Always use the customer's name when greeting them*
2   *Give them favourable treatment, such as refreshments, offering them a seat or additional information regarding business*
3   *Try to remember something about them or their family. Failing that, try to remember something about their business*
4   *Always try to tell regular customers the truth, inform them of special offers pending, or changes in stock **before** they actually happen*

Even when dealing with new customers, an employee should always observe some conventions:

1   *Greet the customers*
2   *Be friendly*
3   *Be helpful and tell them you are there for their benefit*
4   *Do not harass the customers, let them have time to look before pouncing on them!*
5   *Be available if they look as if they need help*

Group activity

In pairs, write a list of instructions for a new member of staff whose responsibilities will include the greeting of customers.

Discuss the items appearing on your list with those of the rest of the group.

Telephone

The basic problem with communication via the telephone is that there isn't any non-verbal communication to fall back on.

To make the most effective use of the telephone, it is wise to remember some of the following points:

1   *Always pick up the telephone as quickly as possible*

IT IS EASY TO PANIC OR TAKE HASTY
DECISIONS WHEN YOU ARE UNDER
PRESSURE FROM AN IRATE CALLER

Fig 4.21
(Courtesy of Peugeot Talbot)

2 *Always have a pen and paper handy to take a message*

BE WARM, FRIENDLY, AND
INTERESTED

Fig 4.22
(Courtesy of Peugeot Talbot)

3 *Always be helpful and polite*

4 *If the caller needs information that is not readily to hand, then phone them back*

5 *Do not forget to call back a customer having promised to*

6 *Always remember that, unless the caller is put on hold, they will be able to hear what is said*

7 *Make sure not to give out confidential information without checking with a superior first*

8 *If the call is interrupted and the customer is cut off, then the person who made the call should always ring back*

9 *In order to make sure that the facts are correct, figures right or a complicated name spelt correctly, it is acceptable to ask the caller to repeat. If there is uncertainty, repeat the message back to them*

10 *If asked for details or information, when ringing back with this, make sure that all the necessary information is to hand*

Fig 4.23
(Courtesy of Peugeot Talbot)

11 *Always quote figures in pairs as they are easier to understand and remember*
12 *Always complete the call by saying 'thank you'*

Fig 4.24
(Courtesy of Peugeot Talbot)

If a caller wants someone who is not available this procedure should be
followed:

1 *Having established that the person they want to speak to is not available, ask if there is someone else who can help them*
2 *Offer to help*
3 *If this is not acceptable then either ask the caller to ring back, or promise to get the person they wanted to call them back*
4 *If necessary, take a message and ensure that it gets to the right person*

If taking a call for someone who is available, this procedure should be followed:

1 *After they have asked for someone in particular, ask the caller who they are*
2 *Ask the caller to hold the line, while you find or contact the person they need*

POINTS NEEDING IMPROVEMENT

Fig 4.25
(Courtesy of Peugeot Talbot)

3 *Contact the person required and say who is calling, and if relevant, what the call is about*

Group activity

In pairs, start a conversation with your partner. After two minutes, change position so that you are now back to back. Try to continue the conversation for another two minutes.

Having done this, quickly write down what differences you felt not facing your partner had on the conversation. Were you able to concentrate? Did you feel you were listening or being listened to? Were there gaps in the conversation? Did you feel ignored?

Now change places and repeat the procedure with your partner making the conversation.

Compare the feelings you experienced with those of your partner.

Written communication

In our day-to-day life, we use written communication, and it is just as important when writing a personal letter to a friend or a note to one of the family, that we ensure our spelling and grammar are correct.

In all organisations, neat, accurate and reliable written communication is vitally important.

Written communication in the business world takes several forms.

Passing on messages

It may be that someone has taken a telephone message for a colleague who is unavailable at the time. It is essential that the information contained in this message is correct and legible.

PEUGEOT TALBOT
MOTOR COMPANY LTD

telephone message

To

From

Message is

Ring back	On telephone no.	
Message taken by	Date	Time

PT 10029 (Rev. 12/85)

Fig 4.26 Peugeot Talbot's personalised telephone message form

Memorandum

Internal memoranda are used for communication between different departments within the same organisation. These are often called 'memos'. An example of a memo is given in Fig 4.28. It is normally shorter than a business letter and usually deals with one particular subject. When more than one point is being made it is normal to number them. (*See* Fig 4.27 and 4.28.)

Memos are not signed in the same way as a business letter, but the person issuing the memo would normally initial it at the end.

Business letters

A business letter, unlike a memorandum, would be sent outside the organisation. It is important then that they are neat, accurate and well presented.

The headed paper used by the organisation for its business letters would form part of their 'corporate image'. The example shown gives the information an organisation would wish each of their customers or clients to see regularly:

1. *The name and address of the organisation*
2. *The telephone number, fax number and/or telex number of the organisation*
3. *The registered address of the organisation, as this may be different from its postal address*
4. *The company registration number*

**PEUGEOT TALBOT
MOTOR COMPANY PLC**

internal correspondence

From (name)	Department	Location
		S09M
To (name)	Department	Location
Subject	O/Ref	Date

Fig 4.27 *Peugeot Talbot use this form for internal communication*

5 *The names of the Directors of the organisation*

6 *Any other companies the organisation may represent or be affiliated to*

The layout or format of the business letter will usually also be part of the organisation's corporate image, and different organisations have their own rules about the way in which a letter should be displayed. It is common nowadays to use the fully-blocked method of display, which means that each part of the letter commences at the left hand margin.

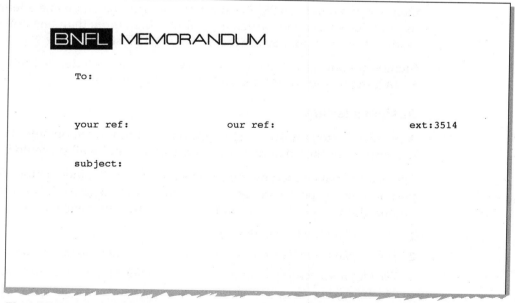

BNFL MEMORANDUM

To:

your ref: our ref: ext:3514

subject:

Fig 4.28 *BNFL's memorandum form*

The following format can be used as a guideline:

1   Our reference – this can be initials and/or numbers which the organisation sending the letter will use for filing purposes.

2   Your reference – this again is usually initials and/or numbers which the organisation receiving the letter has used in previous correspondence.

3   The date – all letters must be dated

4   The name and address of the recipient (the person or organisation to which the letter is being sent) – when using the fully-blocked style of business letter, it is normal to use 'open punctuation' in this section. That means that no punctuation is required in the name and address. (Fig 4.29.)

The name of the town should be in capital letters, and the postcode should be on a line of its own.

5   The salutation – this is the Dear Sir/Madam/Mr/Ms/Mrs/Miss etc.

6   The heading – very often, after the Dear Sir, an organisation will give the letter a title. This is normally either typed in capitals, with initial capital letters only, and may be underlined or emboldened.

7   The body of the letter is then typed. Each line of the paragraph would commence on the left hand margin, and a line space would be left between paragraphs.

If replying to previous correspondence, it is usual to start a letter with 'Thank you for your letter', or 'I refer to your letter dated ...'. The first paragraph would also state what the letter is about.

The subsequent paragraphs would contain the purpose of the letter and what information is required.

The final paragraph would conclude the letter. In this section any enclosures are mentioned. Concluding comments may include things like 'I look forward to hearing from you soon' or 'Should you require any further information, please do not hesitate to contact me'.

8   The complimentary close – this is the 'Yours faithfully' or 'Yours sincerely'. The complimentary close will match the salutation. When using 'Dear Sir/Madam', 'Yours faithfully' is used. When using 'Dear Mr/Ms/Mrs/Miss' at the beginning, 'Yours sincerely' is used at the end.

After allowing space for a signature, the name of the person signing the letter is typed, as well as their title.

9   Enclosure(s) – any enclosed additional information which is mentioned in the body of the letter is usually indicated at the foot of the letter. This is done by typing 'Enc(s)' after the complimentary close.

By indicating the number of enclosures, the recipient is sure that everything needed has actually been received.

```
                                              14 Wellington Road
                                              GREAT YARMOUTH
                                                      Norfolk
                                                     NR30 6BU

                                      Tel No 0493 855677
          19 November 19..

          Hightime Short Breaks
          Princess Street
          NORWICH
          NR1 4TT

          Dear Sir

          HIGHTIME SHORT CAPITAL BREAKS

          As I am unable to come to your offices to book a Short Capital
          Break, I should be obliged if you could complete the booking form
          on my behalf.

          I wish to book a Hightime Capital Break to London, for 3 nights
          commencing 15 June 19..

          My first and second choice hotels are the Washington and the
          Piccadilly Plaza respectively.   I require a single room with
          shower.

          As detailed in your brochure, I would like to reserve a place on
          the Special London Tour on 16 June 19.., and enclose the
          completed form as suggested by you on the telephone.

          I would like to pay by Access and my card number is 5224 0098
          1768, the expiry date is 01/95.

          I look forward to receiving a receipt and confirmation in due
          course.

          Thank you very much for your assistance in this matter.

          Yours faithfully




          MISS C SHORTEN

          Enc
```

Fig 4.29 A fully-blocked business letter

Individual activity

Individually, compose and write a letter of application for the following advertisement which appeared in your local newspaper this week.

COLLEGE LEAVER REQUIRED

- ■ Post available immediately.

- ■ For busy Accounts Department.

- ■ Good communication skills essential.

- ■ Must be competent at figure work.

- ■ Salary negotiable but dependent on age and experience.

Send letter of application to:

Mr T Tucker

Hunt Sportswear, 1 Station Road, Edgware, Middx ED4 5PJ

Invitations

Informal and formal invitations may be sent or received by organisations. When these are being issued in bulk, it is normal that they will be printed by a specialist company and simply prepared for postage within the organisation. An invitation will usually contain the following information:

- ■ The address of the person sending out the invitation

- ■ The date the invitation is sent out

- ■ The names of the people acting as host/hostess at the event

- ■ The date of the event

- ■ The venue of the event

- ■ The time of the event

- ■ The reason for the event (e.g. 18th birthday party)

- ■ RSVP – this is a request for a reply and is taken from the French *répondez s'il vous plaît*. Sometimes a deadline for replies is also given.

Group activity

In pairs, design an invitation for a Awards Evening at your school/college.

The choice of date is yours, but you would like to know who will be attending at least two weeks before the event so that arrangements for the buffet can be made.

Notices

If an organisation wishes to pass a message on to a number of employees, it may place information on its staff notice-boards.

These messages may be formal or informal. Perhaps there is a change to normal organisational procedures, or maybe a social event is being planned by the organisation's Personnel Department.

Notices allow the quick and easy sending of information to a large number of people. Notice-boards can also be used by individuals wishing to inform colleagues of items for sale or events planned.

Group activity

Referring back to the previous activity, when you designed an invitation, now prepare a notice to be placed on all staff notice-boards informing them of the date, time and venue of the Awards Evening. Tell the staff that the Headmaster/Principal would be pleased to see as many staff present as possible.

Reports

Although reports issued by or received by an organisation can be either informal or very formal, both types contain certain common elements, although not necessarily in the same format.

A report may contain research which has been carried out for a specific purpose. It may be the findings and recommendations of work that has been carried out for a specific purpose. Or it may be an account of something which has taken place and been reported on.

A report will contain the following headings:

- *Terms of Reference* – this will state what has been required of the report. It may be that a particular aspect or topic has been researched
- *Procedure* – this will say how the information presented has been gathered
- *Findings* – in this section are stated the facts as found, not statements about recommendations, but simply facts
- *Conclusion* – this would be a general statement about the findings. Again this is not the place to make recommendations, but to conclude and sum up the findings
- *Recommendations* – based on the findings and conclusions, recommendations are made for future research or projects

It is usual to sign and date a report.

Using numbers within a report

Sometimes it is helpful to break down the headings used in a report. This could be done by using a series of numbers. For example:

1   REORGANISATION OF CAR PARKING FACILITIES

   a   Parking permits

      i   Allocation by seniority

or

1   REORGANISATION OF CAR PARKING FACILITIES

   1.1   Parking permits

      1.1.1   Allocation by seniority

Forms

In everyday life, as well as in life in the business world, there are a large variety of forms to complete. When carrying out this task, there are some useful guidelines to ensure that a neat and accurate job of completing forms is made:

1   *If possible take a photocopy of the form to practice on first. If this is not possible, complete in pencil first to avoid messy crossings out*

2   *Read the form thoroughly before even considering starting to complete it*

3   *Be sure to know how to complete the form before starting, and that all the information required is readily to hand*

4   *Check to see if there is any instruction regarding the colour of pen to use. Some forms stipulate 'use black pen'*

5   *Check to see if there is any instruction regarding the style in which to complete the form. Some forms stipulate 'use block capitals only'*

6   *Use neat handwriting*

7   *Try to complete all parts of the form. If there is some information not readily to hand, do not send the form off until it is fully completed*

8   *Check thoroughly that everything is completed before sending the form off. If possible ask someone else to look at it – sometimes one cannot find one's own mistakes!*

(*See* Fig 4.30.)

Preparing a summary

It may be that during the course of your work you will be asked to use the written form of communication called summarising. This means that you are given a long article or report and have to read it and make the information shorter. The original document may be long and complicated to start with, so it is necessary that the information you read is fully understood. You would then take out the unnecessary facts and write a shorter information pack. The following are guidelines for carrying out this task:

1   *Read through the whole document first, rather than trying to understand everything as you go through*

2   *Reread the document more thoroughly. You could highlight the areas of importance at this stage, or cross out the unnecessary information*

3   *Make a list of the items you have to use and that are important to include*

4   *Compare your list with the main document to make sure you haven't forgotten anything important*

5   *Write a draft summary. It may be that a superior could check this for you at this stage. Once you are happy with this draft, you may want to write a final draft*

6   *Once the final draft has been agreed, you can write the final Summary*

TOP COPY | **Request for stationery and forms** | DTI 2003 (12/91) (999–9055)

Note: Please use form **DTI 2088** **(999–9118)** to order items **not** in the Stationery Catalogue.

From: (use CAPITAL letters)

Cost Centre Code

To: FMG – Stationery
Deputy Manager
Room 101
Westfield House
103c Strathville Road
London SW18 4QQ

Name

Address

Postcode

☎

Catalogue Code Number	Quantity in packs Refer to catalogue	For Stationery Staff use only	Catalogue Code Number	Quantity in packs Refer to catalogue	For Stationery Staff use only

Authorised _____ (Cost Centre Manager)

Name (CAPITAL letters) _____

Grade _____

☎ _____ Date _____

Please send the top copy to Stationery Section and keep the bottom copy for your records.

Prepared by the Information Design Team

Fig 4.30 The top copy of DTI's stationery request form

Individual activity

Summarise the following passage:

Franchising encompasses not only physical consumer or industrial goods but also services, particularly those aimed at businesses. To a greater or lesser extent, the franchisor keeps a controlling interest in the franchisee. The franchisor must, above all, make sure that the standard of service offered by the franchisee is consistent with the corporate image of the franchising operation.

Writing a project

Just as you write projects for your college work, so you may be asked by your employer to write a project for them. If this task is new to you, it may be useful to look at some guidelines for completing projects.

Preparation

The first thing you need to find out is the date for completion of the project. Allow plenty of time to research and write up the information. Don't leave things until the last minute – you will not feel good about it and your work will not be of the highest possible standard.

Second, find out exactly what is required of you. How long does the project have to be? How many pages of typing or writing is expected? Is there a limit to the number of words you submit?

Next, do you have to submit the project in a certain format? Are there set headings you are expected to use?

Last, where will you find out the information you need? Make a list of the sources of information you will need to use:

- *Your local library will be very pleased to help you in your research. Facilities the library may offer are:*

  - Photocopying

  - Books and magazines for reference

  - An indexing system that you can refer to in order to find the literature you require

  - Ordering of specific books, or reserving them for you when they are returned to the library

  - Quiet areas when you can carry out research without being disturbed

- *Local and national newspapers*

- *Local and national radio and television*

- *Banks*

- *Building societies*

- *Post offices*

- *Citizens' Advice Bureaux*

- *Chamber of Commerce*

Many other organisations offer assistance in project work. It will obviously depend on the type of research you are carrying out.

Different methods of displaying information

Whether writing a project or preparing for a presentation to a group of people, there are many different ways you could display this information in order to vary the methods already used. It is often said that something is easier to understand if it can be seen rather than verbally described. With that in mind, we are going to mention a few alternative methods of displaying information, maybe for use as visual aids:

Charts, photographs, sketches, pictograms and diagrams

When talking about a complicated piece of machinery or the layout of a new extension, it is obviously easier for you and your audience to see a diagram of the proposed topic. Charts and diagrams not only make something easier to visualise, but are also more pleasant to look at than page after page of script. You know yourself that very often when you pick up a newspaper or magazine, what you tend to look at first are the pictures.

Bar charts, line graphs and pie charts

This method of producing and displaying information is increasingly prepared using computer software. You might use this method to show percentages, to prove an increase or decrease in current trends, or to make comparisons. (*See* Figs 4.31, 4.32 and 4.33.)

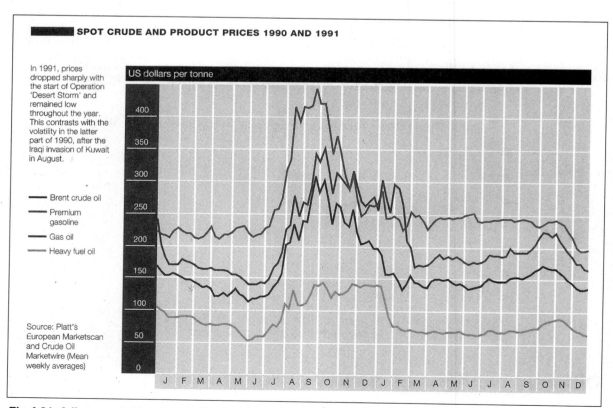

Fig 4.31 A line graph showing the prices of oil over a two-year period
(Courtesy of BP)

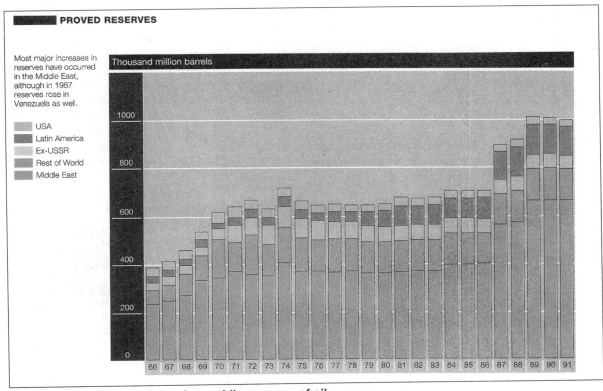

Fig 4.32 A bar chart showing the world's reserves of oil
(Courtesy of BP)

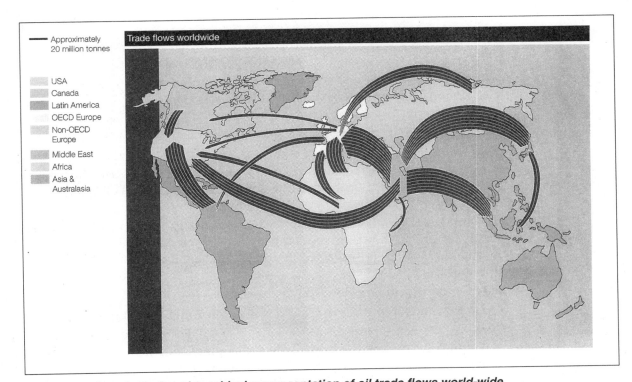

Fig 4.33 A cleverly designed graphical respresentation of oil trade flows world-wide
(Courtesy of BP)

Using the facsimile machine

Another way an organisation would choose to communicate with its customers or clients is by the use of the fax machine. The word facsimile means an exact and faithful reproduction of text, photographs or graphic images. This means that the added benefit of a 'fax' is that an organisation is not limited to what it can send. It is also useful for organisations which may be contacting companies overseas. A fax machine is left on for 24 hours a day, and it does not have to be continually monitored through the night. This means that the time differences between countries is not a problem. The procedure for sending a facsimile message via the telephone line is as follows:

FACSIMILE

TO   ATTENTION OF_____

LOCATION/DEPARTMENT_____
Other destinations listed below

FAX NO._____

FROM   ORIGINATOR   _____

DIRECT LINE_____OUR FAX NO._____

DATE_____NO. OF SHEETS INCLUDING THIS ONE_____

■ IF TRANSMISSION IS NOT PROPERLY RECEIVED PLEASE CALL THE NUMBER ABOVE

Mercury
COMMUNICATIONS

Mercury Communications Ltd
New Mercury House
26 Red Lion Square
London WC1R 4HQ

Switchboard: 071-528 2000
Telex: 910000 Mercom G

Fig 4.34 Mercury Communications' facsimile transmission form

1 Prepare the original document (this may be typed, handwritten, contain graphs, charts, diagrams, etc.)

2 Prepare a covering sheet which will contain a short message, show the name of the recipient of the document, the name of the sender, the fax numbers involved and the number of pages being sent

3 Look up the fax number of the recipient. Often an organisation will keep these readily to hand. If, however, the company is being contacted for the first time, then a Fax Directory is available. This works in the same way as a Telephone Directory

4 Place the document face-down on the machine

5 Key in the number of the recipient. Machines vary slightly, but the machine will give instructions as to the correct procedure to follow

6 Providing a connection has been made, the original document will pass through the machine and you will be informed that transmission is taking place. Should the recipient's line be engaged, the machine will automatically redial the number at intervals

7   Once transmission has taken place, the machine will issue a Transmission Report. This will state the date, time and length of the call, the recipient's number, the sender's number, the number of pages sent and that transmission was acceptable. Should there have been a problem in transmission, the report will indicate this and retransmission may be necessary

(*See* Fig 4.34.)

Individual activity

Using a Fax Directory, look up the fax numbers of at least six market leaders in the area of frozen food production.

Using the telex machine

Although much the same principle as the facsimile machines, the telex is more limited in its use. It is not possible to transmit charts and diagrams via the telex. However, the same advantages apply regarding the transmission of messages to countries overseas. Telex messages can also be prepared and saved on electronic file and transmitted at a later time when they are despatched automatically. The procedure for sending a telex message is as follows:

1   Prepare the text of the telex
2   Find the telex number of the recipient. This will be done in the same way as the fax machine, but using the Telex Directory
3   Make contact with the recipient by keying in the telex number
4   Obtain confirmatory answerback code from the recipient
5   Provide identification in the form of answerback code of the sender
6   Despatch the telex

TYPES OF CUSTOMER

We should consider each customer to be an individual in their own right, and as such, they may display a number of characteristics in addition to some of the more obvious features of an individual. Some of these characteristics may be:

- *Age*
- *Sex*
- *Socio-economic group*
- *Temperament*

4.77

■ *Patience*

■ *Personality*

■ *Confidence*

We will look at some of the different types of customer and offer suggestions as to how to deal with them.

Children

In many occupations, it is unlikely that you will have any contact with children on a day-to-day basis. If we restrict our thoughts to a retail operation, particularly a corner shop, toy shop or record shop, we may well encounter more children than adults. We should first say that children may not necessarily be accompanied by an adult, in which case they may be more difficult to cope with. In any case, they are still customers, and should be treated accordingly. Here are some main points to consider when dealing with a child as a customer:

1 Children may need more help than adults, since they may not have a clear idea as to exactly what they want

everything is made of atoms, you are and so is this book

the centres of atoms are made of neutrons and protons

atoms from a metal called uranium are special

we have called them mighty atoms, this story tells you why

the mighty atom!

Fig 4.35 BNFL's 'the mighty atom' proves that even young children can be a target for publicity

2 Depending on the age of the child, they may not be able to communicate sufficiently to express exactly what they want

3 Younger children do not have a firm grasp of money matters, and may need additional assistance when paying for products or services. In this situation, regardless of the age of the child, tell them exactly what you are doing and

how much money you are taking from them. This will avoid unnecessary complications if they think you have taken too much

4   Always try to treat a child as you would an adult. If the child is a regular customer you should attempt to remember their name and always use it when they visit

5   If you have a disruptive child in the shop, you should take steps to find out if they are with their parents or another adult. It is not advisable to shout at the child, but be firm and they should respond to your directions

6   If you have discovered that the child has become separated from their parents, then you should ensure that you find out their name and address (if possible). Depending on the company policy, you may have to inform the police if you cannot find the parents, but in all cases, you should ensure that the child does not leave the shop

(*See* Fig 4.35.)

Special needs

In this section, we will not only be looking at those who have a handicap, but also foreigners, customers with problems, or those wishing to discuss confidential matters.

Handicapped customers

This broad, and somewhat crude, category includes the deaf, the blind, the disabled and the mentally handicapped. Let us have a look at the ideal and recommended methods of customer care in this area:

Customers with hearing difficulties

You should not assume that a deaf person can necessarily lip-read. You should always be facing them when you do talk. Even those who cannot lip-read may well be able to pick up the 'gist' of what you are saying to them. It is hard to know whether a person is deaf or not, but once this has been established, do not be tempted to shout, but do speak slowly and clearly.

Blind or partially sighted customers

People who are blind, or who have impaired eyesight, are reliant upon sound and touch to compensate for their vision. Many will have enhanced hearing to compensate for their blindness and this should be remembered when approaching a blind customer. Not all will have the customary white stick or guide dog and their blindness may not be immediately apparent. A blind person will rely upon you to guide them to the required section of the store and to describe, if necessary, the product they wish to purchase, and possibly to assist them when paying for goods.

Physically handicapped customers

Hopefully, the premises you work in will provide ramps for use by customers who may be confined to a wheelchair. This will alleviate any problems they may encounter with steps. Disabled customers would appreciate having doors opened for them, particularly if they are shopping alone. It will also be important not to try and rush the customer and to ensure that you are attentive to their individual needs.

Mentally handicapped customers

It is possible that a customer who has a mental handicap could have problems in communicating their needs and wants. It may be that they have a limited vocabulary, therefore it would take longer for them to explain to you what they wish to buy. The main thing to remember is that patience on your part is important.

Foreign customers

It may be that a foreign customer cannot speak very good English. This will mean that they find it difficult to ask for whatever it is they wish to purchase. It would be helpful if you are aware of this and remember to speak slowly and use basic English, rather than long sentences. Be patient with foreign customers and remember that there is no need to shout at them – a mistake we all sometimes seem to make.

Customers with problems

Some people may come into the shop who are unable to communicate easily due to nervousness. Others may have confidential matters which they wish to discuss in private.

In the first instance, when dealing with a nervous or shy person you should always attempt to be friendly and put them at their ease. If they are taking a considerable amount of time trying to explain what it is they want, do not be tempted to finish their sentences for them and be prepared to give them the time that they need. If they appear to be reluctant to accept help or assistance, then let them take their time looking around the shop, but always be aware that they may need help at any time.

Those who need to discuss confidential matters should be given the opportunity to talk privately. In the case of personal or confidential matters, it is advisable to find a quiet part of the shop, or preferably a room off the shop-floor. You should take care to note any information that they may give you and be careful to give them the information which they require. In complicated cases, it is advisable to refer the matter to a senior member of staff.

Satisfied customers

These are perhaps the easiest customers to deal with. They will be valued customers who, having received good service, will return and be willing to recommend your services to other people. It is advisable to always allow these customers time but to be on hand to offer advice should they need it. It is often the case that satisfied customers do not necessarily need as much help on return visits, but should always be treated with courtesy and politeness. (*See* Figs 4.36 and 4.37.)

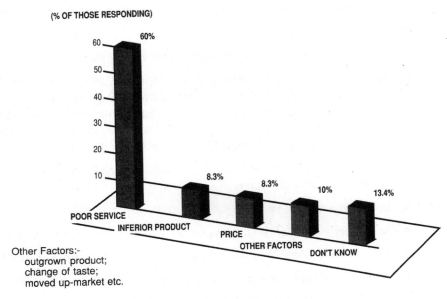

(% OF THOSE RESPONDING)

Other Factors:-
outgrown product;
change of taste;
moved up-market etc.

Fig 4.36 Why customers switch to the competition
(Courtesy of Peugeot Talbot)

HOW CUSTOMERS SEE IT DIFFERENTLY

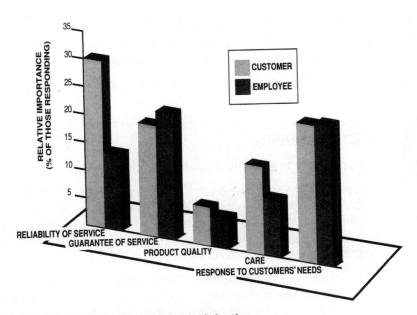

Fig 4.37 The importance of customer satisfaction
(Courtesy of Peugeot Talbot)

4.81

Dissatisfied customers

A customer may be dissatisfied for a number of reasons. These may include the following:

- *The product which they purchased is faulty*
- *They require a product which you either do not stock or is out of stock*
- *They have received poor service*
- *They have a problem which nobody seems to be able to help them with*

In the case of many companies there is a formal complaints procedure for customers who are dissatisfied. It is usual for complaints to be referred to the Manager, who is empowered to act on behalf of the company and make any necessary rapid decisions to help rectify the situation. When dealing with complaints, you should attempt to remember the following:

- *When listening to the complaint do not interrupt, and give the customer an opportunity to explain the situation*
- *Always appear to be sympathetic to the customer*
- *Particularly in complicated cases, make sure you have written down all of the details*
- *When you have done this, check the main points of the complaint with the customer*
- *Even if the customer is abusive, always try to remain calm and polite*
- *If you cannot solve the situation yourself, refer the matter to a senior member of staff*
- *Never give the customer a vague response or an unbelievable excuse*
- *Never blame anyone else directly*
- *Even if provoked, do not lose your temper*
- *Never try to infer that the complaint is not really a problem*
- *Always tell the customer exactly what you are going to do, particularly if this involves having to refer to another person or company*
- *Above all, never make any promises which you cannot personally fulfil*

Group activity

In pairs, try to solve the following problem:

Several customers have visited your organisation in the past two or three days, complaining that they cannot get through to your organisation by telephone. They state that the telephones are constantly engaged and on the odd occasion that they have managed to get through, the staff have been unhelpful. Staff have promised to return the customers' calls, but have failed to carry this out.

Upon investigation, you have discovered that the telephone system has been breaking down periodically throughout the day. Although a service engineer has been called (some two days ago) they have not yet arrived.

Group activity cont.

The customers are irate and not only need their queries answering, but also need to be calmed and assured that the circumstances will not be repeated.

In the role of Assistant to the Sales Manager, you have been asked to write a brief letter to each of the customers, explaining the situation and apologising for the inconvenience they have been caused.

On the subject of unhelpful staff, your Manager, after consultation with the Personnel Director, has agreed to offer a training refresher course to all staff whose duties include telephone answering. Your Manager, in turn, has asked you to identify a correct and recommended procedure of answering telephones in a variety of circumstances.

You should present your explanation and apology to the customers in the form of a correct business letter, preferably mail-merged using a word processor.

For your second task, you should prepare a report in the form of a memorandum to your Manager, detailing your suggestions as to how to solve the staff telephone answering problem.

LEGAL REQUIREMENTS OF CUSTOMER SERVICE

We have already discussed a range of consumer legislation which is aimed at protecting customers from a number of different problems which may occur. Specifically, this consumer legislation will address the following situations:

- *When a customer has been sold potentially dangerous goods*
- *When a customer has discovered that the goods purchased are faulty*
- *When a customer has discovered that the goods purchased are damaged*
- *When the organisation involved has been negligent in some way*
- *When an accident has occurred as a result of action taken by an employee of an organisation*
- *When a customer has been misled by something said by an employee of an organisation*
- *When a customer has been quoted a particular price and charged a higher one*

Health and safety

We have already seen that the Health and Safety at Work Act refers specifically to employees, but in some respects there are circumstances when a customer may be affected by health and safety legislation.

Accidents can occur which may injure a customer. This may be due to the actions of an employee or an injury related to the use of a product. A customer may suffer physically or financially from the actions of an employee or a faulty product. In order to safeguard against potential claims from an injured customer, an organisation will obtain the following insurance:

Public Liability Insurance

An organisation such as a hairdressing salon or a firm of builders would take out such an insurance. This can be a legal requirement, and the policy would cover any claims a customer may make against the organisation. A customer may make a claim if they were caused personal injury caused by negligence by one of the employees or because of defective equipment or building structure.

Product Liability Insurance

This insurance covers an organisation against claims by customers because of an injury caused by faulty goods.

Professional Indemnity

An organisation would take out this insurance to protect itself against any claims a customer may make against it for professional negligence. Professional organisations such as doctors, dentists and solicitors would take out such an insurance.

Individual activity

In the role of the owner of a hairdressing salon, consider the types of claims that may be made against you by your customers. Write down as many possible reasons for claim that you can think of, then compare your list with the rest of the group.

Honesty

At all times, employees should be aware of not misleading a customer in any way. Honesty can relate to descriptions of products, promises of service, promises of delivery or promises of after-sales service. Perhaps the most serious is to lie about the capabilities of a product. If an employee is guilty of this, they may be contravening the Sale of Goods Act, the Trades Description Act and, perhaps, the Consumer Protection Act. This may lead to heavy penalties being paid by the organisation.

An additional point to make is that statements made by employees which may not necessarily be illegal in themselves, can cause a great deal of ill-feeling on the side of the customer.

Group activity

In pairs, consider the following problems faced by an estate agent. Estate agents are now obliged to give purely descriptive statements regarding properties under the Property Misdescriptions Act. In the role of an estate agent, how would you describe the following properties without falling foul of the Act?

Group activity cont.

■ The house is semi-derelict and has been vacant for 10 years

■ The house is a small terraced property which faces a busy railway viaduct

■ The property is a spacious flat which has been recently refurbished after an extensive fire

Compare your considerations with those of the rest of the group.

Element assignment

DEALING WITH CUSTOMERS

In the role of a shop assistant in a retail outlet specialising in sports equipment, detail your actions in dealing with the following customers:

1 A small child who has just received £20 for his birthday, and wishes to buy a pair of football boots. Unfortunately, you do not have a pair which fit him and are unlikely to have them before he needs to play his next game of football at school

2 A customer has returned a broken tennis racquet. The manufacturer's guarantee ran out three months ago. The customer is insistent that you replace the damaged racquet. You suspect that the damage is not the fault of the manufacturer, but that it has been misused

3 A customer, representing a local social club, wishes to purchase 10 pool cues. Each cue is valued at £15.99. He has £150.00 in cash. He will only buy the 10 pool cues if he can have them for £150.00. The Manager is not present and the customer says that unless you are prepared to sell him the 10 cues at his price, he will have to purchase them from another store

You should present your solutions to these problems in the form of an oral presentation to the rest of your group, who will adopt the role of your Manager.

UNIT TEST   Element 4.3

1 Give four reasons why a customer might contact an organisation

2 What is a guarantee?

3 Give six rules for ensuring good verbal communication

4 What is NVC?

5 List five important rules to consider when greeting a customer

6 List five important rules to consider when answering a telephone

7 When would a memo be used?

8 What is a salutation?

9 What is open punctuation?

10 How would you indicate an enclosure?

11 List the main headings of a report

12 What is a summary?

13 Give three services offered by a local library

14 Give three methods of displaying information graphically

15 What do you understand by the term 'answerback code'?

16 List four characteristics of a customer

17 What should you do if you find a lost child in your shop?

18 How should you deal with a foreign customer?

19 Give two reasons why a customer might be dissatisfied

20 What type of organisation would require Public Liability Insurance?

Element 4.4
Customer services provided by business sectors

PERFORMANCE CRITERIA

1 Customer services provided by business sectors are described
2 Ways to monitor customer satisfaction with services are investigated
3 Improvements to customer services are suggested
4 Forms of protection for customers are described
5 Ways to communicate customer protection are proposed

RANGE

1 **Business sectors:** public and private
2 **Customer services:** information, help, care, refunds and after-sales
3 **Ways to monitor customer satisfaction:** sales performance, feedback, complaints and market research
4 **Protection:** contract of sale, Citizen's Charters, guarantees, legal, ombudsman, consumer associations and media

EVIDENCE INDICATORS

Proposals for improvements to customer services in a private and a public sector business with proposals for communicating two forms of protection to customers. Evidence should demonstrate understanding of the implications of the range dimensions in relation to the element. The unit test will confirm the candidate's coverage of range.

CUSTOMER SERVICE BY BUSINESS SECTOR

Many organisations consider themselves to be fully well aware of the needs and wants of their customers. Indeed, all of their activities revolve around the satisfaction of customers. Organisations consider customers to be of vital importance since this is the key to business success. If an organisation manages to keep the customer in mind at all times, then inevitably it will increase its market share, provide better services than those of the competitors, it will maintain its current customers and attract new ones.

The exact nature of customer service may differ slightly depending upon the sector in which the organisation operates. In this respect, we are concerned with two major sectors. We will look at these shortly.

What exactly are customer services? Let us try to identify them:

- *Giving the customer information and help*
- *Processing refunds and dealing with replacements*
- *Handling customer complaints*
- *Giving advice on after-sales service*
- *Taking steps to prove that the organisation is interested in the needs and wants of the customer*
- *Answering the telephone promptly*
- *Replying to all forms of communication made by customers*
- *Trying to avoid releasing any confusing or misleading information*
- *Always being polite and courteous*
- *Offering a quality service throughout all aspects of the business activity*
- *Trying to remember the names of all regular customers*

(*See* Fig 4.38.)

TIDY UP YOUR WORK AREA

Fig 4.38
(Courtesy of Peugeot Talbot)

4.88

Group activity

In pairs, in the role of owners of a fish and chip shop, which of the above would you think are important customer service considerations for your establishment?

Let us now consider the two principle sectors:

The private sector

Private sector organisations are primarily interested in profits. It is a simple equation – the more customers, the more sales, the more profit. An organisation which has this equation in mind will try to find out exactly what a customer wants. It will take all steps necessary to ensure that it can provide everything the customer might need. It will even take account of possible changes in trends and fashions to try to predict what customers might need in the future. As we have already seen, an organisation which takes all of the above into consideration can be known as a market-orientated organisation. (*See* Fig 4.39.)

The public sector

Public sector organisations did not have to consider customer service to any great extent until recently. They did not have to worry about profits since they were financed by Central or Local Government. The situation has changed to some extent, but we have seen great changes in the attitudes of public sector organis-ations, which have become aware of the demands of customers and how this relates to their possibility of survival. Hospitals, for example, now face the prospect of competition from the private sector. Even tax offices have imple-mented a customer service programme which aims to deal with customers courte-ously and efficiently. To ensure that some of the larger public corporations deal with customers in a fair manner, the Government has set up a 'watchdog' or 'ombudsman' to monitor their behaviour. Privatisation may just be round the corner for many of the public sector organisations, so they need to prepare them-selves and adopt the customer service techniques in common practice in the private sector.

MONITORING AND RESPONDING TO CUSTOMER SATISFACTION

Even if an organisation has established a range of customer service provision, it must still try to improve this service. It will do this by constantly monitoring a variety of areas in which customer service is a part. These areas of concern include the following:

TRAINING AND DEVELOPMENT

Name:

Identity Number:

Job Title:

Department:

Manager:

Date Completed:

ACHIEVEMENT OF PAST OBJECTIVES/TARGETS

TRAINING & DEVELOPMENT NEEDS

Method of working

METHODS OF WORKING

Dealing with people

DEALING WITH PEOPLE

Other needs

OBJECTIVES/TARGETS FOR NEXT YEAR

PERSONAL TRAINING & DEVELOPMENT PLAN
To be completed in conjunction with Personnel/Training Function

Proposed Activity/Action*	Responsibility

*Should include preferred timing and priority

INDIVIDUAL'S COMMENTS

Individual's Signature:

Appraiser's Signature:

Date Plan Agreed:

Fig 4.39 *Peugeot Talbot's comprehensive appraisal and training/development programme places great importance on customer care and personal development*

Monitoring the sales performance

Sales will increase if the organisation manages to attract more customers, or if it convinces its existing customers to purchase more products or services. A well organised company will keep a close check on the number of enquiries made by customers and how many of these have been turned into actual sales. In order to facilitate this monitoring system, it may enter all the names and addresses of customers who have made enquiries onto a database. It will then be an easy matter to cross-check actual orders and see what percentage 'conversion rate' has been achieved. Another way of monitoring sales performance is to see how often existing customers reorder products or services.

Repeat purchases are the life-blood of an organisation. They must take strenuous steps to ensure that customers who regularly reorder are treated well and may be offered extended credit facilities to ensure that they stay loyal to the organisation.

Requesting feedback

An organisation which takes customer service seriously will be interested in the attitudes and opinions formed by the customer. The customer may have very valuable things to say about products or service and may offer useful solutions to difficult problems. There are several ways of obtaining customer feedback, these include the following:

1   Employees asking the customer directly what they think about a product or service

2   'Unknown' employees posing as customers who will visit a branch of the organisation to assess the behaviour of the staff present

3   The organisation may choose to set up a consumer panel which aims to obtain feedback in an informal situation. Normally, this will take the form of a group of customers talking about products and services with a selected group of employees. Very valuable information may be gained from this, including new ideas for products or services.

Group activity

In pairs, you have been asked to draw up a list of discussion areas for a consumer panel. Your organisation is involved in the manufacture, wholesaling and retailing of cast-iron park benches. At present, you only offer four different versions in three different colours.

Discuss your list with those of the rest of the group.

Monitoring complaints

The easiest way to monitor complaints is to see how many returned goods the organisation receives. In all cases, these should be accompanied by appro-

22nd March 1993

MERCURY EXTENDS NETWORK TO 90% OF UK POPULATION

Mercury Communications has announced that from the end of April, following recent network extensions, around 90% of the UK population will be able to access the Mercury network for business and residential services.

Over £2 million has been invested in this latest expansion, Mercury's largest ever single extension programme which will provide access for an additional 1.5 million residential exchange lines. In only five years Mercury has been able to expand its access within the UK from under 60% in 1988 to 90% in 1993.

Over 100 new areas, spread throughout the British Isles, will become available with a significant number of these in Scotland and Northern Ireland. New STD codes able to access Mercury services in the first quarter of 1993 include, Kirkcaldy, Perth, Larne and Ballymena. Also included are Doncaster, Tunbridge Wells, Burnley, Lancaster and Worcester.

Mercury has invested a total of £1.9 billion in its network, products and services and will continue this significant investment programme over the next few years. Mercury is signing up over 25,000 new customers a month to its residential service and 99 of the top 100 companies in the UK are Mercury customers.

Mercury Communications is a subsidiary of Cable & Wireless and is licensed as Telecommunications Operator in the UK.

ends

For further information please contact
Richard Prescott, Mercury Press Office   Tel:071-528-2561
                                                    Fax:071-528-2577
For Mercury information   Freephone 0500-500-194

Mercury Communications Limited, New Mercury House, 26 Red Lion Square, London, WC1R 4HQ. Switchboard: 071-528 2000 Fax: 071-528 2181 Telex: 910000 Mercom G

Fig 4.40 Telecommunications services improve the pace as Mercury expands its coverage of the UK to 90 per cent of the population

priate paperwork which details the exact nature of the problem. A customer who returns to the organisation dissatisfied may well now be satisfied after they have received a replacement for their faulty or damaged goods. The organisation will cross-reference the number, type and source of the faulty or damaged goods and see if there are any common features, such as a large number of faulty goods from a single supplier.

Carrying out market research

Market research is useful in discovering what both existing and potential customers think about the organisation and its range of products or services.

Although the information is based upon opinion, organisations place a great emphasis on the reliability of this data and will often act upon it directly. The questionnaire itself must be clear and easy to fill in and in some cases, the organisation will offer an incentive or reward for the customer to complete the document. (*See* Fig 4.40.)

Monitoring after-sales service

Having established an after-sales service, an organisation will be keen to ensure that it is functioning correctly. A series of procedures will need to be in place to make sure that the after-sales service matches the promises made when the product or service was initially sold to the customer. Although a large proportion of customers may not need after-sales service, the organisation will want to ensure that it is available on demand.

PROTECTION FOR CUSTOMERS

Less than 30 years ago, there was little or no protection for consumers under the law. In fact, the phrase that was most often used was 'Let the buyer beware'. In other words, the consumer had to rely on their own common sense and feelings as to whether a product was suitable or fit for use. Nowadays, however, there are certain standards as laid down by law, as well as voluntary agreements and codes of practice adopted by industries or particular businesses.

The consumer can quite rightly expect to receive goods and services which not only match the description, but are not faulty, dangerous or unfit for use. Over the years the law has developed to provide guidelines for transactions and to offer a means of dealing with disputes between the supplier and the consumer. The law further tries to address the imbalance between the power of a large organisation, which will have the backing of specialists and lawyers, and the vulnerability of the individual consumer.

Acts of Parliament relating to consumer protection fall within both the civil and criminal areas of the law.

Civil law

Civil law covers disputes between individuals and suppliers. When a transaction is made, this is, in effect, a contract. If one side suffers a loss in any way from the contract, then the injured party may sue.

Criminal law

Criminal law tends to cope with more wide-spread abuses related to sales transactions. If an organisation sells a product which is harmful or dangerous to the community in general, then it will be the Government (through the Law Courts) which will take action against them. Under criminal law, an organisation or individual found guilty is liable to fines, imprisonment, or both.

Contract of sale

As we have already said, when goods or services are provided, the consumer should expect that they are fit for the purpose for which they were intended. If a product does not meet the consumer's requirements, then they may expect a replacement. If the product is wholly unfit then the consumer may expect their money back. These basic rights form part of the Sale of Goods Act. The companion law is the Trades Description Act. This makes it a criminal offence to wrongly describe a product. In other words, any description of the product must be accurate.

The Weights and Measures Act attempts to ensure that the quantity stated on the box, container or bag matches the weight of the contents inside. It is an offence under this Act to claim a particular weight and supply a lighter one.

The Food and Drugs Act deals with food and medicines specifically. Under this Act an organisation cannot supply a product which is harmful and must always make sure that any instructions are clear as to the use or preparation of the product. For example, uncooked red kidney beans contain a toxic substance which is eliminated by the correct cooking period. Suppliers of this product must ensure that any packaging states very clearly the potential hazards. Also under this Act, rules apply to certain prepared foodstuffs such as sausages. Sausages must contain a defined amount of meat to be called a sausage. If they do not, then they must be alternatively labelled.

Citizen's Charter

The Citizen's Charter sets out consumer rights which indicate that, particularly as far as public services are concerned, the consumer should expect a certain level of service. It further states that if the service does not meet a certain level of standards, then the consumer should expect compensation. This system is regulated by a separate organisation (some of which we will look at later). It is further suggested that once the services reach a particular standard, then they will be able to claim a 'Chartermark'. This Chartermark is hoped to give the consumer clear indication that they will receive a high-quality service.

The first phase of the Citizen's Charter is for organisations to release a list of 'promises'. These promises clearly state exactly what the consumer should expect from that organisation. From this set of promises the consumer should now know what their rights are as far as services provided are concerned.

The main reason for the Citizen's Charter is to control publicly run organisations, such as Local Authorities, to maintain some level of control over 'opted-out' organisations, such as hospitals or schools and colleges.

Group activity

In groups of three, in the role of Manager of the Local Authority's refuse collection service, produce a Citizen's Charter covering your promises of service.

Compare your charter with those of the rest of the group.

Guarantees and other legal protection

A guarantee or a warranty is basically an undertaking by the manufacturer to replace or repair the product, or parts of the product, should they prove to be defective. It further undertakes to do this free of charge, and as quickly as possible. A typical guarantee would include the following:

- *The product will be repaired free of charge if faulty because of defective materials used*

- *The product will be repaired free of charge if faulty because of defective workmanship*

- *The product will be repaired free of charge if found faulty within the first 12 months*

- *The manufacturer will require a proof of purchase such as a receipt or credit card voucher*

- *The product must be repaired or replaced only at the manufacturer's service centre or approved service centre*

- *If it is discovered that the fault is not the result of defective parts or workmanship, but due to negligence by the consumer or retailer, then the manufacturer is not obliged to repair or replace free of charge*

- *Optionally, the consumer may choose to extend the guarantee or warranty period by paying an additional charge. In this case, the manufacturer extends its offer of replacement or repair for the period purchased*

We have already mentioned the Sale of Goods Act and the Trades Descriptions Act, but there are some other laws which similarly protect consumer rights.

Group activity

In pairs, discuss the warranties you would expect to find when purchasing a pocket calculator.

The Consumer Protection Act

This Act is primarily concerned with price and pricing policy of organisations. No doubt many of us have been caught out when purchasing a product to find that the price quoted is not the price in reality. This may be because the sale period has ended, the price quoted did not include VAT, or that the claimed price reduction is untrue. This Act states that the organisation must clearly state the 'real' price of a product, not make unfair or untrue comparisons between products and price, and not make false statements about price reductions.

You will often see, particularly in a sale, one of two statements made on a price ticket:

1 The price ticket will state that the product was available for a period of time at a previously higher price. It may not necessarily have been available in that store, but in an alternative location owned by that organisation.

2 The other statement may read that the product has been specifically bought-in and offered at a low price for the sale period only.

The Consumer Protection Act further covers the consumer in respect of being offered unsafe goods under any circumstances.

Supply of Goods and Services Act

This Act was created to cover loop-holes in the Sale of Goods Act. The older Act did not include services, hired goods or part exchanges. All goods or services 'purchased' under these conditions are now covered. In respect of services this Act protects the consumer against poor workmanship, long delays and hidden costs.

Ombudsmen

An Ombudsman's job is to ensure that any complaints between an organisation and the consumer are fairly dealt with. The Ombudsmen Scheme has been extended from its original form which dealt only with Government departments, to a variety of different business activities. These include the following:

- *The Health Service* – an Ombudsman deals with complaints from both staff and patients

- *Local Government* – an Ombudsman investigates complaints concerning Local Government and services which they provide

- *Legal Services* – an Ombudsman operates to consider complaints against solicitors and barristers

- *Insurance Industry* – an Ombudsman investigates unfair small print on insurance policies, inefficiencies and insurance companies' responses and communications with consumers

- *Estate Agents* – an Ombudsman protects the consumer against false descriptions of properties and 'gazumping' (which is allowing another buyer to offer a higher price after a lower price has already been accepted)

- *Banking* – an Ombudsman attempts to control bank charges, unfair interest rates and generally poor service

- *Building Societies* – an Ombudsman looks at complaints regarding surveys on homes carried out by a building society's valuer

- *Investment* – an Ombudsman considers complaints regarding poor or misleading investment advice
- *Pension Schemes* – an Ombudsman investigates complaints regarding personal, company or state pensions

Consumer associations

Although any truly reputable organisation will go to great lengths to ensure that its products or services meet all the necessary standards and demands, there is a need for independent evaluators. The Consumer Association itself looks at various products and services within a particular area and releases its findings in the magazine *Which?*.

In addition to this organisation, is the National Federation of Consumer Groups, which co-ordinates local consumer groups. These local consumer groups investigate products and services available in the region and like the Consumer Association, publish their findings. They also are very active in campaigning for changes and further protection for the consumer.

Media

Newspapers, television and radio are often at the forefront of campaigns in support of the consumer. They will often bring to the public's notice abuses and dangers in products or services. In some cases, they will be responding to a public outcry concerning a product or a service. At other times, they will be responsible for investigating a product or a service and discovering some aspect which they believe the public should be made aware of.

There are many consumer-orientated programmes and features which have had a very positive impact in changing organisation's attitudes, service and products to the betterment of the public.

Watchdog bodies

Some of the watchdog bodies have been set up by the Government in order to monitor organisation's activities, particularly in their dealings with the public. Others have been set up by the industry to keep a check on their member organisations. This has been done to ensure that standards are maintained and that any adverse publicity resulting from a disreputable trader does not damage the industry as a whole. Some examples of these watchdog organisations are:

1 *Office of Fair Trading* – this is a Government body whose brief is to take care of consumer interests as well as those of traders. It releases a range of codes of practice in an effort to improve standards of service. In addition, the Office of Fair Trading will ensure that organisations compete fairly and that no single organisation controls the sole supply of goods or services. An organisation which does is known as a monopoly

2 *Citizens' Advice Bureau* – the principle duty of this chain of offices is to act as a mediator in disputes between organisations and consumers. They are also responsible for a variety of other advisory matters, not necessarily relating to consumer rights

3 *Trading Standards Department* – this organisation investigates various complaints relating to short weights, false or misleading offers and matters relating to credit

4 *National Consumer Council* – this council is responsible for representing the consumer in disputes and problems with Government departments, nationalised industries, local authorities and other businesses

5 *Environmental Health Department* – this organisation operates a series of local offices which investigate aspects relating to food and hygiene. It has the power to enforce legislation relating to food hygiene and may even close businesses which break the regulations

6 *British Standards Institution* – this organisation, which operates on funds received from the Government and voluntary donations, is concerned with setting minimum standards in all aspects of business and industry. Its most common image is the BSI Kitemark which denotes that a product has been manufactured and reached the standards laid down by the British Standards Institute

7 *Consumer and Consultative Councils* – these organisations have been set up to monitor the operations of nationalised industries, and to ensure that they do not abuse their monopoly in terms of charging too high a price or providing a poor level of service

8 *Trade Associations* – this large number of organisations deal with specific industries or services and offer assistance, information and advice to their members. In addition, they also devise a voluntary code of practice to which all members are expected to adhere. An example of these organisations is ABTA (Association of British Travel Agents). The Association also offers guidelines as to how consumers should be treated, particularly with regard to complaints

9 *Advertising Standards Authority* – this independent organisation is involved in ensuring that all advertisements are 'legal, decent, honest and truthful'

10 *The Chartered Institute of Marketing* – which is another independent organisation that attempts to ensure that its members have high professional standards, particularly in terms of honesty and integrity. Their British Code of Advertising Practice gives the advertising industry a clear set of rules to follow

11 *Independent Broadcasting Authority* – this organisation monitors the activities of television and radio stations and ensures that particular standards are maintained. Recently, it has been concerned with a new marketing technique known as 'placement' which involves popular programmes featuring and recommending particular brand names or products. Although placement is well established in America, the IBA have ruled that it is unacceptable in Great Britain

Group activity

In groups of four, contact and obtain leaflets or brochures from at least six of the above organisations. Having done this, summarise the main areas of activity of each of the organisations and compile your findings in the form of a fact sheets which could be made available via the Citizens' Advice Bureaux and local libraries.

Element assignment

THE CUSTOMER IS ALWAYS RIGHT

In groups of four, your task is to attempt to improve customer services in a private and public sector organisation. In order to do this you must devise a personalised questionnaire for both organisations in order to assess the attitudes and opinions of existing customers. Having designed your questionnaires carefully, focusing on customer service issues, you must then obtain completed questionnaires from at least 50 customers of each organisation.

For the purposes of this assignment, you should use your institution as an example of a public sector organisation. In consultation with the person responsible for customer-related matters, you should obtain permission to carry out this task.

For the purposes of this assignment, you should attempt to obtain permission from a private sector organisation to carry out a survey of their customers.

Having collected all of the data from the questionnaires, you must now analyse the results and present your findings in the form of a formal written report which you can then submit to the individuals from whom you gained permission to carry out the research.

Your questionnaires must be word processed and as easy as possible to complete.

Your written report must similarly be word processed and statistical data should be presented in a suitable graphical form.

UNIT TEST   Element 4.4

1   Give three types of customer service

2   How would an organisation monitor its sales performance?

3   State two ways an organisation might obtain feedback from customers

4   What is the easiest way of monitoring customer complaints?

5   What is civil law?

6   What does criminal law cope with?

7   What is a contract of sale?

8 What does the Weights and Measures Act cover?

9 What is a Citizen's Charter?

10 What is a chartermark?

11 List three undertakings covered by a warranty

12 Briefly explain the Consumer Protection Act

13 Explain the role of an Ombudsman

14 What is a Watchdog Body?

15 What is the Chartered Institute of Marketing?

16 What does the Environmental Health Department investigate?

17 What is the Office of Fair Trading?

18 How could the media assist a consumer in dealing with a disreputable company?

19 Can you name two television programmes that deal with consumer affairs?

20 What is the National Federation of Consumer Groups?

UNIT 4   End Test

1 What is demography?
   (a) The study of population trends
   (b) The study of spending patterns
   (c) The study of buying habits
   (d) The study of the cost of living

2 What is the RPI and what does it mean?
   (a) Real Price Index – production costs
   (b) Regional Purchasing Index – regional price trends
   (c) Retail Price Index – inflation
   (d) Regional Policy Initiators – government development grants

3 What is ACORN?
   (a) A classification of regional newspaper
   (b) A classification of residential neighbourhoods
   (c) A classification of recession news
   (d) A classification of retail numbers

4 What is TAP?
   (a) Trade Advertising Programme
   (b) Total Advertising Policy
   (c) Television Audience Potential
   (d) Total Audience Package

5 Which of the following is an independent national radio station?
   (a) Classic FM
   (b) Radio 1
   (c) Capital Radio
   (d) Radio 4

6 Which of the following would not be used as a form of internal communication?

(a) A memo
(b) A letter
(c) A telephone message
(d) A report

7 What are NVCs?

(a) Non-Vocational Courses
(b) National Verbal Communication
(c) Non-Verbal Communications
(d) Normal Verbal Communications

8 Which of the following is not a watchdog body?

(a) OFWAT
(b) OFTEL
(c) OFCOM
(d) Environmental Health Department

9 What is a Citizen's Charter?

(a) A series of promises made by an organisation
(b) Queen's Award for Industry
(c) A method of hiring equipment
(d) An aspect of the Weights and Measures Act

10 What is the CIM?

(a) Certificate of Incorporation for Managers
(b) Chartered Institute of Marketing
(c) Chartered Institute of Monitors
(d) Consumer Information Magazine

Index